AF512193

Studies in ELT, Linguistics and Applied Linguistics

Edited by
Mohit K. Ray

ATLANTIC
PUBLISHERS & DISTRIBUTORS (P) LTD

Published by

ATLANTIC

PUBLISHERS & DISTRIBUTORS (P) LTD

7/22, Ansari Road, Darya Ganj,
New Delhi-110002
Phones : +91-11-40775252, 23273880, 23275880, 23280451
Fax : +91-11-23285873
Web : www.atlanticbooks.com
E-mail : orders@atlanticbooks.com

Branch Office
5, Nallathambi Street, Wallajah Road,
Chennai-600002
Phones : +91-44-64611085, 32413319
E-mail : chennai@atlanticbooks.com

Copyright © Atlantic Publishers and Distributors (P) Ltd., 2004, 2012

All rights reserved. No part of this publication may be reproduced, stored in a retrieval system, transmitted or utilized in any form or by any means, electronic, mechanical, photocopying, recording or otherwise, without the prior permission of the copyright owner. Application for such permission should be addressed to the publisher.

Printed in India at Nice Printing Press, A-33/3A, Site-IV, Industrial Area, Sahibabad, Ghaziabad, U.P.

Preface

While it is true that English does not and should not occupy the place of 'pride' that it used to in the British Raj, it is equally true, nevertheless, that the importance of English both as a link language, a means of communication and as a medium of instruction has been steadily growing since Independence, so that the total number of learners of English in India today would easily exceed the total populations of many countries of Europe. Moreover, we have now more speakers of English in India than in Britain.

Learning a language is different from learning about a language, but to acquire proficiency in a language at all the levels of listening, speaking, reading and writing, and an ability to express both functional and conceptual meaning it is not enough to know the language. However, since natural use of a language is richly variegated it is only when a good command of the language has been acquired that the learner can proceed to develop his personal linguistic repertoire through a knowledge of how a language works. A student of literature must also know how to apply the insights of linguistics to the appreciation of literature.

Thirty essays that constitute this Volume explore in depth various aspects of the English language, English language teaching, functional, notional and communicative approaches to material production and syllabus design, different kinds of English, different uses of English in literary works, application of linguistic theories to the study of literature, translation and semantics.

In his highly perceptive essay Amiya Basu shows as to how languages often die like human beings, and shed light on the circumstances leading to the death of a language.

Dr Mallikarjun Patil calls attention to the richness, flexibility and resilience of the English language which is now "the most copious, heterogeneous and varied" language of the world.

Dr Sailendra Kumar Mukul treats the same theme from a different perspective and argues with illustrations that the English language "that we speak today directly owes to Anglo-Saxon prose and verse."

Dr Sharad Rajimwale analyzes Elizabethan prose—its gusto and drive—and shows that it has contained the seeds of many literary genres of the future period.

In his sharp and insightful critical survey of the origin and growth of English education in India Professor Avadhesh Kumar Singh argues that the teaching of English literature in India handed down to us by the British has lost its relevance, and strongly advocates for its reorientation towards contemporary Indian situation and experience.

S. Jagadisan and S. Imtiaz Ali try to bring out the salient features of Babu English and Butler English and show how they constitute an interesting variety of Indian English.

Professor Amarnath Jha makes a detailed comparative study of American English in terms of orthography, pronunciation, syntax and usage, and traces the reasons for increasing acceptability of American English in India.

Jaydeep Sarangi in his socio-linguistic study of the Indian Variety of English (IVE) identifies the distinctive features of IVE in Indian Writing in English (IWE) and argues that though IVE makes a significant departure from standard British English it is not a 'pidgin' language; it is both creative and resourceful.

Dr V.K. Jain holds that there are so many regional and climatic factors impeding the correct use of the English living speech in regard to stress, intonation and rhythm that it demands an alert attention on the part of the teacher to the differences to take care of them.

In her well-researched paper Dr Sandhya Rani Sahoo very briefly but succinctly sums up the history of English education in India and pleads that since the most important objective of the instructional materials is to enable the learner to use the English language effectively and competently, both in speech and writing, it is supremely important to prepare instructional materials with utmost care covering "a wide range of themes from delineation of age-old problems of humanity to discussion of contemporary issues."

Dr P. Bhaskaran Nair also holds that the transition from structural syllabus to semantic syllabus calls for a redefinition of the instructional materials in terms of their social relevance.

In another insightful paper Dr P. Bhaskaran Nair recommends the practical application of the concept of "the zone of proximal development" (L.S. Vygotsky) and adaptation of the given instructional materials for a task-based instructional programme by the intuitive teacher.

Dr Meenakshi Raman, in her paper, highlights the relevance of ELT in the present context of increasing globalization and the responsibility of the teacher in making ELT meaningful, effective and relevant.

Dr Prakash Chandra Pradhan learns from his experience of teaching *Macbeth* that critical discussions of the play should be supplemented by some audio-visual performance to bring out the full import of the play as a text and as a play.

Dr Shubha Tiwari shares her classroom experience of teaching *Paradise Lost* and points out the areas of difficulty experienced by the students on account of the differences in cultural hegemony between the world of *Paradise Lost* and the world of *The Ramayana*.

Benson Agarwarker suggests a practical guideline for developing a better understanding of the perceptions and expectations of the learners to make ELT more effective than it is at present.

Dr Pratibha Gupta shows with examples from Maithili as to how an awareness of the socio-cultural factors operating in the speech act of the second language learner is essential both for effective teaching and for second language acquisition.

Dr K. Balachandran shows when learning a language becomes a load and when not, and believes that "the present language education in India needs a thorough overhauling" in the best interests of the students.

Dr R.P. Singh strongly advocates a bilingual approach to ELT, because the mother tongue is "not just a verbal pile. It is a psychology, an environment, a source of cultural and cognitive sustenance, an emotion, a bond and many collateral things." Instead of preventing L-1 interference the teacher should try to exploit the resources of the mother tongue in the pedagogical endeavour.

Dipak J. Barua feels that the methodology used at present for teaching English has lost touch with reality and pleads for a search for a new methodology in the changed social and political scenario of the country.

Dr V.K. Jain makes some useful observations on the methods of teaching comprehension.

Sisir Kumar Chatterjee, in his well-researched paper makes a micro-analysis of Rushdie's use of language in *Midnight's Children* and shows as to how "Rushdie succeeds in abrogating the 'classical' English and linguistically dragging the peripheral to the central."

Dr Santosh Chakrabarti discovers a distinct and not very distant echoes and reverberations of Joyce's linguistic devices in Arundhati Roy's use of language in *The God of Small Things*.

Mukta Mahajan examines the function of linguistic deviations in translation in the light of various translation theories.

Dr Nandini Sahu makes out a case for Indian poetics as a significant body of critical criteria and pleads for their application in judging Western literature.

Professor Rama Kundu in her highly perceptive study examines Hopkins's concept of "Inscape" in the light of the Indian theory of *Dhvani* and sheds new light on the energy dynamics of the language of Hopkins's poetry.

In his scholarly paper on Sanskrit grammar and linguistics Professor Amar Nath Jha shows Panini anticipates most modern linguistic theories.

Dr Madan M. Sarma argues that "the most positive contribution of structuralism is to free literature and the process of literary creation from mystification," but holds that it is an idealist attitude.

Professor R.S. Pathak in his well-researched paper shows as to how the teaching of language and literature attained a high degree of excellence in ancient India.

Dr Bhaskar Roy Barman in his study of the philosophy of language offers a lucid exposition of the different theories of meaning.

I thank all the contributors for their luminous studies. I thank my colleague, Professor Rama Kundu for her valuable assistance in readying the Volume.

I am grateful to Dr K.R. Gupta, Chairman, Atlantic Publishers and Distributors, New Delhi, for the confidence evinced in me and for seeing the book through the press.

MOHIT K. RAY
Editor

Contents

1

The Life and Death of Languages

AMIYA BASU

The death of languages, surprisingly, is no less common than the death of human beings—only it is not reported every day. What surprises one more is the rate at which languages appear to be dying. According to a UNESCO survey (2002), several hundred languages in Australasia and the Americas disappeared without a trace during the 20th century, while a half of the 6000 or so languages spoken in the world today may become extinct in course of the 21st century. Most of these are minority, small-community languages, although languages with large numbers are not necessarily safe (Crystal 2000: 12-13).

The death of a language usually comes in the wake of what is known as language *decline,* a process in which a language is spoken by fewer and fewer people until it is spoken by nobody; the language dies with its last speaker. Any such death will mean snapping of ties with a source of inherited knowledge. A language community stores its collective wisdom in a wide range of linguistic codes and signs and, in the words of Ivanov (1992) [cited in Crystal 2000: 36] it is "a semiotic system" of understanding the world. This is perhaps why social psychologists insist on giving the child access to his mother tongue. This would promote linguistic sensitivity along with psychological security.

The death of a language is to be lamented from another point of view: we need linguistic diversity just as we do bio-diversity. In the language of ecology, the strongest eco-systems are those which are most diverse. The presence of multiple languages in a society—and, consequently, of multiple cultures—leads to a welcome cross-fertilization of thought. Even one fewer language leaves us that much poorer.

Linguistic human rights and minority education are the two emerging demands of the post-colonial, pluralist democracies of the 21st century. Curiously, only a thirty-odd of the world's 192 sovereign countries, including just half a dozen in Europe, have more than one official language. The concept of the monolingual nation-state is no longer promoted, but many observers feel (Skutnabb-Kangas 1981; Smolicz *et al* 2000) that the dangers of state-imposed monolingualism—based on the West's ideology of stability through uniformity—are very real. This is borne out by the West's aggressive marketing of its three principal languages.

The UNESCO survey unequivocally states that it is the pressure from dominant languages like English, French and mainstream Chinese that is drowning out minority languages. The pressure is not always overtly political. As Baker (2001) points out, the world's minority languages are losing out since they have little or no economic value against the majority languages with a stranglehold—through multinational companies headquartered in the West—on international commerce, communication and the media. The process of globalisation has only helped majority languages, especially English, to consolidate themselves, pushing minority languages to largely non-economic domains. The process of marginalisation has been described by Fishman (1989) as the 'folklorization' of a language—the use, in other words, of a minority language in economically low-status and insignificant sectors such as arts and religion, popular entertainment or non-sustainable developments in the rural zone. This often indicates the start of the decline of a language, as it gradually disappears from the 'serious' side of life and its use mainly found among senior citizens.

Sizable linguistic minorities notwithstanding, both Britain and USA follow a one-language policy. Crystal (1997) admits that Britain has done "relatively little" by way of mother-tongue education to its immigrants. Edwards (1985) [cited in Hoffmann 1991: 235] thinks that the 'melting pot' ideology, used in the context of United States, called for complete homogenization or 'Anglo-conformity' which was a reflection of the preferred policies in the English and American colonizing contexts. At the same time, both these countries have promoted the use of English as a foreign language with an eye to their economic interests in the developing countries, and the teaching of English to speakers of other languages has itself become an industry. All applicants to British and American universities from Asia and Africa are required to pass a stringent—and expensive—test of English, conducted by agencies of the two governments. The pressure, in particular, to use English for science and technology—Information Technology is the most recent example—is one of many ways in which the hegemony of an upmarket language is established. Cook (1996: 41) agrees that the pressure to use English for science is a form of "linguistic imperialism," a term first used by Phillipson (1992).

Phillipson argues that English is now the "cornerstone of the world capitalist system." At the core of its perceived status is Phillipson's concept of 'linguicism' which has replaced racism, now aiming at a "continuous creation of cultural inequalities between English and other languages." Phillipson believes that the dominance of English is a direct result of the careful construction of myths about its reach and linguistic powers.

Phillipson sees the imposition of a language from the erstwhile colonial powers as part of an intricate political design. The power, he says, is at the Centre (*i.e.*, the West) which dominates the Periphery (*i.e.*, the underdeveloped world). The dominance is manifested in a variety of ways, one of which is forcing the Periphery to use its languages. Thus English or French as a Centre language is used for trade between Periphery countries and the centre. A sample survey shows* that most former European-ruled colonies have retained English, French or Portugese, and not local languages, enjoying official status even after independence.

The decline and death of languages is often caused by sheer external pressure, but there is no doubt that it may also be the effect of more subtle causes. A minority speech community may, in terms of its own experience, opt not to

* See Cambridge Encyclopedia of Language, 359.

maintain its language but gradually veer to another, a process known as language *shift*. A shift is based on social relocation of a community and the shift of language will be only one in a whole sequence of far-reaching changes. Moreover, a shift is likely to be spread over two or more generations (Hoffmann 1991). The shift from Cornish to English in Cornwall, south-west England, provides an example.

Speakers of minority languages everywhere probably suffer from an inherent insecurity which is reflected in their move towards a majority language, and the majority language media constantly play on this insecurity. In television soap-operas, characters from Periphery communities who learn to speak a Centre language are, as a rule, figures of fun and the butt of jokes (Crystal 2000: 81). Seldom does one come across a speaker of a minority language who speaks the majority language well or correctly. The centre, by implication, has attributes which are way beyond the reach of the Periphery, both socially and intellectually. The destructive effect of the relentless campaign in the media has been likened to "cultural nerve gas" (Krauss 1992).

Combined with the legitimate desire for upward mobility, the psychological insecurity often prompts minority speech communities to assimilate to 'standard' majority languages. In South America, many speakers of Quechua and Aymara are migrating to Peru and shifting, conveniently, to Spanish. In 1998, Hispanic immigrants in the US State of California voted overwhelmingly in favour of proposal to drop the native tongue (Spanish in their case) as a medium of instruction in elementary school and go straightway for English.

Linguists speak of elaborate strategies like language maintenance and language planning when addressing problems such as language death on a major scale. One interesting case of language planning involved Modern Hebrew which was reconstructed from an original 5000-word base and expanded to be Israel's first language. The Basque language of Spain, once under threat from the France regime, provides a good example of language maintenance. It has now been officially recognised and is receiving governmental support. However, the official action apart, in both cases the prosperity of the languages could be directly linked to popular sentiments as well as sustained political campaigns. The support from the government came only as the crest of a powerful wave of nationalism. After all, it is a community's socio-political aspirations that finally decide the destiny of a language.

From a study of number of majority and minority languages, Crystal (2000: 81) coasts to the conclusion that fostering positive attitudes (*i.e.*, being proud of one's language, among other things) could be one of the most important initiatives in the task of language preservation. Evidence tells us that when a speech community develops a negative self-image, when it believes it is linguistically backward, decline sets in. It is then that a minority language becomes vulnerable to all kinds of external pressure. A language does actually live on that bit of pride in itself; it is a question of self-belief, as Prof. Higgins had been saying in Shaw's *Pygmalion*.

WORKS CITED

Baker, C. Review of 'Linguistic Minorities and Modernity'—*Journal of Sociolinguistics*, Vol. 5 No. 4, 2001.

Cook, V. *Second Language Learning and Language Teaching*. London: Arnold, 1996.

Crystal, D. *The Cambridge Encyclopedia of Language*. Cambridge: CUP, 1997.

Crystal, D. *Language Death*, Cambridge; CUP, 2000.

Fishman, J. *Language and Ethnicity in Minority Sociolinguistic Perspective*. Clevedon: Multilingual Matters, 1989.

Hoffmann, C. *An Introduction to Bilingualism*. Harlow: Longman Group, 1991.

Krauss, M. 'The World's Languages in Crisis' in *Language* 68, 1992.

Phillipson, R. *Linguistic Imperialism*. Oxford: OUP, 1992.

Skutnabb-Kangas, T. *Bilingualism or Not*. Clevedon: MM, 1981.

Smolicz, J.J. Nical, I & Secombe, M.J. 'Educational Policies & Language Maintenance: Australia and the Philippines' in the *International Journal of Bilingual Education & Bilingualism*, Vol. 3: 4, 2000.

UNESCO, *The Atlas of the World's Language in Danger of Disappearing*. Paris, 2002.

2

The English Language

MALLIKARJUN PATIL

According to C.L. Wrenn language is an expression of man in words. Language is a medium of expression and as 20th century linguist Prof. Michael Halliday says, it is a semiogenic process, which helps man to understand himself and the world. Language has limitless uses. Its shades of meaning include indicative, emotive and symbolic. Since man is a thinking animal, he is a talking animal too and he has to exploit language to its fullest possible extent.

English is one such language which because of its multifarious facets and universal features, has, these days, become most useful to the welfare of mankind. The general characteristics of English are that it is extraordinarily receptive and it has an adaptable heterogeneousness. However English was a pure language when Anglo-Saxons first conquered England in 5th Century AD, today it is the most mixed of the languages. A second outstanding feature of English is its simplicity of inflexion. Its relatively fixed word—order is its third hallmark. It has round about ways of saying due to the loss of inflexions. It uses prepositions. A fifth quality of English is the development of new varieties of intonations for expressing shades of meaning which were formerly indicated by varying the shapes of words. These five features have made English so much popular that today it is spoken by the largest number of people all over the world.

But it does not mean English is a language very easy to speak. To speak in English means one has to learn it with constant care and industry. English is easy to speak 'badly,' but difficult to master.

A careful study of some elements of world languages drives home the point that at one time in the past, most of language had shared some common elements. For example, the Sanskrit *Pitra* and *Matra,* the English *father* and *mother* and the Latin *Patre* and *Matre* display this element of onetime togetherness. In this light English and Sanskrit bear certain resemblance. Therefore, English is said to belong to the family of Indo-European languages. This is also called Indo-Germanic or Indo-Aryan. The term Indo-European is used as it covers all the major languages—eastern and western. 'Indo-European' world group has eight sub-groups or families such as Balto-Slavic, Indo-Iranian, Armenian, Albanian in the east and Greek, Latin, Celtic and German in the west and English belongs to the Germanic sub-group. The common features of Indo-European languages share a similar structures (Parts of Speech) and common roots in vocabulary.

English like Dutch, Scandinavian and German, belongs to the primitive or common Germanic (Teutonic). These languages have stress system and two-tense system in verb. This stress system makes English words end weak or consonantal.

Well, in the 5th century, the German tribes of Angles, Saxons and Jutes invaded the then Romanised Britain and they spoke 'Low Germanic' whose dialects were Dutch, Flemish and English. Bede says English language of the first millennium was known as Saxon. Later King Alfred called it Englise or Angles. The term old English is referred to as Anglo-Saxon English (Upto 1100 AD). Middle English is from 1100 to the end of middle ages (1500 A.D.) and therefrom starts the era of Modern (New) English.

Old English was homogenous and inflexional. Its word order was relatively free, while in pronunciation it had no silent syllables. Just at the close of 11th century, some Latin and Norse started influencing the language.

Middle English began with Norman Conquest, which along with Scandinavian invasions, influenced the vocabulary of English language. French scribes, the use of Latin for learned work and of Norman French for aristocratic entertainment, reduced English to a set of dialects. So for some time English became a dialect language. But once when London turned into a commercial hub, English gained an upperhand over the French. This period of Middle English ends in 1500 A.D.

King Alfred who ruled England supremely in 9th century came from West-Saxon area and made West Saxon the standard language. But the present day standard English is based upon South-Eastern or East Midland type which we call as RP today, while Alfred's English has become 'Cockney.' Modern English which is greatly affected by Caxton's revolution in printing is divided into Early. Modern and Later Modern English, the former being extended upto Dryden's death in 1700. Later Modern English is characterised by the loss of inflexions, fixation of word-order and greater use of prepositions. Yet the language is constantly fluid, and it needs to be appreciated in relation to thought, feeling and form.

Of all world languages, English is the most copious heterogeneous and varied, because its vocabulary is highly affected by several sources such as Latin Fathers of the Church, Danish and Norwegian invaders, Renaissance, the Italian artists and Men of letters. Certainly the influence of Latin is substantial. Words such as 'street,' 'mill,' 'cheese,' 'minister,' 'mass,' 'bishop' are Latin. Though Aelfric, a medieval English prose writer tried to keep English homogenous, he did not succeed. The same is true of the 19th century Dorset philologist William Barnes. So Latin influenced the grammatical terminology of English. As a Germanic Language, English belongs to a different group of Indo-European family from Latin, but is heavily influenced by Latin. The difficulties related to the usages of 'It is I' and 'who' and 'whom' are due to Latinate complications. Scientific writers like Francis Bacon and Sir Isaac Newton wrote in Latin thinking that Latin was an everlasting language. Even Thomas More's *Utopia* is in Latin. This made Shakespeare and his men criticise them. However the overuse of Latin by 17th century writers like Milton and Sir Thomas Browne resulted into pedanticity, or 'Un-English,' Latin has helped English formidably. For instance, the so-called suffixes like—*ic*, *-ate* and *–al* are Latin.

What is true of Latin influence on English vocabulary is also true of Greek influence on English. It is said many Greek words entered English through Latin and French. Greek medical science has given English much terminology.

Likewise, French too has heavily influenced English. When the Saxon King Ethelred, the Unready (978-1016) married a Norman princess, the links between England and French promoted. Norman nobles, French culture and fashionable way of life, conquest of William of Normandy in 1060, French legal terms, University of Paris, 100 years of war, literature, social intercourse loan words in terms of art, letters, textiles and furniture, diplomacy, Renaissance, French revolution etc. affected the nature of English words and pronunciation. For example, French words like Castle, prison, tower, mercy, passion, image, war, lamp, soup, par excellence, brochure—entered English and there are as many as 18 French words in Chaucer's introduction to prologue. In terms of pronunciation, the Norman French brought into English the sound *ch* in place of English sound *c*(*k*). So we have Chancellor in place of cancellor. (Wicing became Viking). Likewise because of *w* in place of g, we have *warden* and *warrant* in place of *guardian* and *guarantee* respectively. Dryden followed the French literary form of drama called 'Comedy of Manners' in literature and made fun of Frenchified English.

Third important influence on English is Scandinavian. Denmark, Norway, Sweden and Iceland are Scandinavian countries. Some people of these nations invaded northern districts of England in fifth century and some of their words like, egg, fellow, husband, tungsten came into English.

Similar is the German influence. We know English is basically a Germanic language. But it is a 'Low Germanic' language like the Dutch, Flemish and Frisian. English acquired words from these other low Germanic languages.

Italian influence on English is more in terms of art and painting. English men liked to live like Italians in 16th century and Shakespeare and Ben Johnson attacked the same. Some Italian words are stanza, canto and studio.

Spanish words *patato, renegade*; Portuguese words *caste, pagoda, ayah*; Welsh word *bard* have entered into English. One time Cornish, Scottish, Gaelic, Welsh belonged to the Celtic family of languages, while Czech, Polish, Hungary and Russian belonged to Slavonic language which have given us words such as intelligentsia, robot and mammoth. Many Arab words from Indian vernaculars, words from China, Japan, Australia, Borneo, Malaya, Africa, Haiti and South Sea Islands also have entered the stream of English vocabulary.

Besides, cant, slang and colloquial too have gone into the making of literary English. Alfred, the King, William Barnes, and William Morris attempted to add a local colour to English by bringing dialects into use.

Spelling and pronunciation are the two changing facets of English language, because of variations in each. They are like Thunderbolt and lightening of the environment. The reformation of English spelling and pronunciation has been attempted in every age. Aelfric, Chaucer, Shakespeare and others have reformed the system. English, once had been a phonetic language, but later, due to different continental influences, became slightly un-phonetic. For example, word 'curc' became 'church' when English *c* was replaced by French 'ch' and cancellor became Chancellor later. Earlier 'y' and 'u,' 'u' and 'v' as well as 'f' and 'v' were interchangeable. Due to French influence 'riht' became right and 'gost' became 'ghost.' First the suffixes '-s' and 'es' were in the shape of 'th' and 'eth.' But Caxton and Wynken de Worde, the printers and Dr Samuel Johnson, Dryden and Swift, the writers reformed the English spelling system in their own ways. Printing, compulsory education, radio, cinema and computers today have furthered a linguistic reform. English Academy, Society for Pure English, the ELBS etc. have been set up to make English a living world language. Accordingly Noah Webster in America has updated the spelling system. Stress and intonation have enriched English, while dialects are its great wealth. These components give different shades of meanings. Localities have played an important role in making English vivid and expressive. Homophones (ex-red—read) and homonyms (lead-lead) have added an extra dimension. Archaism have brought in a romantic atmosphere and effected mystery. Thackeray, Spencer, Keats have made use of this in literature.

In the course of the history of English language, as we know, some individuals too have contributed to the making of English. These influences are the Bible, William Shakespeare, Chaucer, Milton, Pope, Dr. Johnson, Wordsworth and others.

The Bible work done by Wyclif, Tyndale, Coverdale, Calvinists, Jesuits, the King James people have brought in diverse elements into English.

English language today has been different because of modern happenings. American speech is one of them. Radio, Cinema, TV, Newspaper, Computer, Internet, discoveries and inventions in the fields of science and commerce, pop-culture and the process of globalization have modernised the language.

We must aim for good English which is clear, intelligible, uniform in spelling and pronunciation, rhythmic and good in intonation. For maintaining speech standards, the BBC along with its Advisory Committee on spoken English has made the language pleasing and natural. Societies like ELBS, have been set up to train speech habits. Speech therapies make the speakers' use of language clear, natural and extremely effective. So 'proper words in proper places.' Today, we have to make use of linguistic discipline and self-controlling. Basic English spelling reform and phonetic spelling is prepared and taught to make English a Global Language just with 850 words.

3

English in Beginnings

SHAILENDRA KUMAR MUKUL

When we look at the large fabric of English literature, we find in it a mosaic of many colours. It is because it bears the different shades of racial characteristics. "The prismatic fancy of the Celt, the sombre passion of the Teuton, the golden gaiety of France, Scandinavian grey's Italian purples"[1] and so on, all with the passage of time have gone to its making. But among all these characteristics the most predominant is the characteristic of the Anglo-Saxons who gave England its name, its language and its culture.

The history of British islands goes far back to the Palaeolithic and Neolithic ages when dark curly-haired primitive race lived near the Thames and used tools and weapons made of stone. Then these islands were subject to a series of invasions by Celts, Britons, Angles, Saxons and Jutes. The Celts drove the original inhabitants to the West and North but thoroughly intermingled with them. The Britons came to Britain in about 300 B.C., settled largely in the south-west and were later known as the Welsh. In the 5th century A.D. three Germanic tribes Angles, Saxons and Jutes—came to Britain from the low-lying country in the East. These tribes originally lived on the shores of the Baltic and the North sea in the eastern lowlands which the Roman historian Tacitus called by the general name of Germania. They were heathens and lived a pastoral life on the shores of the sea and in the clearings of the forest. They worshipped not Christ but Odin and their earlier literature had been oral. It consisted of songs and stories heroic and stirring in character.

But with the passage of time, these tribes gave up their old ways of life and came under the influence of Christianity. Rome was already the seat of Christian religion and in the 6th century A.D. monstery in Iona, one of the British isles, was established by an Irish missionary, St. Columba. The sixth century A.D. witnessed not only the foundation of monastery in Iona but also the landing of St. Augustine, the Roman missionary, in Kent and the conversion of its Anglo-Saxon King Ethelbert to Christianity. In the seventh century A.D. the Anglo-Saxons were converted to Christianity and began to cultivate new culture and learning. The Venerable Bede, a scholarly churchman, produced in Latin a monumental work *Ecclesiastical History of English People* in the 8th century. In the same century *Beowulf* (750 A.D.), "the greatest of Germanic epic poems,"[2] was composed in Old English. Besides this heroic poem, there are also some short elegies like "The Wanderer," "The Seafarer" and "Deor." These elegies are lyric laments—the laments of an exile, a hungry sailor on the wintry seas and a wife parted from her husband. The following is the refrain of "Deor":

That was overcome so may this be.[3]

Beowulf is a long narrative poem composed by an anonymous Christian scribe in Britain. But the material of which it was composed belongs to the distant, pagan land of earlier times. The poem, therefore, is a mosaic of pagan tales placed in a Christian setting. It falls into two major parts. In the first part, Beowulf, a mighty warrior of royal Swedish blood, comes to the court of King Hrothgar of Denmark in order to save him from a man-eating monster, Grendel. The monster often comes to the King's great hall of Heorot to prey upon his warrior. Beowulf fights with this monster and wounds him to death. When monster's mother comes to take revenge upon Beowulf, he follows her to her under-water home. After a desperate struggle he fortunately finds a huge sword with which she is slain. The second part takes place fifty years later when Beowulf, the nephew of King Hygelac of the Geats, is now himself the king of the Geats. A dragon guarding a hoard of treasures has been disturbed and is, therefore, wreaking "slaugther throughout the land."[4] Beowulf fights with the dragon and kills it. But he receives its venomous poison during the struggle and dies a heroic death. At the time of his death, he speaks boldly of his valour:

> I have held the people fifty years; there was not any king of my neighbours, who dared to greet me with warriors, to oppress me with terror [...].[5]

Beowulf, the oldest surviving epic of the Teuton people, contains more than three thousand lines. Though its scenes and people are Scandinavian, the language is purely Anglo-Saxon, the English language at its early stage. Beowulf is held in high esteem and regarded as "the early English ideal of virile courage and nobility."[6] He is to the English what Achilles is to the Greek, Romulus to the Roman and Charlemagne to the French.

Caedmon is the first Anglo-Saxon Christian poet. He sang of the Creation, the Exodus from Egypt and the passion of Jesus Christ. Bede in his *Ecclesiastical History of the English People* said that Caedmon was a lowly lay brother in the monastery of St. Hilda at Whitby. He had no gift of songs and, therefore, always withdrew from the singing ceremony of the hall. Once in the night one came to him in his sleep and commanded him to sing. At his bidding Caedmon sang verses and in the morning he remembered what he sang. As he was unable to read the Bible, it was read to him by monks and he went on to turn its passages into verse. These stories in verse known as *Caedmon's Paraphrase* were written in the 7th century and marked an early stage in the development of Anglo-Saxon religious poetry.

Cynewulf is the second Anglo-Saxon Christian poet. He is a Northumbrian who lived at the close of eighth century and signed his work by means of runic letters woven into the poem. His four Christian poems, *Christ, Juliana, Elene* and *The Fates of the Apostles*, are distinguished by their genuine religious passion and remarkable craftsmanship. *Christ* deals with the three-fold coming of Jesus Christ—the Advent, the Ascension and Doomsday. The Dialogue between Virgin Mary and St. Joseph creates a dramatic situation and serves as the earliest extant dramatic passage in English literature. Anglo-Saxon religious poetry in the hands of Cynewulf moves from the mere biblical paraphrase to the didactic and the mystical.

However, all Christian poems of the Anglo-Saxons are not contained in the biblical paraphrases and the lives of saints and apostles. There are some others also, such as *The Phoenix* and the *Didactic Poems. The Phoenix* is a short Latin poem composed by the fourth-century poet Lactantius who derived his subject from Ovid and Claudian and transformed the mythological phoenix into "a symbol of Christ and the Christian soul."[7] It is a work of eighty-five distichs, conventional in style and spoilt by its dryness and much enigmatic turn. But the poet who has elaborately treated the theme in seven hundred lines has the advantage over his model. Here, Anglo-Saxon plenty successfully relieves the effects of a Latin drought. The poet brings new moving warmth into his treatment of a subject which mythological memories and terms had frozen to lifelessness. His endearing description of the paradise in which the phoenix dwells is preferable to the cold brevity of Latin. It is true that either northern impotence or Anglo-Saxon rhetoric has made the poet unequal to painting a flowery and sunny place of delights. It is also true that he is most at ease when he is paraphrasing the list of the scourges which this Eden is spared. But even in this too negative description there is more charm than the poets of his country were wont to put into their pictures. His smooth and ample uses succeed in suggesting the marvellous harmony of the songs of the Phoenix. The poem ends with the ardent homily whose unctions and melody make it one of the most attractive of the alliterative verses.

Among the didactic poems, *Gifts of Men, Weirds of Men,* and *Ten Instructions of a Father to his Son* are noteworthy. In these, Anglo-Saxon poetry is sententious. *Dialogues between Solomon and, Saturn* is more curious where the fantastic varies the didactic. These dialogues are imitations of a lost Latin original as well as the prototypes of the dialogues between Solomon and Marcolf, very popular in the Middle Ages. Saturn is a Chaldean prince who comes of a family of demons and has nothing in common with the god of mythology. He is acquainted with all books except *Pater Noster* which Solomon explains to him. It is not that Christian morality always finds expression in such amusing fictions. It also loves to create the lugubrious images of death and decomposition to humiliate the body which tempts the soul away from the path of salvation. Hence the struggles between body and soul attracted the Anglo-Saxon poets. In *discourse of the Soul to its Body* the soul inveighs against the body which now suffers the pains of hell for the sins committed by it. The soul feels revengeful and, therefore, describes with savage joy the decomposition of the fatal body.

It is not that the Anglo-Saxons wrote only poetry: some of them came out as good prose-writers of their time. King Alfred of Wessex (871-899) was a remarkable genius indeed. There was in him a rare combination of the warrior, the patriot and the patron. He fought against the Danes, united all the kingdoms of Southern England and translated a series of Latin prose-works into Old English. He either translated Bede's *Historia Ecclesiastica* (Ecclesiastical History of the English People) in Latin into English prose or inspired its translation by another hand. He instituted the great Anglo-Saxon Chronicle, a continuous record of important events in England.

Aelfric, the pupil of the monastic school founded by Aethelwold at Abingdon, wrote *Colloquium* for teaching Latin by conversation. He produced a vocabulary which was the first Latin-English dictionary. But he made his name by *Homilies*, his compilations and translations from the Father of the Church which form two series of forty sermons each. Aelfric's prose, unlike that of Alfred, is written not to be read but to be spoken to the people in the conventional sermonic tone of a priest. Hence, its rhythms are nearer to verse and sentences are divided into sections, more or less equivalent to the metrical line. Because of this reason, scholars were for long uncertain whether to call Aelfric's writings either prose or verse. This poetic prose marks a great advance on that of Alfred. It aims at beauty, measure and harmony. There is much less awkwardness and effort in the connection of phrases than in Alfred's prose.

Wulfstan, the Archbishop of York from 1002 to 1023, was first of all a preacher. The most remarkable of his homilies dates from 1012 when the English were suffering the evils of the Danish invasions. In his homilies he deplores the irreligion and immorality of his people and proclaims the near advent of the great chastiser, the Antichrist. Though Wulfstan as an artist is inferior to Aelfric, the popular emphasis of his language gives it rich colour and lively tones.

English language that we speak today directly owes to Anglo-Saxon prose and verse. Our use of similes, metaphors and alliterations is not new. It is derived from the poetical method employed in our earliest verse where the sun is described as "the candle of heaven"[8] or "the jewel of the sky."[9] In Anglo-Saxon verse a line is normally divided into two parts by a strong caesura; and each part carries two stresses where one or two of the stressed syllables are alliterated:

> Flód under fóldan nis that féor heonon.[10]

There is nothing new about it as all English verse is stressed and has alliterations here and there. But the sledge-hammer Anglo-Saxon stress at times mars the metrical effect and the verse becomes quite unmelodious. The harsh combination of consonants do help in destroying the rhythms of poetry. For example, the "raven" sounds hoarser when it is used as "hraefn." Hardly is there any stanza-form in Anglo-Saxon verse; and rhyme occurs only by accident. However, we have an example of so-called *Rhyming Poem*.

The poetry of the Anglo-Saxons is archaic. Generally, it reverts to traditional turns of expression, to words almost consecrated. But the case with the Anglo-Saxon prose is quite different. It tries to observe the rules of ordinary speech unless it has to copy the Latin prose of the clerks. Its object is not to move but to instruct and inform. Since it educates our understanding, it obviously turns to future. Therefore, it is not surprising to find that the prose-writings of the Anglo-Saxons are much nearer to our speech. No revolution seems to separate Alfred's pages from those of Caxton, Aelfric's from Wyclif's. There is a change but no break. National and linguistic continuity seems to exist right from the days of the Anglo-Saxons to the present.

Still, Anglo-Saxon, English has some grammatical features which distinguish it from the English of the rest of the periods. For example, "p" in Old English stands for both voiced and voiceless sounds represented by O in "this" and θ in "thin." It is known as "thorn." Besides "*thorn*," there is also "yogh" in Old English which is symbolized by "3." It represents "y" and "hh" sounds. Short vowels in Old English, such as a, e, i, o, u are pronounced respectively as in French "patte," English "pet," "pit," "pot" and "put." Final unstressed "e" is generally syllabic and has a sound akin to "schwa" as in "China." Long vowels in Old English, such as a, i, u are pronounced respectively as in father, feel and fool. Among the vowels, "e" and "o" pose some problems because these letters fail to distinguish between open "o" and close "o" and between open "e" and close "e." The usual inflexions in Old English are –e, -en, -ene (plural), -er (comparative): and –est (superlative). There are also verbal inflexions, such as –ep, -ede (-de, -te), -ed (-d, -t), -ynge (-inde, ende). The nominative plurals generally end in –es as in "workes," –is as in "wittis," –en as in "Chyldren." The past form of weak verbs generally lose the final –e and therefore, end only in –ed instead of –ede. Strong verbs in plural number generally end in –en. But there are a few instances when the plural form –eden also occurs as in "lyueden."

Anglo-Saxon poetry has peculiar charm. Its movement is slow and leisurely. Its rhythm does not allow readers to hurry on rapidly but to linger deliberately on each line and pause before going on to the next. Nor are the poet's thoughts too light and swift; and he often says the same thing twice or thrice. Where a single "he" can suffice, he prefers to describe a person in several ways, such as "the brave prince, the bright hero, noble in war, eager and spirited."[11] Though these descriptions contribute very little to the mental picture, they impress us artistically and work upon our emotions, very much like repetitions and variations in music. These effects are chiefly produced by heaping synonym on synonym. For example, in *Beowulf* there are at least thirty-six words for 'hero' or 'prince,' twelve for 'battle' or 'fight,' eleven for 'ship' or 'boat' and so on.

The verse rhythm of Anglo-Saxon poetry is not regular. It undergoes several variations and responds to the nature of the subject. There are no definite number of syllables which neither make rhyme nor form a stanza. Yet, poetry in Anglo-Saxon period was sung. In early times poetry and music were one and indivisible and the minstrel was free to modify the movement of the verse. But the modification made by minstrel was not wanton. It was based on certain rules; and there were always four accented syllables and three alliterative syllables. The form of poetry used in Anglo-Saxon period was generally epic. It suited both the subject and style and lent itself to the treatment of heroic deeds. William Morris's translations of the Scandinavian Sagas is an important work suggesting the characteristics of early English poetry.

REFERENCES

1. Arthur Compton-Rickett, *A History of English Literature* (London: Thomas Nelson and Sons Ltd., 1958), 1.
2. M.H. Abrams, *A Glossary of Literary Terms* (New York: Holt, Rinehart and Winston, Inc., 1971), 117.
3. Cited by Herbert Grierson and J.C. Smith, *A Critical History of English Poetry* (Middlesex: Penguin Books Ltd., 1962), 11.
4. David Daiches, *A Critical History of English Literature* (Bombay: Allied Publishers Private Ltd., 1979), 9.
5. Cited by Compton-Rickett, 5.
6. *Ibid.*, 6.
7. Emile Legouis and Louis Cazamian, *A History of English Literature* (London: J.M. Dent and Sons Ltd., 1957), 47.
8. Cited by Grierson and Smith, 14.
9. *Ibid.*, 14.
10. *Ibid.*, 14.
11. Otto Jespersen, *Growth and Structure of the English Language* (India: Oxford University Press), 47.

4

Elizabethan Prose: A Note on Its Contribution to the Growth of English Prose

SHARAD RAJIMWALE

Whenever Elizabethan literature is mentioned names of Christopher Marlowe, Michael Drayton, Edmund Spenser, Samuel Daniel and Shakespeare come to mind in all their poetic-dramatic splendour. The spirit of poetry, 'a divine gift and heavenly instrument, not to be gotten by labour and learning, but adorned by both, and poured into the wit by a certain *enthousiasmus* and celestial inspiration' presided over the age. Who talks of Elizabethan prose but as a feeble stream, a loose tradition of unruly outpourings catering to the low taste, and so forth?

Yet it seems Elizabethan prose writings represent a continuation of the tradition that had its origin in Anglo-Saxon times, in Boethius, for example, and laid the foundations of such *genres* as novel, serious philosophical tracts and pamphleteering that by the beginning of the eighteenth century engaged nearly all great literary figures. In the fifteenth and sixteenth centuries English almost completely regained its lost prestige under the force of such writers as Sir Thomas Elyot (1490-1546), Roger Ascham (1515-68), Richard Mulcaster, John Lyly (1533-1606) and others. Though classical languages and authors, mainly, Latin and French provided the ideals in thought and literature, more and more Englishmen had begun to realise 'our language did not have at its birth such enemies in gods and stars [...].' A great deal of literary activities was carried on in English. We must clearly understand here that English prose in the age generally sought to address the common man, whether in the form of translations of the Latin-Green-French tracts or such romance works as *Reynard the Fox* (1481) or *Certain Tragical Discourse Written out of French and Latin* (1567), or composed originally in English. Even during the period of almost complete Norman predominance, English continued to be used by general masses as vehicle of communication. Movement towards greater increase in the use of English was facilitated by the sudden rise in prose writings. There can be located five major domains of prose writing:

(i) Religio-philosophical debates
(ii) Romance and fiction
(iii) Pamphleteering
(iv) History
(v) Explorations overseas

The great religious-theological controversies of the Reformation movement spill over into the Elizabethan period. Efforts to translate the Bible needed tremendous courage and grit as was shown by William Tyndal and Miles Coverdale, Hugh Cranmer, John Jewel, John Knox, John Foxe. Their persecution, sacrifices and later on acceptance of the translated versions are too well-known to need mention here, what needs must be emphasized however is that English was chosen as the medium in which to carry on this long-drawn out battle of wits. Even such a staunch supporter of Latinate style as Sir Thomas More had to use English to counter his opponents. English was forging a refined argumentative style characterised by rational thinking. Reginald Pecock's (1395-1460) rationalism, John Leland's (1506-1552) dignified use of polemical approach, Archbishop Cranmer's tenacious search for clear, firm and confident English, Bacon's laborious endeavour to transform English into a language capable of conveying transparency of thought and scientific outlook—they all represent the sudden release of manifold forces that swelled the stream.

A spate of translations that began with the Bible continued in all fields, philosophical and scholarly tracts were rendered by Lord Berner (Froissart's *Chronicles*), Sir John Walsh (Erasmus's *Enchiridion*), John Bale and Edward Hall and a host of others. All kinds of translation were done: historical (Raphael Holinshed ranks foremost), scientific, works related to geographical exploration, etc.; but what captured the masses most were the Italian and French novellas and stories. Malory's *Morte'd Arthur* had already awakened an interest in fiction which from the opponents met with angry protestations ('these ungracious books set out in print [...] which is most to be lamented'). But the growing interest in 'the lighter and, it must be allowed, looser continental writings' could hardly be stemmed. So we have Geoffrey Fenton, Belleforest, Launay, William Painter and Arthur Brooke doing the spade-work for establishing a tradition of fiction which really took off in a big way in the eighteenth century. In this way while windows were being thrown open to Romance fiction, John Lyly, Sir Philip Sidney, Robert Greene, Thomas Nash, Gascoigne, Deloney and Heywood were producing their own fictional work in what has been described—as 'homely prose [...] sharp, witty, earnest, with such gusto and drive, such wealth of language and imagination, such compelling rhythm that burns with life.' They were loose and shapeless, presenting scenes and incidents that were drawn from the common life of a society tossed around by historical controversies and political turmoil. So rich is this wealth that dramatists like Shakespeare, Spenser, Marlowe and later Ben Jonson derived inspiration for their plots, characters, scenes and even speeches from these narratives. Thomas Lodge's *Rosalynde: Euphues Golden Legacy* gave plot for Shakespeare's *Winter's Tale*, Shakespeare liberally used Elizabethan pamphlets and jest books such as *Scoggin's Jests* (1566), *Tarlton's Jests* (1592) and *Skelton's Merry Tales* (1567) to pepper his comedies and histories. Thomas Deloney's *Thomas of Reading* must have provided a lot of stuff of which Lady Macbeth is made. Great historical books of Raphael Holinshed, Richard Stany Hurst and William Harrison and the wonderful accounts of the great geographical explorations of Richard Haklyut (1553-1616) and Francis Drake (1540-96), Sir Walter Raleigh (1554-1618), and Richard Eden filled the imagination of such contemporary poets and dramatists as Michael Drayton who wrote of 'a thousand kingdoms' to be discovered, Daniel, George, Chapman, Barnfield and Shakespeare. *The Tempest* and *The Merchant of Venice* clearly suggest how deeply Shakespeare was indebted to the explorers' accounts for his scenic and verbal beauty. It is Marlowe who directly transformed Haklyut into poetry whether we take Faustus's flight to India for gold or Tamburlaine ever aspiring to new discoveries and conquests. It is not just for information that the prose works were used; but instances can be found when works like *The Unfortunate Traveller, Jack of Newbury* and *Alarm of Usurers* so rich with tales of mystery and murder, colourful expressions and idioms, often were used by poets and playwrights. *Thomas of Reading* for instance, has scenes and situations that remind one of *Macbeth*. It is surprising how the English prose of the period brought into print common man's language and stylistic manners and made them popular among renaissance playwrights. Perhaps in no other period writers enjoyed so much using ever new words, inventing and bandying them around; as Helen Morris says, 'Writers enjoyed stringing together long lists of words, potentially abusive ones [...]. Even ordinary unliterary people became intoxicated with 'words, words, word's; [...] Elizabethans exulted in their freedom, playing with language for its own sake, revelling in what Spenser called, "the brightness of brave and glorious words." They were truly intoxicated with the exuberance of their own verbosity, as was Shakespeare's Armado

> One whom the music of his own vain tongue
> Doth ravish like enchanting harmony.

It is only in the Victorian period that one comes across in such writers as Charles Dickens a true and crazy delight in the use of words.

But the Elizabethans were also very concerned, very careful to give a high status to their 'vulgar tunge' which had suffered so much during the great ascendancy period of Latin and French. 'But for the uttering sweetly and properly the conceit of the minde, which is the end of speech, that (English) hath it equally with any other tongue in the world,' said Richard Carew in *The Excellency of the English Tongue* (1595). He was not alone in his anxiety for the language which often through comparison with Greek and Latin was relegated to subsidiary position and now needed to be elevated. 'If physicians be angry, that I have written physicke in englische, let them remember the grekes wrate in greke, the Romans in latine, Avicenna and the other in Arabike, which were their own proper and maternall tongues,' wrote Sir Thomas Elyot in *Castle of Health* (1534). Roger Ascham, Richard Mulcaster, Thomas Drant, George Pettie, John Hart, Thomas Smith, Richard Stanyhurst, Charles Butler, William Bulloker, were all engaged in the raging discussion over improving English. Smith's *Dialogue concerning the correct and Emended Writing of the English Language* (1568), Hart's *An Orthographie* (1569), Bulloker's *Booke at Large, for the Amendment of Orthographie for English Speech* (1580), George Pettie's *Civil Conversation* (1586) and Charles Butler's *The Institution of Letters, Syllables and Words in the English Tung* paved was for later writers like Jonathan Swift, and Dr. Samuel Johnson to initiate a vigorous movement for what Swift called 'ascertaining and fixing' English spelling and standardizing its vocabulary and syntax.

It is curious how in foregrounding the poetic and dramatic genius of Elizabethan age we tend to overlook the achievements and endeavours of its prose writers. Elizabethan prose indeed presents a highly variegated and many-sided output that containing the seeds of several literary prose genres of the future period.

WORKS CONSULTED

Baugh, A.C. and Cable Thomas. *A History of the English Language*. London and New York: Routledge and Kegan Paul, 1987.

Chambers, E.K., *English Literature at the Close of the Middle Ages*. London: Oxford Clarendon Press, 1947.

Entwistle, William and J. Gillett Eric. *The Literature of English, A.D. 500-1950*. London: Longmans, Green and Co., 1952.

Lewis, C.S. *English Literature in the Sixteenth Century, Excluding Drama*. London: OUP, 1973.

Morris, Helen, *Elizabethan Literature*. London: OUP, 1958.

Snell, F.J. and Hales, John W. *The Age of Transition, 1400-1580*. London: G. Bell and Sons, Ltd., 1931.

5

Between the Metro & Municipality: Contemporary Teaching of English Literature in India*

AVADHESH KUMAR SINGH

I am not Prince Hamlet, nor was meant to be:
Am an attendant lord, one tha't will do
To swell a progress, start a scene or two.

—*T.S. Eliot*

The title of my paper "Between the Metro and Municipality" may appear to be a poor parody of R. Williams' much-acclaimed work *The Country and the City* (1975) with slight deviation, of course. Williams had put the country before the city whereas I have placed the Metro before the Municipality, for there is no space for the country or municipality in teaching of English literature; and the non-metro or municipality is in practice subservient to metropolitan priorities and prerogatives.

"[...] And we must read our literature by it (the sense of the past)," thus informed Lionel Trilling (Ramaswami and Seturaman 1986: 1). It is truer in case of teaching of literature—be it British or Indian literature, contemporary or otherwise. Colonial considerations and post-colonial compulsions need to be understood here as part of politics that condition and govern, as they did then, various aspects of our lives including teaching of literature in India. The introduction of English literature in India was a part of colonial strategy of establishing its supremacy and legitimizing itself. The Dispatch of 1824 by the Court of Directors of John Company noted:

* Reprinted from *The Critical Endeavour* with permission of the publisher.

> In teaching mere Hindoo or mere Mohammedan literature, you bound yourself to teach a great deal of what is frivolous, not a little of what was purely mischievous, a small remainder indeed in which utility was in anyway concerned. (Mishra 1961: 153)

T.B. Macaulay, as was natural to him, in his arrogant and now much infamous pronouncement, considered a single shelf of European books of greater worth than all the learning in Sanskrit, Persian and Arabic put together. Macaulay's words should not matter much for us at least now, for he did not know any of the languages referred by him, say the least about literatures in them. However, he indirectly suggested the necessity of introducing English literature to the colony.

Macaulay considered it necessary to make natives of the country good English scholars, and form a "class who may be interpreters between us and the millions whom we govern" (Young 1967: 729). It subsequently led to the establishment of universities in India and introduction of English literature as a means of social control—a less abrasive secular hegemonizing source in consonance with Charles Grant's advice to the state to maintain certain neutrality, else a blow will be struck at our power in India which in the course of time may prove fatal. But the introduction of English literature had less to do, as K.R.S. Iyengar had observed, "with the glories of the English 'canon' and rather more with a definitive course of hegemonic incorporation" (1962: 27).

To measure our attitude towards English literature in the pre-Independence era one may, to avoid an elongated discussion, take recourse to Gandhiji's views, however debatable they may be, for he was of our leaders most concerned and conscious of Indian situation and its dilemmas. His views on English as a language and English language as the medium of instruction are well-known to us and do not demand discussion here, for we have separated literature from language teaching or learning. He, however, had something equally pertinent to say about English literature, as he spoke of the impact of English literature:

> A word about literature. We had to learn several books of English prose and poetry. No doubt all this was

nice. But that knowledge has been of no use in serving or bringing me in touch with the masses. (*Young India* 1-6-21)

The difference between colonial and post-colonial function of English literature is easily discernible here, as Gandhiji laid emphasis on 'serving' the masses and bringing him in touch with them, whereas the Dispatch of the Directors kept 'utility' in their agenda. Further, Gandhiji was candid enough to suggest, to much of our embarrassment, irrelevance of teaching and learning of English literature, "I am unable to say that if I had not learnt what I did of English prose and poetry, I should have missed a rare treasure" (*Harijan*, 9-7-38).

Munshi Premchand, neither a political leader nor an active freedom fighter, but a renowned Urdu/Hindi writer, was conscious of enslaving influence of English language. Echoing Gandhiji he said, "It is the English language, so to say, grinds every segment of our literate society into submission [...]. The English language has so enchained our will and our intelligence that neither is left with the least initiative. Our educated classes are obliged to regard that yoke as a precious garland round their necks (Premchand 1957: 150-51). In the pre-Independent India, English language and even literature were associated with colonial rule. Hence, to throw off the yoke of thralldom, it was considered necessary to get rid of them. More than this, according to Gandhiji, it (English language) had "unfitted us for true national service" (Prabhu 1958: 8). English language suited Nehruvian model of secular modern India. As its consequence English anchored itself in the post-independent India. Rammanohar Lohia, a socialist and severe critic of the Nehruvian model, critiqued Nehruvian/Congress model including his/its attitude towards English. He said that Nehru knows "full well that English is a most potent of instrument of such a caste rule and that abolition of the public use of this language would of a sudden release the shackled mass of the people (Lohia 1972: 255-56). In continuation of English, he saw continuation of neo/colonial purpose in India. Terming it as 'an unmitigated curse' he said, "The chasms that separate man from man on account of birth, riches, caste, or education become terrifying and wholly unbridgeable on account of the public use of a foreign language. Some kind of a secret learning or secret magic comes to prevail [...] which is utterly comprehensible to the people, as they were listening to some charms and invocation of superstitious lore" (*Ibidem*: 327). Though he felt that English language "helps to cut the tongue and deaden the ear of ninety percent of the people (*Ibidem*: 106-07), yet he noted with dismay that English has come to stay in India and only a revolution can remove it (Lohia remarked).

At the beginning of the 21st century and even after celebrating the golden jubilee of our Independence, we find that revolution is yet to take place. If that happens, what shall become of us? We shall be jobless. Does the anxiety of the teachers of English hinder the advent of the 'impending' revolution? Are we 'really' capable of bringing about or hindering the arrival of a revolution?

English language and literature, fortunately or unfortunately, at least for our sake, survive and thrive in our country. It seems that Macaulay knew the fate of his language and literature in the alien land better than Mahatma Gandhiji or Lohia did the fate of an alien language and literature in their own land.

II

Macaulay in his "speech of 10 July 1933" had remarked that the British even after India's independence would leave a never decaying empire in India and that would be imperishable empire of our arts and our morals, our literature and laws" (Young 1967: 717). The pre-Independence teachers of English literature regarded themselves as representative of English, "British" and Western culture. Barring a few distinguished exceptions, pre-Independence teachers of English hardly strove to relate their laboriously acquired knowledge of English literature to Indian experience, thought, literature and culture. The teacher of English had a sense of pride in playing an ape to his British counterparts and replicating the Ox-bridge drawal. Without being rooted in his own environs or even willing to do so he lacked in inner strength and did nothing more than mouthing agreement with the English critics. Even at his best, he could not go beyond minor disagreements. He read and taught without relating his reading and teaching to the Indian situation. He longed to see the Albion's shore and be a part of it. And this was the best and the easiest way. Yet, to be honest, some of them could inspire generations of students and teachers. Though his impact was limited, yet he had not contracted the obtaining virus 'Publish or Perish' that plagues us now.

The role of English literature changed in the post-Independent period as a means of social or cultural organizer from what it was in pre-Independent era as a means of social control. The post-Independence era witnessed a radical change in situation but no substantial change in teaching English literature. Majority of our English teachers, as some of us still do, continued to work in isolation without realizing diverse expectations from them in the new situation. There has, however, been phenomenal quantitative growth in the number of universities and post-graduate departments and colleges. In 1947, there were only 19 universities as well as 636 colleges with total enrolment of about 2,50,000 students. Now there are over 225 universities, 6,000 colleges and over 4 million students. The quantity prospered, but in the process quality suffered. To fathom and eradicate the ill and evils of the higher education system quite a few committees and commissions came into existence. Two decades after the Kothari Commission in the Mid-1960s, the "National Policy on Education" (NPE of Rajeev Gandhi) initiated a nation wide debate through the document "Challenge of Education: A Policy Perspective" (1985). The policy makers paid lip service to teachers by mentioning that "whatever merit there is in the present system flows essentially number of teachers who have become deeply involved in the welfare of their pupils and have, despite the heartaches and poor rewards available in the system given their very best" (*Challenge of Education,* 55).

However, one can easily discern the conspicuous neglect of humanities in the NEP. They were abandoned carelessly in the category of General Education by the myopic policy framers who intended to envision the future social and cultural goals of the country without sparing proper place and thought to Humanities. They forget, and they still do so, that if science and technology provide provision, then humanities and social sciences provide vision. For true manifestation of knowledge and realization of wisdom science and human sciences should complement each other. Excessive emphasis on any would lead to lop-sided development. The science-intoxicated policy makers and bureaucrats should know it well. Not caring for holistic planning even after knowing it amounts to a national crime. The question that crops up here is: Where would English literature stand in this scheme of things obsessed with science and technology, for it is most likely to treat human resources in the same manner as they do with natural resources? Another question is: where would the teaching of English stand in the world of humanities where teachers of regional literatures, for reasons absolutely non-literary, grab a good chunk of whatever is spared for humanities? The teachers of English language and literature do not, in good measure, deserve exoneration, for they have also contributed to this situation, for the majority of us remained unconcerned with literatures in Indian languages. And if we did not care of our Indian literatures, why should they?

I must leave it to you imagine the position and priority that English literature is likely to earn for itself in the obtaining situation. In a state of 'academic' confusion and dismay, we have tried quite a few things that we could lay our hands on but not with much success. For instance, to take the case of language not literature teaching in the last 5 decades we have shifted our English language teaching approaches and course contents, and designed our syllabi in different ways suggested to us, imported or imposed by/on us. Our ELT methodologies in the late 50's and early 60's were hitched to foreign language strategies. Then we shifted to second language strategies and later to teaching English as a library language. We tried to adapt the structural method, then the bilingual method and then the communicative English. We separated language learning from literature, splitting them unnaturally, reducing it to objective type-comprehension exercise and grammatical skills. Fortunately, teaching of literature in our country did not see so many changes. Barring the Curriculum Development Committee Report, no comprehensive and concentrated effort has been made to streamline teaching of English literature in India.

But what will laboriously envisioned CDC Report achieve if our classrooms remain as diverse as are with us. Our classrooms of literature are as diverse in terms of space, standard, or strength and type and quality as the students or classrooms themselves. Our students join English courses for varied purposes—to enhance their social mobility, status, matrimonial prospects, prepare for competitive examinations and the few to enter and appreciate magical world of English literature and thereby enrich their literary sensibility. A good number of them are 'immigrants' or 'leftovers' from other faculties—would-have-been scientists, doctors or engineers. Some universities in some of our state allow admission to P.G. Courses in English literature to such students as have never been even briefly exposed to English literature at the Under Graduate levels. When I asked my Head of the Department, more than a decade earlier, in a university in M.P. where I taught for some time, "Why do we admit such students?" His sympathetic and humanitarian answer was, "Where else will they go?" Fed up with my persistent questions and counter remarks like, "let them, wherever they wish; why should we entertain these 'leftovers?'" My sage Head of the Department en/lightened me, "where shall we get students from?" These immigrants and leftovers keep you—all of us in job? At least half of the departmental faculties will become redundant in their absence?' It silenced my remarks and counter remarks forever. Surprisingly these 'immigrants' and 'leftovers' on good number of occasions earned placed for themselves in the merit list, for the kind of system that we have, 'methods' matter more than matter, and who has time for 'matter' in the 'central assessment?' For better or worse, I left that Department to the present one in the state of Gujarat where B.A. with Special English (as literature is often called here) is compulsory for admission in M.A. (English). However, I do not see much qualitative difference between the M.A. classrooms in M.P. and Gujarat.

Further, the most accommodating and sweeping statement like 'English is not an alien language but our own by now' remains a sort of mental itching. Do they help us—the teachers and learners of literature—in honing their skills or in enhancing their responsive capacity? Our learners approach a literary text—a poem or a novel—at best with a sense of reverence, not for the experience that the text contains, or at worst with a sense of fear of the language of the literary text, of the impending examinations and of the threatening tone of their teachers. Excepting the few who have thwarted complacency and burden of alien theories, the most of us have forgotten that literature is to be enjoyed. The usual and considerably legitimate charge often levelled by the teachers of English literature is that enjoyable texts are hardly prescribed. And to top it, all teachers of English are obsessed with 'completing,' 'finishing' and 'covering up' the course in the given time. Only God knows what prevents us from teaching at least one unprescribed yet enjoyable poem or short story (in the entire term) that would help our learners in overcoming fear or the mental block that often hinders close interaction of our learners with the text on equal terms. Healthy interaction of/between the learners and literature is possible only in a state of fearlessness.

Despite all experimentations in our teaching methodologies and re/shuffling in our syllabi, barring a few instances of patch work in the form of an optional paper on Indian writing in English or by incorporating couple of Indian writers or works in certain institutions, English studies in India do not relate themselves to the Indian situation or context in a desirable measure. Here I need couple of hind-shots to buttress my argument. The majority of our students in English literature classrooms particularly at the under graduate level come from non-English medium institution. Even the standard of English medium students is not very healthy or even on all occasions. They bring with them comparatively better language skills but not so good literary sensibility. A good number of students coming to literature classrooms do not bring with them much knowledge and even less capacity for independent literary study. The students from non-English medium schools and colleges bring with them not so good language but a certain literary sensibility forged by their folk, cultural and literary traditions. Of course they do not know much about English literature and care even less for its appreciation. But even the poorest students come with a few fragments from the rich reservoir of their collective sensibility with which they can receive or appreciate certain literary works. They can do so because they approach the literary works without any sense of fear, for the poems to which they have to respond shall be in their own language. Since they have been exposed to soil and dust, water, air and environs that constitute and surround a text, it becomes easy to locate and identify the culture-smeared items. This faculty of these non-English medium students can be made use of by pairing, comparing and contrasting literary texts from Indian literature with English texts. Syllabi in B.A. and M.A. English are still not framed with texts from English and Indian literatures in such a way as to facilitate healthy interaction between the learners and the literary texts. Further, poems and plays can better be taught by culturally displacing and recontextualizing them. Keeping this in view I am very uncomfortable with a flat term like TELI (Teaching English Literature in India) which not only oversights Indian literatures but also the Indian learners' strength. In comparison to this Teaching Literature in English in India (TLIE) and comparative studies between literature in English and Indian literatures seem to be more relevant and meaningful. Unfortunately that is still not happening the way it should.

III

With my infidelity to the topic of the paper, I must have earned enough displeasure and impatience of my readers. This infidelity was a consequence of my concerns with the relevance of contemporary English Studies in India, and even more with its contemporary teaching which to anybody's pleasant surprise, is shifting, though slowly, from 'English' to 'British.'

Even a fleeting glance at our syllabi will reveal that the syllabi of English literature are titled heavily in favour of British (read English here) literature. About 70 to 90 per cent of syllabi deals with British literature in which the works of English authors form the core and the periphery with some space spared for non-English writers like Swift, Shaw or Yeats. Further, our contemporary teaching of English literature at the Under Graduate level in India remains 'sicklied over' with not yet pale cast of Shakespeare, 'daffodilzed' or 'prufrocked.' With an Austen or Hardy novel it is garnished with Indian hues—with some poems of Tagore or an R.K. Narayan, Anand or Raja Rao novel to 'nativize' it a little, superimposed with some prose, and plenty of grammar or general English. Our P.G. courses in English do not present a different picture. They are framed period or movement-wise, century or genre-wise with a paper of literary criticism beginning with Aristotle and ending with Eliot and in some advanced places with Jacques Derrida, Lacan, Stanley Fish or Stephen Greenblatt with a paper or two on American literature or Indian writing in English, or literature in Translation, or ELT and linguistics. The metro universities and some of their non-metro counterparts teach papers like commonwealth literatures, or African literature, or Latin American writing, Comparative literature or Canadian or Australian literature or a paper like 'Politics, Ideology and Teaching literature' or Black literature. Not content with teaching Shakespeare at the Under Graduate level there may be a couple of plays of Shakespeare at the P.G. level at the cost of contemporary literature. The last paper may be sprinkled with the works of William Golding, Philip Larkin. The writers like Graham Swift, A.S. Byatt, Charlotte Keatley, Caryll Philips, Andrew Motion, and Glyn Maxwell are spared for research after they have been re 'searched' by different awarding institutions or agencies. Some writers like Rushdie or Rohinton Mistry or David Davydeen or Philips enjoy multiple existence—as a British and Indian writer as well, as a Canadian and an Indian writer, as a British and a Caribbean writer respectively. Whatever has taken place in the name of decanonization is not very assuring. Most of our syllabi present an image of salad bowl with lot of borrowed vegetables. Our contemporary syllabi can best be described by taking recourse to a Gujarati term *oondhiyu* (a mixed vegetable dish) with addition of some home grown vegetables added to other vegetables grown elsewhere but without the native flavour or relish that it gets from slow but careful cooking—absorbing, assimilating each other's properties yet retaining its own distinct character.

The preceding observation notwithstanding, contemporary TELI has to take note of a few facts. Call it British or English, British literature with suitable representation from Irish, Welsh,

Scottish and English literature would form substantial part of TELI. It should, because whether fortunate and otherwise it has been with us for long. But TELI has to be contemporanized, for Caryll Philips or Davydeen or Gurnah are more relevant than Austen or Dickens not because they are irrelevant but because they have already been taught at Under Graduate level. Should we have them again at the P.G. level at the cost of relevant contemporary writers. Instead of having a paper or two works of Shakespeare or of Milton it is better to have just one play or drop them altogether to accommodate some contemporary writing dealing with the experience and reality more pertinent to us at the P.G. level.

Our TELI has to relate itself to Indian situation and experience. It is nothing but tragic that in our M.A. syllabus, we teach Greek, Roman, English, German, French and Russian critics and their works in the compulsory paper of 'Literary Criticism,' but not Indian poetics. We teach Ferdinand de Saussure, the progenitor of the second French revolution in the 20th Century, and a host of French critics like Claude Levi-Strauss, Roland Barthes and Derrida whom he had influenced, but not Panini or Bharutihari who had influenced de Saussure. This lack of self-respect for one's own traditions and self-confidence in examining them in an upfront manner suggests that our intellectual de-colonization is yet to take place. Else why should we wait for the 'papal' approval of our rich Indian poetical traditions—ancient, medieval, and contemporary, elite (shastriya) and folk (lok) by the West? We should prescribe the texts of Indian poetics, teach them to our students in the compulsory paper of 'literary criticism' so that our students can locate themselves between the Indian and western critical traditions and interact with them.

Further, the English studies (and its teaching) in India has to relate itself to Indian literatures particularly to contemporary creativity. The departments of English must keep the Indian literatures in different Indian languages in mind, while framing their syllabi, lest they should become dinosaurs. We must note the healthy shift from English to British which is recognition of multiplicity of voices from Scotland, Wales, Ireland, China, Japan, Caribbean islands, Africa and India among others, along with England. If that is the case, why can't TELI accommodate Indian literatures through translations or comparative studies or something like TLIE (Teaching Literature in English) or TIWET (Teaching Indian Writing in English and Translation)? It should, however, not be done ritualistically by dumping them in an optional paper, but by incorporating in the core paper(s) or by having a separate compulsory paper(s) for them. If there can be one or two papers on European classics, why can't there be a paper on Indian classics? Or there can be a paper on classics with at least half of the texts as the Indian classics in it. Mere tokenism, however, will serve no purpose—neither of English studies nor of Indian society.

Can I exculpate myself for presenting not so pleasant a picture of contemporary TLIE in our country, for in the course of my submission I have voiced my personal impressions? I still do not know for certain if the "I" of the epigraph from Eliot stands for the teaching, of Contemporary teaching of English in India, or TELI or TLIE or TIWET or for all. However, all the while I did in tone W.H. Auden during the course of organizing my distracted thoughts on TLIE:

"If I could tell you
I would let you."

WORKS CITED

Gandhi, M.K. *Evils Wrought by the English Medium.* Ed. K.N. Prabhu. Ahmedabad: Navjeevan Publishing House, 1958.

Iyengar, K.R.S. *Indian Writing in English.* Delhi: Sterling Publishers, 1962.

Macaulay, T.B. "Minute on Indian Education." *Prose and Poetry.* Ed. G.M. Young. Cambridge, Mass: Harvard UP, 1967.

Lohia, Rammanohar. *Notes and Comments,* Vol. 1. Hyderabad: Lohia Samatavidyalaya, Vyas Prakashan Vibhag, 1972.

Mishra, B.B. *The Indian Middle Class: Their Growth in Modern Times.* Bombay: OUP, 1961.

Munsi Prem Chand. "National Language Hindi and its problems." *The Purpose of Literature.* Ed. Shivani Prem Chand. Allahabad: Hans Publications, 1957.

Trilling, Lionel. "The Sense of Past." *English Critical Text.* Eds. S. Ramaswami and V.S. Seturaman. Madras: Macmillan, 1986.

6

Babu English and Butler English

S. JAGADISAN and S. IMTIAZ ALI

We have heard of British English, American English, Australian English, Indian English etc. But, has anyone heard of 'Babu English' and 'Butler English'?—Yes, there was one such form of English in India during the Raj days. In reaching out to the different parts of the world and becoming global, English has developed a variety of forms. Each one of these forms is correct within its own context. These varieties of English are classified as National, regional, social, occupational and so on. The national variety is English as it is used, particularly in the spoken form, in different countries. The regional variety includes the dialectical forms within England—Yorkshire dialect, Lancashire dialect, London dialect etc. The social variety is related to the social and educational background of those speaking English. Occupational variety is English for special purposes satisfying the linguistic requirements of the field of activity one is engaged in.

Babu English and Butler English are a subvariety of Indian English. 'Babu,' in a limited sense, is a term of respectful address, like Master or Mister. (This term of address is particularly common in Andhra.) In Bengal, among Anglo-Indians, it was used with a touch of disparagement. In the *Oxford Encyclopaedia Dictionary* (Vol. I), Babu is defined as "an Indian Clerk or Official, with superficial education, who writes English." "A form of address in Hindi equivalent to Mister, placed before a man's full name or after his first name. A Hindu Clerk, possessing a prerequisite degree of literacy in English. A native of India who has acquired some superficial education in English" (*Readers Digest Universal*

Dictionary). The term came to be applied to the clerks who had a smattering of English. 'The pliable, plastic, receptive Babu eagerly avails himself of the system of English education partly from a desire to please the Sahib, and partly from a desire to obtain a Government Employment' (Hobson Jobson). The term also was applied to 'English Officers who have become de-Europeanised from long residence among undomesticated natives. Such officials are what Lord Lytton calls White Baboos' (Hobson Jobson).

A 'Babu' tried to impress his British employer with his command of the English Language. In Babu English verbosity is more pronounced than context and he was described as 'Bombastic Baboo.' His attempt to measure up to the level of his master in the use of English often resulted in the misuse or corruption of the language for example, he would say 'Simpson and Delilah.' Babu English is amusing. A book of ready made letters containing an ideal letter to a newly married girl says, 'You must have adjusted yourself in the family of your in-laws. Always give good impression and impact to them by your every action.' The girl's reply is 'They treat me first like their daughter. Really they are affectionate and fondling.' Babu English smacks of obsequiousness. 'Hoping to have the honour of throwing myself at your goodness's philanthropic feet.' The term Babu, if not his English, now refers to the bureaucrats, but not in a complimentary sense.

The butler was an important member of the British household in India. He was the male head servant. He purchased provisions and vegetables, was in charge of domestic stores and attended on the master and his lady at the table. He was the steward controlling the domestic staff. An application calling for the post of a butler said "wanted a person to act as Steward or Butler in a Gentleman's House." 'He must understand hairdressing.' Butler English has come to signify the broken English spoken by the native servants in the Madras Presidency. While Babu English suffers from bombast, in Butler English, the emphasis is on content and language is reduced to its barest essentials. The present participle without the auxiliary is used to signify the future indicative. 'I telling'—I will tell. The past tense is formed by using the form 'done'—I done tell. I have told'; 'I done come'—I have arrived. Peculiar meanings are attached to words. 'My family has gone to the village'—means my wife has gone to the village. The English masters often used this form of English while speaking to the servants. Even now we come across instances of butler or broken English. 'Mother dead,' 'Off the fan,' 'apply apply no reply,' "I long son, no father, no mother, no wife, no issue."

7

The Acceptability of American English in India

AMAR NATH JHA

Once condemned as Americanisms, American variations in orthography, pronunciation and usage find their respectable places in standard British dictionaries and grammars of current or contemporary English. Like BBC English, 'General American is that form of American which does not have marked regional characteristics' (A. Cruttenden 1994: 84). Likewise General Indian English also pleads for the use of the form of English intelligible and acceptable both nationally and internationally. English language used in the U.S.A. and India has attained its own distinctive features in lexis, phonology, and usage. Both American and Indian English differ from the parent stock of British English in all these areas. But despite their differences, they are mutually intelligible in their educated forms.

Am E, as also Indian English, has certain affinities with Scottish English, which is rhotic, and has no diphthongs such as |ɪə, eə, ʊə|. The diphthong |er| is a monophthong in Am E, and |əʊ| is also pronounced as a monophthong in some areas (Nihalani *et al.* 1979: 209) and as |oʊ| in General American (Wells 1990: xvi). The lateral |l| is dark in both Scottish and American English. Scottish English is 'most frequently accepted as an alternative standard to RP' (Cruttenden 1994: 83). Nihalani *et al.* (1979: 204) point out that 'Scottish or Welsh influence in the English spoken by Indians in certain parts of' of India has been traced 'and these influences have been attributed to the Scots and Welsh teachers who worked in these regions.' This also brings out the affinity of Indian English with

American, as, 'indeed, the general speech of both Scotland and Ireland is nearer to the pronunciation of American English' (LDCE 1978: xvii).

While British and American English have thoroughly been recorded in all their linguistic aspects, Indian English has, perhaps, not been done so as yet. Despite the pioneering works by Bansal and Harrison (1974), Bansal and Brasnett (1976), Nihalani *et al.* (1979) as well as Braj Kachru (1983) among others, the complete corpus of Indian English is not as yet easy to be found. The samples of pronunciation of a few words selected here have been picked out from observation of the speeches of educated Indians, educated in the country, having little formal knowledge of the phonology of English. For certain points of lexis, grammar and usage, the print media have been relied on.

Orthography

Indian English follows the British model of spelling. Nevertheless, newspapers and magazines also follow the spelling conventions on the American model. In words such as *age, eye, like, mile* the final-*e* is dropped before the addition of suffixes beginning with a vowel to give forms like *aging, eying, likable, milage* in American English and also sometimes in Indian English, especially in newspapers. American English uses single (l) in cases where BrE has double (l) and also *vice versa*:

Br.E.	*Am.E.*
tranquillity	tranquility
tranquillize	tranquilize
tranquillizer	tranquilizer
woollen	woolen
gold-medallist	gold-medalist
all right	alright
jewellery	jewelry
skilful	skillful
benefited	benefitted
embed	imbed

enclose	inclose
ensure	insure
sceptical	skeptical
speciality	specialty
raquet	racket
cannot	can not
moustache	mustache
waggon	wagon

For the British—*our* AmE substitutes—*or. Color TV* is invariably spelt with *-or* even in IE. The other spelling differences relate to the use of *-re—> -er, -ence —> ense, -amme —> -am, -ae- / -oe —> -e-*. Indian English generally follows the British spellings but American spellings also are not uncommon. AmE has popularized the *-ize* forms of verbs in BrE and IE. Spell-checks in word processors may not approve the British spellings. Sometimes even the uncommon American variants in spelling are used. For example, Ms. Madhuri Dixit's Los Angeles-based husband, an NRI surgeon, is called an 'ornery guy' (TOI Nov. 6, 1999: 14) for an 'ordinary guy' and that too with the change of the current meaning of the word which in AmE means 'tending to get angry and argue with people' (CIDE). American spellings are coming into vogue in the newspaper articles, supplements and advertisements.

Pronunciation

Both AmE and IE have deviations in pronunciation from the British parent stock. These phonetic deviations depend 'on geographical, social, cultural and other conditions' (M. Hari Prasad 1990: 89). It is, however, to be stressed 'that AmE as well as IE have more similarities than differences from BrE' (*Ibid.*: 90). Nevertheless, there are some points of similarity in pronunciation between AmE and IE, especially in the area of vowels. British English diphthongs |er| and |əʊ| are pronounced as monophthongs in both IE and AmE. The BrE diphthong |əʊ| may also be realized in AmE as |oʊ|. Most Americans may use |ə| for |^| and |3:| as in Indian English. American English has no |ɒ| phoneme which is realized as |ɑ:| in a few cases like that in the Western U.P. speakers of English, who pronounce 'God' |g ɒ d| as |ga:d|, 'congress'

|'kɒŋgrəs| as |'ka:ŋgres|. AmE has no diphthongs |ɪə, eə, ʊə| and the first element of the diphthong is immediately followed by |r|. IE, on the other hand, has these diphthongs, but these are not used for all the words having them. In a few words |ɪə| is realised as |I|, |eə| as |e| and |Uə| as |ʊ| followed by |r|:

|ɪə| —> |I|-zero |'z ɪro:|, hero |'hIro:| souvenir |'suvnir|

|eə|—> |e|-area |'erɪə|, grammarian |grəm'erɪən|, various |'veɪəas|, aerial |'erɪəl|

|ʊə| —> |ʊ| pleurisy |'plʊrɪsɪ|, tour |tʊr|, jury |ɪdsʊrɪ|

These cases of diphthongs pronounced as monophthongs are like those in American English. AmE pronunciations of *thorough* and *borough* are closer to those in IE.

The vowel (a) after (w) is pronounced |wa:| both in AmE and IE, as in *war, water* etc. In the consonant cluster *wh* -, as in *when, what,* etc. except *who, whose,* and a few others, the spoken realization is |hw|- in both AmE and IE. *Clerk* is pronounced |kl3:rk|, *sample* as |'sampel|, *wrath* as |nr.o| *with* as |wio|, *gratis* as |'grjrtls|, *booth* as |bu:e| *leisure* as |li:3ar| in both AmE and IE. These pronunciations are variants from the British. *Iron* is the only example in BrE where (r) is silent even before a vowel, but this is pronounced in AmE and IE.

Some of the words in American English have spelling pronunciation and also pronunciation spelling. These are also characteristic features of Indian English as well. The novels of Mulk Raj Anand, in particular, are full of examples of pronunciation spelling. *Lieutenant* has a spelling pronunciation in American English, but not in Indian English. The abbreviated form *O.K.* has a pronunciation spelling, which is also given another pronunciation spelling *Okay. K.O.ed* and *xed* are instances of abbreviated spelling pronunciation. *Chassis* is pronounced with the initial |tç| in AmE and IE. The final <s>, silent in AmE, is pronounced in IE. The IE realization of *caricature* for its final syllable is akin to AmE variant pronunciation |-tçər| (LPD). <L> in AmE is dark in all the positions and <t> is voiced between vowels, but not so in IE. *Can't* and *shan't* in IE are pronounced like those in AmE. *Slander* in AmE has |æ| for the first vowel sound. *Banal* is pronounced in AmE way in IE. It is strange how the first vowel in *grammar* is pronounced |ɑ:| in IE as against BrE and AmE |æ|. The personal name *Anthony* in AmE is pronounced with |θ| as in IE. Yet, despite a few differences, the articulation of vowels in AmE is closer to that in IE.

In stress and intonation AmE has certain resemblances with those in IE. In BrE lots of words change their stress when these words are used as nouns and verbs and as adjectives and verbs. But in a few words this pattern in the change of accent with functional shift is not followed. The following nouns, when used as verbs, are not accented upon the second syllable in AmE (CIDE):

combat	contrast	contract	export
frequent	insult	protest	recall
survey	transfer	transport	

The recommendations of Bansal and Harrison (1972) are not heeded to in the use of stress pattern in such words in the spoken form of IE. *Cigarette* in IE is stressed upon the last syllable as in AmE. *Corollary* is accented on the second syllable in BrE but on the first in AmE. IE generally follows the AmE pattern.

The rhythm of AmE is what H.L. Mencken calls 'predominantly *staccato* and *marcato* as against the British trend towards *glissando* (qtd. Simeon Potter 1968: 166). The metaphors from music in the above communicate that the rhythm of American English is sharply detached from the others and is played with emphasis, while that in BrE is 'a continuous slide of adjacent notes upwards or downwards' (COD 1990). The rhythm of connected speech in IE is not much different from that in AmE.

Vocabulary

The vocabulary of both AmE and IE is conditioned by geographical, social, cultural and other conditions. Both rely on the resources of their respective other native languages by way of loan-words and translations of words from other languages of the region, the use of hybrid forms and neologisms. The typical vocabulary of AmE is popularly used in IE. Most of these words belong to the area of food, clothing and transport. The following observation is worth quoting:

> American words are frequently taken into British English, but it is less common for American speakers to use new British words. Australian English uses words from both British and American English. (CIDE 1995)

IE, like Australian English, uses such words from both AmE and BrE in most of the cases. It is also true that many of such words used in IE are from AmE. The use of their BrE equivalents is less popular in IE. The following words belong to the former category:

BrE	*AmE*
engaged	busy (telephone)
biscuit	cookies
trousers	pants
flat	apartment
injection	shot
sweater	jumper
rubber	eraser
aerial (transistor)	antenna (TV)
queue	line
market	mart

The following words come under the second category in which American words are preferred to the British in IE:

BrE	*AmE*
plait	braid
Alice band	hair-band
lead	cord (electric)
dialling code	area code
demist	defog
rota	roster
ironmongery	hardware
paraffin	kerosene
cotton wool	cotton
Maths	Math
sparking plug	spark plug
carrier bag	shopping bag

underground	subway
pen lid	pen cap

A few of the words used in AmE have different nuances from those in BrE. Likewise, a few of the American words used in IE have different meanings. *Cheap* is used disapprovingly in AmE and also in IE. BrE form *car* is in use in IE but the clipped form of AmE *automobile* is used in the sense of an autorickshaw. The words such as *prophylactic* and *hunkeydory* have come into vogue in IE. The *faculty* of AmE is used in IE for 'the members of the department.' The names for teaching ranks such as *assistant professor* and *associate professor* used in the academic field in IE are from AmE. AmE *panhandle* communicates more than 'to beg.' The use of the non-sexist language in IE is mostly from AmE. The use of *Ms* is replacing *Miss* and *Mrs. Chairperson* has replaced chairman/ chairwoman.

Syntax and Usage

There are only minor syntactic differences between AmE and BrE or between AmE and IE. The use of double negatives in AmE is acceptable neither in BrE nor IE. The use of the objective forms after 'than,' 'as' and 'like' in AmE is now acceptable not only in IE, but also in BrE. A few of the grammatical patterns of AmE are used in IE but labelled 'Americanism' in BrE. *Have,* in the stative sense of possession, is constructed as an auxiliary in BrE while 'AmE prefers the *do*-construction' (Quirk and Greenbaum 1973: 35):

I { haven't / *don't have* } any books.

In IE, AmE pattern is used along with the British.

In AmE the indefinite pronoun *one* is followed by *his* and *himself* for the BrE *one's* and *oneself.* IE users are very prone to using the AmE forms, besides the BrE ones. The uses of prepositions in IE, different from those in AmE, with some verbs and adjectives have become acceptable in IE. *Different than* and *preferable than* are common in AmE and are also used in Indian English, though not usual in BrE. AmE may drop a preposition used after a verb. In AmE, as also in IE, the verb *protest may* be followed by its object ignoring the use of *about/against*:

A group of students were protesting research cuts.

Besides the BrE *aim at,* AmE *aim to* is not uncommon in IE. IE prefers AmE *cater to* BrE *cater for*. In AmE, and also in IE, *at* is common with *furious/angry/livid* when the 'stimulus' is a person or an object (Quirk and Greenbaum 1973: 160). *Notary public,* used in IE, is from AmE. *Aplenty* is postposed in AmE and IE. Among health adjectives, the attributive use of *sick* is common in AmE (Quirk and Greenbaum 1973: 160). This use is very common in IE. Past tense forms ending in *-ed* are more common in AmE than those ending in *-t*. The former are also more common in IE. Americans may greet their friends with *Have a nice day.* This may sound irritating to a British but not to an Indian. Typical AmE forms such as *gotten, roomed together, drink and eats* etc. are occasionally found in Indian English fiction. Analogical plural forms in *-s* are replacing the foreign plural forms in non-technical senses mostly under the impact of AmE. The verb *avail* is used without a reflexive pronoun in AmE and also frequently in IE in cases where it is obligatory in BrE. Goods in India and US are put *on sale* and not *in the sale* like those in the UK.

More countries worldwide are now following the model of AmE and 'General American is the standard model for the pronunciation of English as an L_2 in parts of Asia (*e.g.* the Philippines) and parts of Latin America (*e.g.* Mexico)' (Cruttenden 1994: 84). Among the European countries, as A.H. Marckwardt (1963) points out, Italy may be closer to England in distance, 'but the amount of contact with the speakers of American English is surprisingly great' (Allen and Campbell (eds.) 1965/77: 235).

With the rise of the U.S.A. as a superpower, the British lexicographers and grammarians talk of 'the influence of America' (Gowers & Fraser 1973: 268) even on British English. IE has borrowed some of the American influence via BrE, while much of the impact has come direct from the U.S.A. There may be chance similarities as well.

The liberal educational facilities granted to India by the U.S.A. motivated the Indian students' and teachers' interest in

American language and literature along with American history, culture and politics. Moreover, the globe-trotting Indian bureaucrats and technocrats, scientists and engineers, journalists and advertisers, businessmen and top executives as well as creative writers etc. have accelerated the American impact on IE. The popularity of standard American textbooks mainly on applied science and computer technology reprinted in India in economy editions has made Indian learners familiar with AmE to such an extent that American English seems to have attained acceptability and intelligibility in India as much as in Britain. 'Consequently, the National Council of Teachers of English (NCTE) has shown increasing interest in the objective study of American English both for its own sake and for the potential improvement in the teaching of language and literature' (N.R. Shastri 1990).

WORKS CITED

Allen, H.B. and R.N. Campbell. *Teaching English as a Second Language.* 1965; New Delhi: TMH, 1973.

Bansal, R.K. and J.B. Harrison. *Spoken English for India.* Madras: O.L., 1972,

Bansal, R.K. and Clive Brasnett. *An English Phonetic Reader.* Calcutta: O.L., 1976.

CIDE (*Cambridge Interantional Dictionary of English*) Cambridge: CUP,1995.

COD (*The Concise Oxford Dictionary*) Delhi: OUP, 1990.

Cruttenden, A. *Gimson's Pronunciation of English.* London: ELBS/Edward Arnold, 1994.

Gowers, Sir Ernst and Sir Bruce Eraser. *The Complete Plain Words.* London: ELBS, 1973.

I.J.A.S. (*Indian Journal of American Studies*). No. 2. Summer, 1990.

Kachru, B.B. *The Indianization of English,* Delhi: OUP, 1983.

LDCE (*Longman Dictionary of Contemporary English*). London: ELBS/ Longman, 1978.

Marckwardt, A.H. 'American and British English.' In Allen and Campbell (eds.), 1963: 234-42.

Nihalani, Paroo, R.K. Tongue and Priya Hosali. *Indian and British English.* Delhi: O.U.P., 1979.

Potter, Simeon. *Our Language.* 1950: Harmondsworth: Penguin, 1968.

Prasad, M. Hari, 'Indian English and the American Language.' In *I.J.A.S.* 1990: 89-92.

Quirk, R. and Sidney Greenbaum. *A University Grammar of English.* London: Longman, 1973.

Shastri, N.R. 'Mencken on American English: Some Observations.' In *I.J.A.S.* 1990: 83-88.

T.O.I. (*The Times of India*), 1999, November 6: Editorial (Runaway Bride).

Wells, J.C. *Longman Pronunciation Dictionary* (LPD). London: Longman, 1990.

8

Indian Variety of English: A Socio-Linguistic Study

JAYDEEP SARANGI

In the linguistically and culturally pluralistic Indian subcontinent English is used as the Second Language (L_2) which is acquired after one has learnt the First Language (L_1). This co-existence of English, the Foreign Language (FL) and the First Language results in interference from one's First Language in the Second Language. Through the large-scale socio-cultural interaction with regional contexts English became Indianized. A variety of English albeit non-native, lexically, morphologically, syntactically and stylistically different from the standard British form has come to be known as 'Indian Variety of English' (IVE). 'Indian Variety of English' is not at all the vulgarised form of English but creative and resourceful with distinctive individualistic socio-linguistic features.

India is a vast and almost endless country. It is a multi-cultural and multilingual country too. As there is no comprehensive homogeneity in the use of language, 'Indian Variety of English' is not sufficient enough to describe all the regional variations of English in respective of geographical identities. For definite geographical boundaries, socio-linguistic backgrounds and several other decisive reasons, several regional varieties of IVE such as Gujarati English, Bengali English, Tamil English have come into existence. Each kind of IVE has certain individualistic marks. But when we have considerable number of differences is it really possible to prepare general characteristics of IVE? It is a topic to be debated time and again. To pin point my discussion, I consider

English used in India spread over a continuum. And I prefer the use of General Indian English (GIE) to regional varieties. If we analyse the varieties of IVE, we can trace out certain phonological, lexical, morphological, syntactic and stylistic features of several varieties of IVE together.

> GIE is meant a certain variety of English spoken by educated Indians. General Indian English is free from regional features. It is both descriptive and prescriptive model.[1]

GIE model is used to common, shared phonological properties of several varieties of IVE. For example, in GIE the voiceless plosives are unaspirated in all positions, whereas in RP they are aspirated when they occur at the initial position in stressed syllables.

Through this paper I propose to capture some of the features which are used in a distinctive manner by a majority of educated Indian speakers of English as well as in the 'established' Indian Writings in English (IWE). Therefore, I've used both the literal and the non-literal (spoken) data in my analysis of IVE. My paper does not claim to establish a comprehensive description of English as it is used in the politico-geographical identity of India. I'm well-aware that a valid and more acceptable description of Indian Variety of English can be prepared only after a large-scale survey with the basis of literal and non-literal data.

Pronunciation really matters among the speaker of English in India. The gross regional characteristics render the English speech of Indians unintelligible and sometimes unacceptable even to fellow-Indians. Since India is a polyglot country there is no real possibility of something called IVE in the same sense as German Variety of English or American Variety of English. There are, of course, many varieties of English spoken in India, each being influenced by the mother tongue of the speakers of these varieties of English. The influence of the mother tongue on English (as L_2) is known as 'mother tongue pull.' We may consider the following examples to support the fact:

(i) Most Malayalees pronounce the /p/ in 'temple' and 'ample' as [b], the |t| in 'canteen' as [d].

(ii) Many Bengalees pronounce 'sip' and 'ship' alike. As in Bengali, there is hardly any difference in short and long vowels. The Bengalees tend to pronounce 'sit' and 'seat' alike.

(iii) The Bengalees often pronounce /f/ as bilabial plosive when the actual sound is a labio-dental plosive. In Bengali, /f/ is always bilabial. Whereas, in English /f/ is labio-dental.

(iv) Telugu speakers often add an extra /u/ at the end of words (mainly when the words end in consonants). Therefore, 'fan' is pronounced as 'fanu.'

We may count numerous examples of such mother tongue interference influencing the speakers of English in India.

A large number of Indian words (from different regional languages or Hindi) pass into 'Indian Variety of English' register. This register is an index of a rich culture and a great tradition of indigenous languages. We can cite a few examples of Indian words which are frequently used in Indian Writings in English as well as in the conversations of English (IVE):

Indian words/expressions		*Meaning*
Dhotis	:	Hindu loin-cloths about four yards long and a yard wide worn by men in India.
Burra	:	Big.
Biri	:	Indian equivalent to a Cigarette; Tabacco wrapped in dried leaf.
Chapaties	:	Indian pancakes made of wheat-flour.
Vilayat	:	Foreign land; mainly used for England in contemporary India.
Hakim	:	Native doctor.
Gol Kamra	:	Living-room.
Kum kum mark	:	a kind of mark ladies take in their forehead.
Pahlwanji	:	Term of respect and fear for a wrestler.

Bastis	:	Colony.
Bibiji	:	A term of respect for a Hindu wife.
Babu	:	An well-versed man; term generally used for a clerk.
Angrezi Sarkar	:	The English Government.
Dakdar	:	Doctor.
Swadeshi	:	National.
Harijan	:	Untouchable/downtrodden.
Namaskar	:	Traditional Indian greeting (generally used at the beginning of a conversation/meeting).

This list of Indian words/expressions used in Indian Writings in English and in Indian English conversation (spoken) is really a big one. It covers all the aspects of life. The words are taken from the socio-political life, socio-cultural life, philosophical life and the social life of the Indians. These words/expressions also project the 'Indianness' in particular.

There are some typically Indian affixes which go into the derivation of IVE vocabulary. For example: -wallah, -ji, -sahib are class maintaining derivational suffixes:

Congress + wallah	—	Congress-wallah.
Rickshaw + wallah	—	Rickshaw-wallah.
Bibi + ji	—	Bibiji.
Pahlwan + ji	—	Pahlwanji.
Major + sahib	—	Majorsahib.

If we analyse the morphological structure of the hybrids/ nominal compounds of 'Indian Variety of English' we can easily locate the marks of Indianness. (See chart on next page)

The IVE compounds/hybrids are frequently used in the Writings of Mulk Raj Anand, Raja Rao, R.K. Narayan, Bhabani Bhattacharya, Jayanta Mahapatra, Girish Karnad and other established Writers of Indian Writings in English:

(i) "What do I know of the sahib-log's life?" [from *Coolie*]

(ii) "'Doe double roti!' the bearer said." [from *Coolie*]

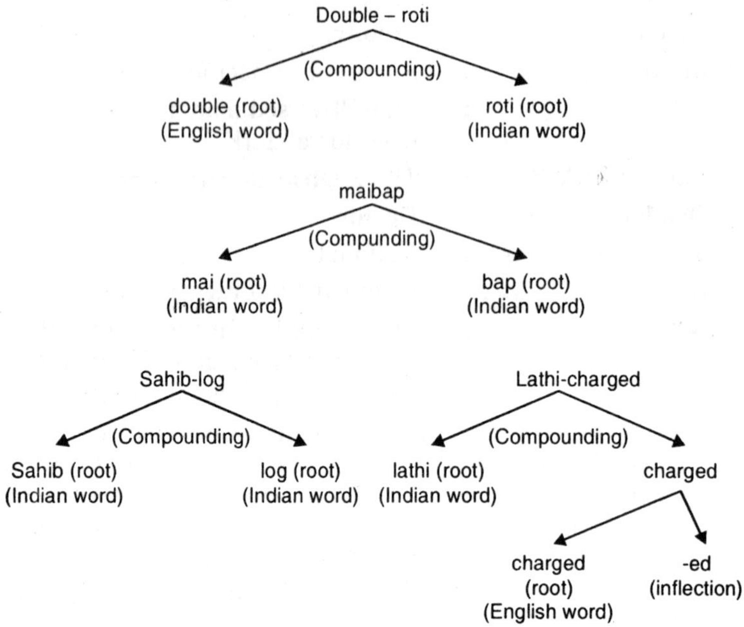

'Indian Variety of English' allows (individualistic) differences with standard British English at the syntactic level and the lexical level too. But these deviations are "not idiosyncratic or unsystematic." Earlier, IVE was "used in a derogatory sense."[2] Now things have changed. In IVE, reduplication[3] is used for the sake of emphasis or to highlight a continuation of an on-going process. Indian Writers in English have explored this resourcefulness to a great extent:

(i) "See it go higher, higher." [from *So Many Hungers*]

(ii) "Go home! Go home! It is only a base rumour spread by our enemies." [from *Coolie*]

(iii) "Money, Money, where to get Money. [from *The Railway Clerk*]

(iv) "With these very eyes, with these very eyes, [...] all killed by magic, by magic [...]." [from *Kanthapura*]

In IVE, sometimes present progressive (continuous) is used instead of simple present tense to denote habitual action:

(i) "I am doing my duty." [from *The Railway Clerk*].
'be do + ing' form is used instead of only 'do.'

(ii) "I am discharging it properly." [from *The Railway Clerk*].
'be discharge + ing' is used in place of only 'discharge.'

'Indian Variety of English' has a tendency to use present continuous tense instead of present perfect continuous tense as well. In the spoken variety, people often use sentences like:

'I'm living in Kolkata for three years,' or 'I am working here for ten years.'

Instead of 'I've been living in Kolkata for three years' and 'I've been working here for ten years.' We can locate this characteristic of IVE in IWE too:

"I am living far off in Borivli." [from *The Railway Clerk*]

The VG (Verb Group) is "am living" instead of "have been living." Here the 'Aspect' is incomplete. The structural difference between the two forms is shown below:

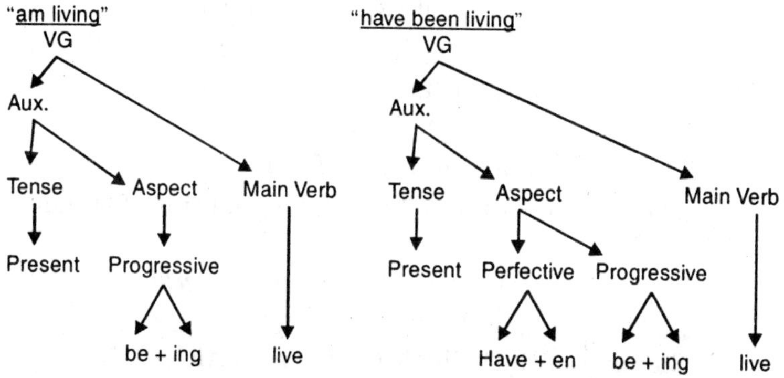

In IVE, simple sentences are converted into their respective interrogative forms only by the use of a mark of interrogation at the end of the statement, such as,

"You are pleased, Onu?" [from *Music for Mohini*]

"You are wed, Kajoli?" [from *So Many Hungers!*]

"Lions here?" [from *The Guide*]

"You have finished with the image of Mother Durga?" [from *Inquilab by* Asif Currimbhoy]

Behind the mark of interrogation is implied the rising tone of the speaker in asking questions whereas a level tone or lowered tone (falling tone) might mean a statement or an answer. This is an established practice in the conversation form of most of the Indian languages.

While framing the interrogative constructions 'Indian Variety of English' speakers do not necessarily follow the subject-auxiliary inversion rule. They tend to follow the non-inversion of auxiliary. Therefore, people often say, 'where you are going?' instead of 'where are you going?'

"How long this can go on?" [from *The Railway Clerk*]

In the above example 'can' remains unchanged even in the interrogative form. The general form can be:

This can go on ... (Statement)
Subj. Aux.

How long can this go on ? (Interrogative)
Aux. Subj.
(After Subj. – Aux. inversion)

IVE makes room for the study of idiosyncratic use of articles. Sometimes (in IVE) articles are not used when mandatory in British English. For example:

"I'll be getting married in near future."

('the' before "near future" mandatory in British Standard English)

"I wish I was bird." (from *The Railway Clerk*)

In the above example, an article before 'bird' is a must in Standard British English. In IVE, articles are often added when not necessary too.

In Indian Writings in English, we find several examples of proverbs, legends and concrete imagery in Indian context. In the similes and metaphors familiar animals and birds figure most:

(i) "Money is a winged bird. It will fly off." (from *So Many Hungers!*)

(ii) "[...] and yet he was as honest as an elephant." [from *Kanthapura*]

Numerous Indian regional proverbs pass into Indian Variety of English. IVE is saturated with Indian idiom, Indian imagery and rural colour. Sometimes there are literal translations from different languages like Kannada, Punjabi, Bengali and so on:

(i) "The police men are not your uncle's sons." [from *Kanthapura*]

(ii) "You cannot straighten a dog's tail." [from *Kanthapura*]

(iii) "Through their fingers money goes pouring like water." [from *Kanthapura*]

(iv) "One must wear painted plumes in the company of peacocks." [from *Shadow from Ladakh*]

(v) "Munoo thinks that the taste of the fresh cotton thread in the factory vickening, like bile in the mouth." [from *Coolie*]

(vi) "[...] and mother and wife and widow godmother went up to their lighted lizard-clucking homes." [from *Kanthapura*]

(vii) "Postman Subbayya, who had no fire in his stomach, and was red with red and blue with blue." [from *Kanthapura*]

Sometimes Indian Writers of English use expressions which are obviously not English and which have no counterpart in 'source language' (SL). This is a falsification of English. For example:

(i) "He gave her a very warmful bed."

(ii) "[...] deep breathful of meditation." [from Raja Rao's Novels]

Similarly, Bhabani Bhattacharya coins diminutive of a thing by adding "-ling" to the root/stem, such as:

Child + ling — Childling.

Wife + ling — Wifeling.

He is also inventive coining adjectival forms by adding class changing derivational suffix "-ful" to nouns; for example:

sky + ful — skyful.

pride + ful — prideful.

Indian sensibility gets reflected "in a language not one's own the spirit that is one's own." Onomatopoeic words (Indian) are often used in IVE. These words add regional/local fervour to the language in use. We may cite a few of these words:

Words		*Meaning*
khit-khit	—	useless talk.
shup-shup	—	sound of a book,
phut-phuti	—	motorbike,
mush-mush	—	sounds of shoe.

Some Indian Variety of English collocations (a technical term which refers to the way in which certain words tend to go in the company of other words) differ from the British English. For example, 'milk' collocates with 'cow' but not with 'tiger.'

> "He has evaporated, the eater of his master!" (Said Lady Todar Mal) [from *Coolie*]

'Evaporate' does not suit to this statement. 'Evaporate' collocates with something that can take gaseous state. 'Vanish' instead of 'evaporate' would have been a better choice in the said example from Mulk Raj Anand's *Coolie.* In the spoken variety of IVE we often use 'light coffee.' 'Light' does not collocate with 'coffee.' The standard British English would be 'weak coffee.'

If we go deep into the conversation of IVE, we can easily locate the individualistic as well as creative trends which are different from British English conversations. Actually, conversation build up with, psycholinguistic guesses. 'Topics,' 'Domains' and Role-relationships of the communicators play decisive role in conversations. 'Domains,' 'Situations' (Topics), 'Role-relationships' are Fishman's Constructs (1971). 'Domains' are socio-cultural constructs abstracted from topics (themes) of communication, relationships or bonds between communicators and locals (settings) of communication.

In running communication, social situations are governed by 'topics' connected with particular situations. Thus social situation is a construct that is of great value in socio-linguistics. In Indian Writings in English as well as in IVE conversations the topics are in most cases Indian. And the very 'congruent' (when domains, situations and role-relationships 'go together' in socio-culturally expected way) reflects 'Indianness' both in theme and style, Role-relationships are implicitly accepted sets of mutual rights, obligations and shared feelings between members of the same socio-cultural system. Teacher-student, husband-wife, father-daughter are some of the examples of the role-relationships that exist in speech community. Now let us examine the above-mentioned socio-linguistic constructs (Fishman's constructs) from the point of view of IVE:

Type of text — literal.

[The text is an extract from Mulk Raj Anand's famous novel *Untouchable.*]

'Eh, eh, boy, come here. Go and get a bottle of soda-water.'

Bakha came back with a start and stood staring at the dignitary who had called him. The man wore a monocle in his left eye and Bakha, who had never seen anything of that kind, wondered how a single glass could remain fixed on the eye without a frame.

'Don't stare at me!' shouted the gentleman, while Bakha was wondering who the man could be, too sallow-faced for an Englishman, too white for an Indian, and clad in such fine clothes, yellow gloves on his hands and white cloth on his buckskin shoes.

'Ham desi sahib, don't stare at me,' said the man deliberately using the wrong Hindustani spoken by the English, but becoming kinder for a moment. 'I have just come from Vilayat. Is there a soda-water shop near here?'

Bakha had been taken unawares. He couldn't adjust himself to this Phenomenon. So he moved his head to indicate that he didn't know. Fortunately for him, the man's attention was switched off to his friend, a young man with a delicate feline face, illuminated by sparkling, dark eyes and long, black curly hair, who stood next to him dressed in flowing Indian robes like a poet's. Bakha's

> inadequate answer did not, therefore, evoke the insolent flourish of the barrister's cane as it might have done.

The above is a fitting example of IVE conversation. Bakha and the 'desi sahib' are the communicators here. The 'Domain' is typically an Indian social life where two different cultural identities co-exist. The situation (topic) is connected with the 'Bakha's staring at the desi sahib.' This is an .example of Sahib (master) and dalit/harijan (servant) role-relationship. The conversation begins with Indian Variety of English: "Eh, eh, boy [...]." All three socio-linguistic constructs reflect the very feeling of Indianness.

Indian Variety of English is known for 'code switching' and 'code mixing.' India is a multicultural land where different cultures exist side by side. Each culture makes its impact on the other cultures. People speak more than one language. They tend to mixup their codes in their conversations (both writing or spoken):

> "Mahatma Gandhi Ki jai! Mahatma Gandhi Ki jai!" the cry went thundering up into the smoke-scented evening. (from *Untouchable*)

In the above extract from *Untouchable* Hindi code and English code are used together. This is a typical characteristic of IVE. This feature of IVE is more prominent when the Role-relationship is friend-friend, the topic is related to sports or film. In these cases the communicators tend to mix up their codes every now and then to add special intimacy among themselves. Apart from all such reasons, the communicators find their topics easier for communication when they use mixed code.

In 'Indian Variety of English' the communicators use a different style in 'rule of address.' 'Socio-linguistic status-based dimension' go into the making of 'rule of address.' Indian society has several classes, based on economy and professions. Each class has individual rules of address. 'Babu,' 'Huzoor,' 'Sahib' are the general terms sociologically lower-class people use to their respective higher-class people. '-ji' is an IVE suffix that go with people with social recognition. For example:

> Gandhi + ji — Gandhiji.

Actually, 'status' (economic or sociological) determine the socio-linguistic rules of address of the communicators. British intrusion in India "was military and exploitative."[4] It also made a deep impact on Indian sociological structure. In Indian 'status-based dimension,' people address their superiors (sociologically) with some Indian address words like—'babu,' 'sahib,' 'huzoor.' This tendency is not so routine-wise in British 'socio-linguistic rule of address.' And in standard British English conversation the communicators don't use the status-based address words so often. So, what happened in India, as in several other Asian, African and American countries, was that as a result of socio-cultural interaction with regional topics/contexts English became 'X-ized'. And IVE is the outcome of the Indianization of English.

Raja Rao in his *Preface* to his novel *Kanthapura* says, English is not a "foreign tongue in India, but it is only the language of our intellectual make-up, not of our emotional make-up." Indian Variety of English is used in Indian Writings in English to express Indian sensibility, *i.e.* to convey/translate the 'feel' of the cultural, philosophical and emotional life of the Indians to the readers. Raja Rao refers to a problem generally troubles the Writers of Indian Writings in English:

> [...] We are all instinctively bilingual, many of us Writing in our own language end in English. We cannot Write like the English. We should not. We can write only as Indians. We have grown to look at the large world as part of us. Our method of expression, therefore, has to be a dialect which will some day prove to be as distinctive and colourful as the Irish or the American.[5]

Indo-Anglian writers tend "to bring the hangover of the mother tongue [...] into their expressions."[6]

In this context I'm reminded of Meenakshi Mukherjee's comment "using the English language in a way that will be distinctly Indian and still remain English."[7]

We cannot deny the fact that Indian Variety of English is a great departure from the standard British English. We are but to accept it. But IVE is not a 'Pidgin'[8] Language. It is creative as well as resourceful. 'Indian Variety of English' is a socio-liguistic reality today.

NOTES & REFERENCES

1. Balasubramanian, T., *A Textbook of English Phonetics for Indian Students.* New Delhi, Macmillan India Limited, 1999.
2. Kachru, B.B., *Indian English: A Socio-linguistic Profile.*
3. A device generally we find in Indian languages. It means the repetition of words/phrases in statement/sentence.
4. Parasher, S.V., *Indian English: Certain Grammatical and Stylistic Features.* Published in *English Worldwide,* 1983.
5. Rao, Raja. *Preface to Kanthapura.*
6. Anand, Mulk Raj. "*Pigeon—Indian: Some Notes on Indian English Writing.*" The Karnataka University *Journal Humanities*, Vol. XVI (1972), 14-15.
7. Mukherjee, Meenakshi, *The Twice Born Fiction.* Arnold-Heinemann Publisher, 1974, 165.
8. 'Pidgin' is a contact language: a mixture of elements from different languages. Its used is restricted to certain groups, traders, seamen etc.

9

Teaching of English in India: Problems and Prospects

V.K. JAIN

In the present age of globalization and liberalization English is the only lingua-franca for the entire world but students and teachers of English face numerous problems related to the study and teaching of the language. Initially it enjoyed the status of the first language (Pre-Independence era). Then its status was changed into that of a second language used for official work throughout the country. Then it was demoted to the position of an optional second language. Though, today it is well-known to the sizable number of people in the country, it is on the way to become a foreign language.

The learning of English as second language is bound to pose a number of difficulties both the teachers and the learners. Even among the linguists there have been differences of opinion as to how to proceed to teach the language; on what place to place the stress and what sort of text should be prepared for the students? While according to some scholars the real difficulty of learning of foreign language lies in mastering its vocabulary. There are others who hold that the real problem his in mastering the sound system and the structure of the language. Similarly the problem is posed by differences in culture between L_1 and L_2.

In order to achieve these, a number of methods have been developed and distinct kinds of planning such as selection, grading and presentation have been advocated. But whatever method is adopted the goal of a teacher of English language is fairly clear. The student is to be taught to read, write, speak and to understand. These cover the entire gamut of language learning. Phonetics, phonology, grammar and vocabulary are the four constituents of English language. A few observations on each of them may be made.

The mother tongue of a student learning English as second language is bound to have different phonology. And their English is much more affected by their regional accent and it is rather difficult to avoid the pull of one's mother tongue standing in the way of correct pronunciation of English. In order to give effective teaching the teacher must have a good knowledge of L_1 and L_2 and the differences between the two.

English, as it is internationally spoken, has more than one accent. Apart from two standard models (American English and British English) there are native speakers of this language in Canada, Australia, New Zealand and South Africa. But British RP (Received Pronunciation) still enjoys world-wide recognition.

In India we may have English speakers from Assam, Bihar, M.P., U.P., Delhi and Tamil Nadu with variations. Some Bengali and Bihari speakers, for instance, replace /v/ by /b/ (instead of pronouncing 'Vinay' they pronounce 'Binay') and some speakers from U.P. and M.P. replace /s/ by /ʃ/ (sh), instead of pronouncing 'Shobha' they pronounce 'Sobha.' There is a section of Indians, who, by efforts and training, have achieved the approximation to the British standard pronunciation. It may be made clear that it is neither possible nor necessary for everyone to get mastery over the British RP. But to aim at international intelligibility, approximation to the above standard can be tried out. Within India, the model of GIE (General Indian English) which is the desirable model to achieve intelligibility within India, would suffice.

The school teachers of today don't know better pronunciation. They are also not aware of RP. In such condition it is futile to hope that students would catch the right pronunciation. Only the BBC programmes and Doordarshan news readers, may help in forming habits of speaking English correctly.

In this age of globalization, international tourism, travel and trade, exchange of resources and knowledge, spoken form of English is getting due importance. Therefore, international intelligibility of spoken English should be the learner's aim. Here are some tips towards learning correct pronunciation of English:

(i) The first thing that the students should be taught is naturally concerned with the English *sound system,* i.e. without teaching phonetics to the students, he must teach them the correct pronunciation of various English sounds both individually and when they are used in connected speech. The discrepancy between written symbol and actual pronunciation of various English sounds will have to be made known to the students.

One must know all the 44 English speech sounds and their symbols. 20 of these are vowel sounds and 24 are consonant sounds. Key to the phonetic symbols can be found in Daniel Jones's *English Pronouncing Dictionary* (EPD). With knowledge of these sounds and symbols, a learner can easily distinguish /s/ from /ʃ/.

(ii) *Voiced and Voiceless Sounds*

In articulating the vowel sounds and the consonants b, d, d_3, v, ȝ, z, 3, m, n, l, r, j, w our vocal cords vibrate. All these sounds are called voiced-sounds. Rest of the speech sounds *i.e.*, p, t, k, tʃ, p, θ, s, ʃ, h are called voiceless sounds. This information is very useful and is part of training in spoken English. Adding 's' to <u>cut</u> gives /s/ sound: cuts /k^ts/. But adding 's' to <u>pen</u> gives /z/ sound: pens /penz/. Reason is clear if inflection of 's' follows a voiced sound (*i.e.*, /n/ in <u>pen</u>) it sounds /z/.

(iii) *Accent on the right syllable of a word*

Knowledge of syllable structure is also helpful in the direction of achieving the correct pronunciation. Though theory or definitions of syllable are not advisable to the students of first year yet this much can be told that syllable is a word or a part of word which has one vowel sound. For example the word CAT/Kæt/has one vowel sound that is /∂e/ and the first and the last sound in this word are consonants.

Accents of English pose a great problem. There is no fixed rule regarding which syllable in a polysyllabic word should take the accent. In addition to this, suffixes often change the accentual patterns of several English words. For instance:

a'cademy (stress on the second syllable)

aca'demic (stress on the third syllable)

acade'mician (stress on the fourth syllable)

Accent also depends upon words function in the sentence *i.e.* whether the word is a verb or a noun/adjective. For instance

Verb	*Noun /Adjective*
Convict /kən'vikt/	Convict /'kɔnvikt/
Export /iks'pə:t/	Export /'ekspɔ:t/

Also pronunciation of the sound changes

Verb	*Noun*
Use /ju:z/	Use /ju:s/

All these features are totally new to an Indian learner because he doesn't come across anything like this complexity in his native language so very often he places the accent on the wrong syllable of a word with disastrous consequences. Bansal illustrates this point with following examples:

Word	*Indian Pronunciation*	*Understood by native speakers as*
Character	[kəe'rektə r]	director
Decay	['dike:]	ticket
Defence	['difɛns]	difference

Through drilling and practice it would be learnt that in a word with more than one syllable which particular syllable is to be stressed or we can say that the syllable is said with greater force. Placing stress on a wrong syllable or not stressing anyone makes our pronunciation bad.

(iv) *Aspirated Sounds*

Aspiration is an important feature of native English. Most Indians substitute unaspirated /p/ /t/ /k/ for aspirated [pʰ] [tʰ] [kʰ] at the beginning of accented syllables. For instance in the word '*paper*' the first /p/ is aspirated and the second is unaspirated so the word is pronounced ['pʰeipə] by a native speaker of English, whereas it is pronounced /'peipər/ by most Indians. It is interesting to note that unaspirated voiceless plosives at the beginning of accented syllables sound like voiced plosives to the ears of a native speaker. The following table illustrates this point:

Word	*Pronounced by an Indian as*	*Understood by a native speaker*
touch	[t^tʃ]	Dutch
twelve	[twɛ lv]	dwell
pack	[pəek]	back

This clearly illustrates that communication positively breaks down if the initial voiceless plosives in accented syllables are not aspirated. Aspiration of plosives should not be a problem to Indian speakers because in most Indian languages the aspiration of plosives is distinctive. The only trouble is that in English the same letter ρ is used for [pʰ] and [p].

(v) *Pronouncing /θ/ and /ʒ/*

Indian speakers substitute the dental plosive [t̪ʰ] (Hindi sound थ) or [t̪] for English /θ/ and [d̪] (Hindi sound [द] for English /ʒ/. In English there is no [थ] or [द] sound. When articulating /θ/ sound, tip of the tongue is placed between upper teeth can lower teeth and the air passes through places of articulations with friction ./θ/ is voiceless and /ʒ/ is voiced.

/θ/ and /ʒ/ sound do not exist in Indian languages. This cause a problem in intelligibility because there are many minimal pairs contrasting /t/ and /θ/ in English like <u>taught</u> and <u>thought</u>, <u>tree</u> and <u>three</u>, <u>tin</u> and <u>thin</u>.

To a native speaker of English [t̪ʰ] or [t̪] sounds more like an alveolar plosive /t/ then a dental fricative /θ/. Similarly they understand [d̪] as /d/ and not as /ʒ/. Hence as Bansal observes they misunderstood <u>themselves</u> as <u>damsels</u>.

(vi) *Substitution of /ʋ/ for English /v/ and /w/*

In English /v/ and /w/ are different phonemes. This distinction is lost in Indian English and both <u>west</u> and <u>vest</u> are pronounced [ʋɛst] by most educated Indians. The students should be asked to make their /v/ fricative and to articulate /w/ properly with rounded lips.

(vii) *Substitution of /s/ for /z/*

There is no one to one relationships between spelling and sound. *House* has /s/ as the final sound whereas noise has /z/. The letters ss are pronounced /s/ in essence but /z/ in scissors. The letter /x/ is /ks/ in except but gz in exact.

Plural endings are pronounced /s/ by most Indians and peace and peas are thus homophones in their speech. Some other homophones used by Indian learners are fans and fence, peas and piece, knees and niece, falls and false, eyes and ice.

Thus our English (*i.e.*, Indian English) is much more affected by our regional accent and it is rather difficult to avoid the pull of one's mother tongue standing in the way of correct pronunciation of English. In order to learn correct pronunciation one should keep all these points in mind and he should be a keen listener to good English. So far as vocabulary is concerned he may be directed to seek the help of a dictionary. But even then he will have to be directed in using the words in an appropriate way keeping in view the spirit of the English language into account. So by and large a practical teacher is bound to face many challenges when he tries to teach this language to whom it is a foreign language.

WORKS CITED

Allen, W.S. *Living English Speech.* London: Longmans, 1954.

Baker, A. *Introducing English Pronunciation.* Cambridge: Cambridge University Press, 1982.

Balasubramanian, T.A. *Textbook of English Phonetics for Indian Students.* Madras: Macmillan, 1981.

Bansal, R.K. and J.B. Harrison. *Spoken English for India.* Madras: Orient Longman, 1983.

CIEFL, Exercises in Spoken English, Part 1, 2 and 3 OUP, 1994, 1977, 1981.

Daniel Jones. *Outline of English Phonetics.* New Delhi: Kalyani Publisher, 1979.

Hocket, C.F. *A Course in Modern Linguistics.* New Delhi: OUP, 1970.

Kachru, B.B. *The Indianisation of English.* The English Language in India. New Delhi: OUP, 1983.

Sethi, J. and P.V. Dhamija. *A Course in Phonetics and Spoken English.* New Delhi: Prentice-Hall of India, 1989.

10

Innovation in ELT and Instructional Materials: An Indian Context

SANDHYA RANI SAHOO

Introduction: Language Education in India

India has over a billion people. It has 1652 mother tongues, and 44 languages (1990) are used for schooling. Between 34 and 52 per cent of the school time is devoted to language-teaching. In a multi-dialectical and multilingual country of such huge dimension, language planning poses a very serious challenge (Pattnayak, 1997). A Report on the Study of Languages (1986) says that more than one language is necessary for greater mobility and employment opportunity within the state and the country. Evidently innovative and creative experience of a pluralistic society demands cultivated use of more than one language. Knowledge of more than one language encourages appreciation of other's point of view and is conducive to national integration. Study of languages enables the learner to gain knowledge, skills and dispositions to communicate and make comparisons across languages and cultures. Learning and using a language, be it L1, L2 or L3, fosters the development of children as communicators. Along with the acquisition of communicative ability, the learner will also acquire the understanding of culture and the diverse ways of thinking and valuing. This goes a long way in understanding themselves; widening their network of

(Paper presented at the RELC International Seminar on 'Methodology and Material Design in Language Teaching: Current Practices and their Implications,' 22-24 April 2002, at the SEAMEO Regional Language Centre, Singapore.)

interaction to contribute positively and productively as citizens in the linguistically and culturally diverse nation in which they live, and also as global citizens.

The 'three-language formula' recommended by the Education Policy of India (1968) and re-iterated in the Policy of 1986 is an operational device to capture the multi-lingual reality of the country in the educational system. A student during his ten years of schooling is required to learn a minimum of three languages: a state language, a national official language and the national associate official language. The first language should be the mother tongue/regional language. The second language may be Hindi or English in the case of non-Hindi speaking states, and English or one of the modern Indian languages in the Hindi speaking states. The third language in the non-Hindi speaking states will be either Hindi or English, whichever has not been studied as a second language. Similarly in the Hindi speaking states the third language should be English or any modern Indian language whichever has not been studied as a second language.

Our Policy documents emphasize effective language education. All language teaching at the school level should systematically develop those cognitive linguistic abilities in the learner which are acquired naturally by a native learner of a language. Once these abilities are developed in the learner they can be transferred from one language to another. Education in language should be used as a potential instrument for independent training among the learners from the very beginning. Learners should be positively encouraged to come up with their own opinion and interpretation of events around them and events in the past (Frame Work, 1986). Educationists, Linguists and Psycholinguists are of the view that early education should be imparted through mother tongue as it aids concept-formation and promotes creativity.

Pattanayak (1997) reinforces the idea that mother tongue is that language with which one is emotionally identified. It is the language through which the child recognises and organises his experience and environment around him. It is the language through which one expresses one's basic needs, ideas, thoughts, joys, sorrow and all other feelings. It is the language which, if lost and replaced by another language, renders a person intellectually alive but emotionally sterile.

Status of English in the World Scenario

With the advent of Information and Communication Technology, *English* has become a 'living' language, a language of communication. Enormous increase in the educational and academic opportunities and upward social mobility has made English acquire a permanent place in the third world countries.

A press release from the British Council says that in the mid 1990s world-wide, there were over 1,400 million people living in countries where English had official status. One, out of five of the world's population speaks English at some level of competence. By the year 2000, it was estimated that over 1 billion people would be learning English (Graddol, 1996). Kachru observes, 'For the first time a natural language has attained the status of an international (universal) language, essentially for cross-cultural communication' (Kachru, 1983). It is the main language of international commerce and trade. It has more cultural resources, in the sense of works of literature, films and television programmes. The literature of the world is available and read because of English translations. *The Economist* (1996) has described it having 'impregnably established as the world's standard language: an intrinsic part of the global communications revolution.'

English in India

Policy Documents (1968, 1986, 1992) and reports of various Commissions reiterate the importance of English language in India which was earlier studied as a library language. English will continue to enjoy a high status as long as it remains the principal medium of education at University stage and the language of administration at the Centre and in many of the states. It will continue to function as the associate official language of the country. English language has been one of the potent factors for the maintenance of unity in the country. Further, for all practical purposes, it will continue to remain our principal means of establishing contact with the outside world.

Although colonization was responsible for the first stage of spread of English in India, some new forces and processes provided a basis for its further development. Technological development, economic globalization and informed communication have all played a role in the rise of *English* in India. English is an international language and if catastrophic events do not alter the present alignment of world-forces, it will soon be the world language. It has a great socio-functional purpose in a multilingual and the new socio-cultural environment of India. No other Indian language has become so much a part of our natural habit.

This makes the popular mind in India equate education with the knowledge of English. A person who uses English in transactional interaction is considered to be part of the elite group of the society and commands a greater respect. This attitude and motivation for the study of English constitutes 'instrumental motivation,' *i.e.* the desire with a utilitarian objective such as to obtain admission in a particular course or to get a better job (Gardener and Lambert, 1972). On this basis, Khanna and Agnihotri (1982) and Khanna (1982) modified Gardener and Lambert's motivational orientation and divided the motivational reasons into two parts: 'Complementary motivation' which refers to the motivation to learn English to get a better job or study further; and 'Supplementary motivation' that refers to the motivation to learn English to read foreign literature, see English movies or feel superior. This complementary motivation persuades the parents to send their children to English-medium schools even if they are economically deprived so that the children will communicate in English. Many states have now decided to introduce the study of English from class I or class III, particularly because English has become a language of future prosperity and technological breakthroughs have shrunk the globe. Though introduction of English in class I or III is educationally unsound, there is a demand for it.

Innovations in ELT in India

Even if English starts in class I, the role of the language will not differ from that of a second language. The objective of teaching and learning a second language is similar in Asia and the Pacific. It will always be a conscious effort on the part of the student to learn this language, as opposed to the natural mode of acquisition of his mother tongue. In practical terms English does not and cannot express his basic needs, ideas, thought, emotion and feelings. To search for self-affirmation, to establish group-identity and to satisfy the normal urge for cultural 'rootedness,' the student will always fall back upon his mother tongue. Therefore English will always function as a service-subject in its role either as L1 or L2 in India.

To teach English language, various methods have been developed and some of them have proved to be extremely influential at different times. Prabhu (1995) enlists quite a few: classical scholastic procedures, grammar-translation method, direct method, structural method, communicative language teaching, reading methods, task-based language teaching etc. These teaching methods have been tried and evaluated. Some of them have been praised, adopted and then rejected to try new methods that promised successful learning by learners.

Since English has become a 'link language,' a language of communication, the main objective of teaching English is not merely to develop in learners the ability to use grammatically accurate language with some deliberations. It should further develop the ability to produce socially appropriate spontaneity. English language teaching, for that matter, should be based on a syllabus of social functions, rather than of grammatical structures. A learner with proficiency in English grammar fails to use them in real life situation. He lacks in articulation and confidence. Learning of structural items only limits his ability to operate in the world outside the classroom.

The shift from structural approach to communicative approach is a shift from language learning process to language learning purpose. Learning of isolated terms will not enable the learner to communicate appropriately and with excellence in real life. The learners need to rehearse the 'social roles' that they will perform in real situations. The demand is a paradigm shift from the structural exercise to group work, pair work, direct imitation and play-acting etc.

To develop the communication skills in English which has the status of the second language needs a lot of thinking.

In India, in most of the cases the learners are first generation learners, and the opportunities like peer group interaction; guidance of the parents and elders are not available. The reinforcement from the immediate environment is insufficient. The absence of such conducive, intellectually stimulating environment at home and in the surrounding milieu puts pressure on the learner of the second language. This can be overcome by providing a stimulating environment in school, by using appropriate method of teaching and specially designed instructional materials. There is a great need for a change in the methodology of teaching language from a unidirectional, teacher-centred, knowledge-oriented activity to learning through an interactional activity, involving sub-activities like problem solving, group-work, drawing inferences, making generalisations and participating in a variety of other activities with the help of L1, L2, and L3 (Verma, 1987).

Changes in the Curriculum

The recent trends in second language education in India are shaped in the context of the country itself, reflecting its heterogeneous social background and the needs of the learner. The significant reasons for the reforms in ELT are due to increased mobility both within and between the countries; the ethnic and linguistic diversity; harmonious living with cross cultural understanding and tolerance in pluralistic society. NIER-Japan, Seminar Report, 2001 says that the effective communication becomes important because of globalization and closely integrated World Economies. The pressure for economic growth leads countries to give priority to developing the skills of their people. These skills include linguistic capabilities and intercultural understanding. The increasing access to and use of information technologies provides immediate links between people and sights across the world. It opens the doors to information in a variety of languages, bringing the world closer than ever before. These trends provide a background to interpreting and synthesizing the recent trends in foreign/second language education.

A change in the curriculum is called for keeping in mind the knowledge explosion due to advance information and communication technology and pedagogical considerations.

Curriculum, an ongoing process, has to be 'sensitive and responsive to the entire gamut of societal, pedagogical and other changes at all levels.' In fact curriculum is a device to translate national goals into educational experiences.

Affirming the issues related to language education and medium of instruction, the National Curriculum Framework for School Education, 2000, visualises the integration of environmental education with languages in the first two years of primary stage *i.e.* desired skills of listening and speaking. This necessitates some change in the language curriculum. The mastering of an instrumental subject like English tempts the learner to better his communication and comprehension skills for further learning. The function of the language is more important than form. Language should be used profitably and effectively in the real life situations. The curriculum emphasises creative expression and the ability to think on one's own which must be encouraged and nurtured through language teaching with the oral form of language finding important place in language curriculum. The capacity to use the language in speech and writing whenever needed in life and to read it with reasonable speed for information and pleasure would be the most important objective. Grammar is not to be taught as a theoretical subject *per se,* but it would be taught as practical or functional grammar contextually with minimum theory.

Thus, more and more aural and oral skills of language are to be emphasized at the primary stage, all the skills *i.e.*, listening, speaking, reading and writing and thinking are to be aimed at in a balanced manner by the end of the upper primary stage, and slightly more attention is to be paid to the skills of reading and writing at the secondary stage. The most crucial and ultimate task of language education at all these levels remains to prepare the learners to use the languages effectively in either mode (spoken/written) whenever and wherever required in their day to day life-situations of all sorts. However, at the higher secondary stage (+2 level) the objective of language learning is to nurture advanced communication and negotiation skills, higher order reading, writing and study skills and to imbibe a humane, appreciative and futuristic approach to life among learners. The study of language enables the students to learn and use language effectively in the classroom, the community and the workplace. Study of language would ensure better mental health for the learners through exposure to finer human emotions, sentiments, mental conflicts and their resolutions.

Focus of the Syllabus

Communication through second language (mainly English) has become increasingly important in the present global community. Language education (both foreign and second language) is important all over the world at present. The recent global trends have dramatically increased the need for functional communicative competence in languages both for social interaction and, increasingly, for international co-operation (NIER-Japan, Seminar Report 2001). The basic school curriculum has recently incorporated a new emphasis on functional communicative competence in second language teaching. The syllabuses for various stages of school education have been designed keeping in mind the curricular needs specified in the English language curriculum. This establishes a link between educational objectives and the expected developmental goals in a systematic and graded manner. Syllabus plays an important role in transacting the basic recommendations of the Curriculum Framework 2000 based on the National Policy on Education, 1986.

Integrating diverse curricular concerns, relating education to the world of work, reducing curriculum load, making a case for culture specific pedagogy, and nurturing aesthetic sensibilities are some of the other concerns which have been addressed adequately while developing the syllabuses. English fulfils the functional (communicative), literary (aesthetic) and cultural (sociological) needs of the learner. The main thrusts of the new syllabus are to equip the learners with communicative skills, to enable them to perform different language functions, and to help them to develop their cognitive and affective faculties.

According to Verma (1969), the objective of teaching English is not to simply make the learners learn the language skills, but to enable the learners to play their communicative roles effectively and to select languages/registers/styles according to the roles they are playing. "Teaching a second language is a process of helping our pupils make appropriate register choices out of their total register range [...]. Register-shift, *i.e.* the ability to shift registers according to shift in situations, is one of the crucial conditions of success in handling a second language effectively."

Instructional Materials

Instructional Materials provide opportunities for learning. 'A good language learning depends on at least three variables: aptitude, motivation and opportunity' (Rubin, 1979). Opportunity includes materials and the activities within and outside the classroom. The instructional materials are of various kinds: textbooks, audio and video cassettes, handouts, charts, teaching aids of various kinds etc. Keeping in view the vastness of the country, the socio-economic conditions of the people and the constraints in reaching the remote villages, the accessibility of audio and video materials in language teaching across the board is a rare possibility. The textbook is the only important source of information and knowledge available to the teacher as well as to the learner. Therefore this instructional material should be designed according to the needs of the learner. The activities should be woven around the environment of the learner so that the second language learning should not be a burden. Since the emphasis is on the development of the skills, teaching of language should be structured and adequate. The approach should be multi-skilled-activity-based and learner-centred. Taking clues from these requirements the teacher can create new activities to supply language needs which will enable the learner to achieve a level of reasonable competence in using English in appropriate social situations.

Teacher should help the learners to 'learn how to learn,' and to engage them in activities that help them to investigate and analyse, infer, internalise and apply. For a learner to apply language fluently in different social situations, the child must be exposed to 'a variety of language in action.' The teacher and the learner should both be active participants. This interaction will not only give the child opportunity to use the language appropriately, but also to boost his confidence, self-assurance and competence to use English effectively according to the demand of the situation and his roles in it.

The purpose of education is not only to instruct but also to stimulate thinking. Instruction involves factual information whereas education draws out the real potentiality of individuals in such ways that they can access the meaning of the given facts and formulate their own, possibly new, ideas on the subject. So subject matter must be selected and organized with a view to its possible contribution in stimulating and guiding learner's experience which will result in the desired growth.

It must be selected with a view to providing all types of learner's growth—social, physical, moral and emotional and intellectual. The materials should try to realize the main objectives of ELT like: equipping the learners with communicative skills; handling language effectively while performing different language functions; helping them to develop their cognitive and affective faculties; promoting the skill of reading the text intelligently and imaginatively; and enriching the active and passive vocabulary of the learner. Importance is given to the mastery of an instrumental subject like English to develop communication and comprehension skills for further learning.

Instructional materials constitute an important element in the teaching-learning process. The methodology for preparing the instructional materials is based on a multi-skill-activity-based learner-centred approach. The enriched multi-skill course is both innovative and need based. The materials are designed in a manner so as to encourage self-learning. The most important objective of the materials is to develop the capacity to use the language in speech and writing whenever needed in life, and to read it with reasonable speed for information and pleasure. Grammar is not to be taught as a theoretical subject, but it should be taught as practical or functional grammar in the specified context with minimum theory. The language activities should be woven around the child's environment and experience for learners' motivation.

The teacher is the facilitator of learning who presents the communicative tasks through contrived situations in order to equip the child to use English for purposes of communication and expression. The instructional materials have a variety of exercises and activities based on the child's actions and experiences, because "children's use of language is closely related to the things they do with hands and bodies and the objects they come in contact with" (Krishna Kumar, 1994). The listening activities will sharpen the listening skills of the learner and make them conscious of different sounds, stress and intonation patterns of English. The communicative tasks, the dialogues, the role-plays and discussions etc. will help the learner to develop communicative skills and use language profitably and effectively in natural, everyday situations like seeking information, making request and suggestions, and some learning of the niceties of language, such as, polite expressions. There is a shift of emphasis from studying the textbook to learning the language and the stress is laid on the ability to use the language in speech and in writing. To keep alive the student's interest in learning English a variety of activities have been incorporated. These activities have been contextualized and they present language in natural situations. There is nothing artificial and contrived about them. The Projects will enhance learner's active participation; develop team spirit, reference and study skills; and collect information and put them in logical order.

It has been already assessed how relevant the materials are in teaching English language and literature in our teaching situations with the optimal use of available resources and materials in the classroom. The role and scope of materials is to create opportunities of learning. Mindfully put constructive exercises and tasks aim to change passive reading into productive learning. The purpose of designing these tasks is to develop the integrated skills—LSRW thinking/study and reference skills. These materials are based on content and skill, and the questions are both for formative assessment as well as summative assessment. Some questions given in the instruction materials will enable the learner to monitor and assess his own progress and thereby work towards a kind of learner autonomy,' which means that the learner will have full control over his own learning.

The comprehension exercises aim at the teaching of factual comprehension and deepening students' understanding of the lessons besides teaching interpretative/inferential/

evaluative/extrapolative comprehension. The vocabulary exercises are for teaching of spelling and vocabulary enrichment and development of reference skill. The exercises on language functions/functional grammar aim at developing the learner's ability to use the language effectively and accurately. 'Composition' is exploited to develop curiosity, imagination and creativity in the learners; and teach evaluative and extrapolative comprehension. The writing tasks, which are functional or imaginative types, are either controlled or semi-controlled leading on to free composition.

The poems are meant to be read aloud for the students to enjoy a different kind of language use which is creative and imaginative and which can achieve more total communication through a fuller utilization of various resources of language. The exercises at the end of the poem aim at helping the learners to appreciate and enjoy reading the poem.

The supplementary reader is designed to promote in the learner a love for reading by exposing him to good samples of English literature ranging from fables to stories of mystery, adventure and romance which hold the mirror up to different facets of life; to encourage the learner to read extensively on his own. The exercises given after each piece highlight the important points in the story. Some exercises are designed to deepen the student's understanding of the piece. The 'discussion' questions will generate discussion among the learner so as to inculcate effective communicative skills; to make them aware of the world around them; and to make them sensitive to the various aspects of life.

Language education has a greater potential as a means of developing attitudes and values related to all the ten core components reflected in the National Policy of Education, by incorporating appropriate themes and adopting suitable teaching-learning strategies. Language not only nourishes the basic and cognitive skills but also plays a definite role in the society, in the development of interpersonal interactions. It transmits culture and national values. So the instructional materials provide a wide range of themes from delineation of age-old problems of humanity to discussion of contemporary issues. These themes will not only enable the learners to gather information, to make them aware of the happenings in India and round the world, but also make them sensitive to human beings, human emotions and human problems. They will inculcate values for peaceful coexistence in the multilingual, multicultural, and multi religious society. These learning experiences will promote social cohesion and national integration, so essential to a diversified and great land called India.

REFERENCES

Agnihotri, R.K. and Khanna, A.L. *English Language Teaching in India.* Eds. Agnihotri and Khanna. New Delhi: Sage Publications, 1994.

Graddol, David. 'Global English Global Culture?' *Redesigning English New Texts, New Identities.* Eds. Sharon Goodman and David Graddol. 1982; London: Routledge, 1996: 181-82.

Kachru, B.B. *The Other Tongue: English Across Culture,* ed. 1983; Oxford: Pergamon, 1996: 51.

Khanna, A.L. and Agnihotri, R.K. 'Some Predictors of Speech Skill: A Socio-Psychological Study.' *Socio Psycho Logical Perspective on Second Language Learning.* Eds. Agnihotri, Khanna and Sachder. Delhi: Sage Publication, 1998.

Krishna Kumar. *The Child's Language And The Teacher.* New Delhi: National Book Trust, 2000.

National Policy on Education. New Delhi: M.H.R.D., 1986.

National Curriculum for Elementary and Secondary Education—A Framework. Revised version. New Delhi: NCERT, 1988.

National Curriculum Framework for School Education. New Delhi: NCERT, 2000.

Pattanayak, D.P. *Language Curriculum for Teacher Educators.* NCTE Monograph Series. New Delhi: NCTE, 1997.

Prabhu, N.S. *Second Language Pedagogy.* New Delhi: Oxford University Press, 1987.

Report of the Seminar on 'Trends in Foreign/Second Language Education in Asia and the Pacific,' National Institute for Educational Policy Research (NIER), Tokyo, Japan, December 2001.

Ribin, J. "What the good language learner can teach us" in J.B. Pride (ed.) *Socio-linguistic Aspect of Language Learning and Teaching.* Oxford: Oxford University Press, 1979.

'Study of Languages—A Report.' New Delhi: NCERT, March, 1986.

The Economist, 21 December 1996: 39.

Verma, S.K. 'The Changing Roles of Asian Languages: A Study in Register Creation.' Faculty Lecture No. 5. Singapore: National University of Singapore, 1984.

——. 'Language in education in multilingual society.' Presidential address delivered at the All India Conference of Linguists, 1986.

——. 'Teaching English as a Second Language in India: A Socio-Functional View,' *Second Language Acquisition.* Eds. Agnihotri, R.K. and Khanna, A.C. New Delhi: Sage Publications, 1987.

11

Instructional Materials: A Social Perspective

P. BHASKARAN NAIR

In spite of the abundance of researches and new development in Second Language Acquisition (SLA), the average second language classroom remains more or less textbook-dominated. That is to say, in an acquisition-poor-environment the only means of exposure to the target language is the instructional materials, and in our present day set up, they are reduced to a coursebook or a reader. The scope of freedom for the teacher to step out of the so-called prescribed textbook is limited in the sense that neither the methodology he/she is exposed to, nor the evaluation pattern that dominates the whole instructional system permits the teacher to do so. In that case, the significance of the instructional materials becomes more prominent.

Learning a second language in the formal classroom for using it in future was the practice, which had been followed over decades. It has also been found that the gap between the terminal point of such learning and the actual situations in which the target language is to be used could not be bridged. Learning a second language results only in an awareness raising of its formal grammar. It is in this context, an attempt to redefine the role of instructional materials becomes pertinent.

The transition, at the conceptualisation level, from structural syllabuses to semantic syllabi has not got truly reflected in the production of instructional materials. The apparent inability of the second language learner to transfer the knowledge of the target language to situations outside the classroom cannot be reckoned as a linguistic phenomenon; on the contrary it is a social as well as psychological problem of the learner. The psychological potentials of the individuals remain unexploited on the one side, whereas the frustration resulting out of the inability to meet the social requirements remains on the other. Here the apparent inability is not in the mastery of the rules of the language but in the use of that language about which the learner knows much. The problem may be seen, therefore, not as one of lack of transfer but of lack of opportunity to develop inside the classroom some of the skills that will be required outside it.

One major obstacle for the learners in the way the acquisition of communicative competence is the over-reliance on the instructional materials. The majority of the textbooks still present the target language in terms of grammatical structures artificially made 'meaningful' by their being situationalized. Widdowson (1972) has pointed out the futility of an approach, which focuses on language forms and ignores ways in which these forms are appropriately used to realize communicative acts.

Such an approach leads only to the learner's production of grammatically correct but unrelated sentences in a communicative vacuum. All Wright (1975) has questioned the feasibility of eliciting in the classroom the kind of discourse learners will encounter in the target language so long as the basis of classroom production are materials originally produced for language teaching.

How can we replace teaching materials written for use in the classroom? One way of substituting the inadequate materials is redefining materials from the point of view of the learner rather than that of the teacher. That is to say, instructional materials should be more or less learning materials than teaching materials. An approximation of the learning materials of the first language learning situations can be attempted in the second language learning situations too, even though such an approximation will still be remote. A textbook, which provides ample opportunities for classroom interaction, will be an improvement on the one that limits its own scope of being used as the teacher's monologue. In that sense, a change in the function as well as the structure of the learning materials can bring about certain desirable improvements in the quality of learning too. Instructional materials, thus become interactive materials—that is to say, materials which make interaction imperative in the classroom.

The conventional way of treating materials as a means for teaching the grammatical items has been proved inadequate. On the other hand, the use of materials, which serve the purpose of fitting in a communication vacuum, has been found more effective. In the former the progression of language learning is from within the classroom to the world outside, that is to say those language items, which are learned in the classroom, are supposed to be made use of in actual life, later. The progression in the latter is just the opposite; what happens outside is brought to the classroom and presented in the target language, as a result the language embedded in the social situation is led to real life. The question of learning how to do in the first language learning situation is replaced by 'learning how to mean' in a second language (Halliday, 1975). Therefore, the social context of instructional materials which has hitherto been pushed to the background of instructional processes has to be foregrounded and the pedagogic relevance of materials is to be considered only secondary to their social implications. All pedagogically acceptable materials need not be socially relevant, whereas all socially relevant materials are to be made pedagogically useful too. Language is a product of, and the means by which we have access to, the systems of meaning relationship that constitute culture (Halliday, 1975). Therefore, any attempt to the mastery of that alien code will be closer to the target only when the learner starts learning how to mean in the target language. That is to say, the materials which are interactive in structure, can function more effectively since they unravel systems of meaning relationships.

Since the instructional materials are the only text with which, and context in which interaction is made possible in an acquisition-poor environment, the more the interactive potentials in them, the more effective they will be. Defining language development as an interactive process, Halliday asserts that

> The Social semiotic is the system of meanings that defines or constitutes the culture; and the linguistic system is one mode of realization of these meanings. The child's task is to construct the system of meanings that represents his own mode of social reality. This process takes place inside his own head; it is a cognitive process. But it takes place in contexts of social interaction, and there is no way it can take place except in these contexts. (Halliday 1975)

Instructional materials become more effective when they draw their raw materials from social situations, and the ESL classroom is a place where these raw materials are being processed. The very acts of processing are the processes of learning too. A social situation with a cluster of communicative acts in them is brought to the classroom and the communicative acts are performed in the class as if they were performed outside. The enacted communicative function is more or less similar to the one the learner is expected to encounter back in real life. Instructional materials, which are interactive in nature, leave enough scope for language using options, such as "either this, or that, or the other" and not "this alone." Such an open-ended material bridges the gulf between the knowledge about the language gained in the classroom and the use of it outside.

WORKS CITED

R.L. All Wright. *Learning Language through Communication Practice.* Paper presented at the 4th International Congress of Applied Linguistics, Stuttgart, 1975.

M.A.K. Halliday. *Learning how to Mean; Explorations in the Development of Language.* London: Edward Arnold, 1975.

H.G. Widdowson. *The Teaching of English as Communication,* English Language Teaching 27, 1 (1972): 15-19.

——. *Teaching Language as Communication.* London: Oxford University Press, 1978.

12

ADAPTING INSTRUCTIONAL MATERIALS FOR TASK-BASED LANGUAGE CLASSROOMS

P. BHASKARAN NAIR

Quite often teachers complain about the unsuitability of instructional materials such as course books in general or a particular prose piece, in particular. However, as they are 'prescribed' for study, the teachers are forced to teach those books or lessons. How does a teacher know if a particular prose piece or poem is suitable to his/her learner? Are there any specific criteria with which we can evaluate the suitability of instructional materials? Or is it just based on the teacher's intuition or experience?

Learning can be viewed as a self-initiated exploration. Through a series of interrelated processes, the learner moves ahead step by step to the realm of the unknown. Neither at the starting point nor during the course of the expedition does the learner know fully what he is exactly going to find out or where his expedition is leading him. In fact, this obscurity of the realm of the unknown forms the nucleus of the journey. Once the 'unknown' turns into the 'known,' once the curiosity is settled, the charm of the expedition is lost for ever.

Look at a different situation in which the explorer is unable to move forward, since his progress is constantly blocked by obstacle after obstacle of various sort. In such a situation, any explorer of an average calibre gives up the job, since the anticipated ecstasy of reaching the unknown or the flame of curiosity is extinguished for ever. The journey comes to an end where it began. An expedition becomes an interesting experience only when there are challenges ahead and only when those challenges are overcome by self effort. Learning too, becomes interesting when there are challenges to meet and when the learner overcomes those challenges by himself. It is needless to say, the first success leads to the second.

What purpose should instructional materials serve in making learning interesting by sustaining motivation? They should lead the learner ahead by inviting him to do the tasks step by step or one after another. Each stage in the learning material should be slightly above the learner's cognitive ability so that he will be attracted by the charm of reaching the next higher point. Once he reaches there, he is attracted by the next higher point. Such a series of graded tasks keeps the learner's interest sustained. L.S. Vygotsky, the famous Russian psycholinguist has coined the term 'the zone of proximal development,' to denote the higher stage in the child's mental development to which instruction should be geared. If instruction is pitched at too high a point, the learner gets disappointed because none of his efforts takes him to the target point. If the target point is fixed too low by the teacher or materials-producer in standards of teaching and production of materials respectively, learning becomes too dull and monotonous for the learner to move forward. As a result boredom results and learning is altogether given up in the absence of challenges.

How can a teacher choose the instructional materials suitable to his/her learners, on the basis of the theory of the zone of proximal development? In a task-based approach the teacher gets the freedom to split the instructional materials into numerous learning task, big and small. A systematic gradation based on the teacher's knowledge about his/her learner's mental development will help to redesign the instructional material in such a way that it retains the content of the lesson and the special characteristics of the language employed in the lesson. But at the same time, it provides ample opportunities in the form of optimal challenges for the learner to 'function' in the target language. While the learner is meeting the challenges designed to reach his zone of proximal development, he is not mechanically answering a question, but functioning in the language and thereby reaching a higher point in his mental development.

As pointed out earlier, teachers in general, do not get the freedom of choosing instructional materials to be used in the classroom. Moreover, in an examination-oriented set up as we do have in our country, the teachers do not get the freedom to move away from the prescribed books either. In such a situation, an intuitive teacher should be able to make the best use of the available materials so that instruction could be made fruitful. The graded, integrated task-approach will be one way of improving upon the given instructional materials.

WORKS CITED

Vygotsky, L.S. *Thought and Language.* Massachusetts: MIT Press, 1962.

——. *Mind in Society, The Development of Higher Mental Processes.* Eds. M. Cole, V. John-Steiner, S. Scribner and E. Souberman. Cambridge: Harvard University Press, 1978.

Wertsch, J.V. ed. *Recent Trends in Soviet Psycholinguistics.* New York: M.E. Sharpe, 1977.

13

Relevance of English Language Teaching (ELT) in Professional Education

MEENAKSHI RAMAN

It may not be an exaggeration to say that education in India has become synonymous with English, taking into cognizance the pervasiveness of this prestigious language in almost all fields of education. Starting from the lowest till the highest level of education, the importance and dominance of English cannot be ignored. It is a fact that no educational system in India can survive without English language. The same may be the case with many other nations. This link language is the language of all sciences, engineering and technology. To be more specific, the increasing demands for proficiency in English in almost all these fields makes it imperative that the teachers of English language come to the fore, keep themselves abreast of the latest innovations in the teaching methodologies and equip themselves with all those strategies necessary to make ELT more functional and meaningful than ever before.

With its emphasis on the role of the teachers of English language in professional education, this paper addresses itself to the task of identifying and emphasizing the following:

1. the need for ELT in professional education,
2. the strategies which could make ELT more meaningful and functional in professional education and
3. the ELT projects which could be taken up involving the students of professional education.

Need

Professional education is the process by which men and women prepare for exacting responsible service in the professional spirit. It is that process of education that grooms a student towards achieving his specific professional goals and enables him climb the ladder reaching into his chosen profession. The foundation of professional education should be not only technical skill but also a sense of social responsibility, an appreciation of social and human values and relationships and disciplined power to see realities without prejudice or blind commitment. While professional men largely set the pattern of national life, the pattern is much influenced by their earlier intellectual and moral experiences, especially their professional training. The standards and motives of professional practice in the coming years are largely being made in the institutions where they had their professional education. So it is imperative that the students of professional education acquire not only technical skills but also soft skills—communication both oral and written, motivation, creative thinking, self-management etc. Of all these soft skills communication occupies the topmost priority. English, being the link language, provides the basis for this most important soft skill.

By and large, professional education begins after the high school education and it doesn't stop with a graduation. It continues further. While some of the students pursue higher degrees in professional education either in India or abroad, some of them take up professions in academic or research institutions, various Industries such as software, chemical, pharmaceutical, electronic etc. So the process of learning goes on and on. The role of English in all these processes is extremely relevant and significant.

Since a student joins a professional institute after completing his high school English, which he learns or rather, develops during his professional educational process is in the advanced level. His needs in the area of English language learning at school differ from those at a university or college. A student of professional education needs both communicative competence and skill in English. He should develop his passive (listening and reading) skills to become more competent and active skills (speaking and writing) to become more proficient in English. So, it is appropriate to say that at this stage, the role of English teachers is to develop all the four English language skills in the student rather than teaching English language. These skills, besides making the student proficient in English, also helps him face all the competitive examinations such as GRE, TOEFL GMAT, etc. where he has to compete internationally with more confidence. All these exams at the international level and also various other exams at the national level invariably have a valid English component encompassing all the four language skills. Further, proficiency in English unquestionably moulds him as a desirable personality in the professional world. To become a perfect persona, he needs many soft skills out of which communication is very important.

It is needless to say that developing skills in communication is never possible without developing English language skills. Most of the students of professional education occupy executive posts in organizations. Their everyday professional life requires proficiency in English. Starting from giving instructions to participating in high-level meetings they have to perform various tasks each one of which requires effectiveness in the use of English.

Its ability to cope with the language demands of a range of scientific, technical, commercial and industrial topics with both accuracy and interest has also ensured that the English language is a universal tool of communication.

So the ability to use English competently and confidently matters enormously—not only to desk-driving managers and office personnel—but also to the many and varied professionals. They cannot escape the need to listen, speak, read or write English at work and rely on it in their social lives—in their ability to apply for a passport or for higher education, buy a car or attending an interview etc.

With these convictions in mind and with the knowledge that a professional student's skill in using English can be dramatically improved if the will and effort are present, we shall now embark upon discussing the related strategies.

Strategies

As discussed earlier, the needs for developing English language skills and hence English communication skills during the course of professional education are many and varied. But the basic requirement underlying all these needs is the same; that is improving the student's English skills of listening, speaking, reading and writing. This would make the teaching and learning English more meaningful and functional. Here are a few essential strategies that would lead us towards accomplishing this goal:

- to design well structured courses
- to focus mainly in the areas of vocabulary, pronunciation, accent, word order and composition
- to be diligent in choosing and framing the word lists
- to give practice through language games, role play and other innovative methods
- to provide additional practice in language lab and through computer based courseware
- to select appropriate teaching material not only from textbooks but also from internet sites specially dealing with English language
- to initiate more group activities rather than person-centred ones
- to include interesting and useful evaluation components
- to motivate the students through rewards
- to involve students in ELT projects

So at every stage—planning, designing, developing, implementing and monitoring—appropriate strategies need to be adopted play in the process of professional education. Courses such as English Language Skills, Technical Report Writing, Business Communication, Effective Speaking etc. are not only essential to the students of professional education but also are well received by them. With the increasing academic pressure in their professional education at the universities or colleges, today's youth find such courses both important and interesting. The role of the teachers of English is therefore to structure these courses in such a way that the students learn how to communicate effectively their ideas, facts, feelings, attitudes and courses of action to others in their future professional careers.

The purpose of acquiring proficiency in a language is mainly to communicate in that language. It is essential therefore that the student should develop both the receptive and the productive skills. While the former enables him become more competent, the latter equips him with more proficiency. Teachers of English have a significant role to play in the process of professional education. For example, they can help students become better listeners by adopting various strategies in the listening comprehension exercises. Various listening activities such as role-play, informal talks, conversations, certain drills and exercises etc. can be planned (Venkateswaran 1995: 81). As listening and speaking go hand in hand, every listening activity is accompanied by a speaking activity. The teachers, therefore, can develop conversational ability and presentation skills in the student by providing adequate opportunities through participation in role-plays and professional presentations. In addition, the ability to speak can further be developed through various other activities such as interpreting a picture or a graph, discussing in groups and completing a story etc. Introducing Language Games helps further in this direction (Wright 1984: 72). Moving on to the next skill, namely reading, much need to be done at the university level because, with lot of distractions today, the students have almost forgotten the value of reading. Reading comprehension involves understanding the value of each utterance. The practice passages have to be constructed or chosen with utmost care. They should present a wide spectrum of topics ranging from simple real-life experience to complex technical topic. As professionals, the students may require to write various reports, proposals or research papers. The English teachers are the main source of providing suitable guidance in this direction. English language classroom is one place which can make them read and which can strategically improve their reading speed. Not only India, but also the entire world is available to the teachers of English today through computers and television.

The evaluation components need to be a combination of oral as well as written components. Each student is to be tested for the skills he has acquired in all the four language skills. Picture interpretation, informal conversation, impromptu and extemporaneous speeches are certain means through which their oral skills can be evaluated. There are innumerable ways in which their written skills can be tested.

There are a number of Internet sites dedicated to the teachers and the learners of English. These can be effectively used to broaden their horizons in the area of English usage. Mentioned below are a few sites:

www.languagegames.org
www.englishpractice.com
www.planetenglish.com
www.wordcommand.com
www.toefl.org
www.encarta.com
www.eltnewsletter.com
www.cup.cam.ac.uk
www.oup.co.uk

Projects

Growing together is more fruitful than growing in isolation. The interdisciplinary approach is very essential and highly valued in professional education. The students of professional education have greater opportunities of growing together. The marketability of computer-oriented projects motivates them towards engaging themselves in such projects. The competence and strategic planning potential of the teachers of English combined with the interest and technical skills of students can develop various course packages for ELT.

The teachers of English can first decide the teaching or practice material to be developed through multimedia and with the help of interested and skilled students can gradually develop course material for all the courses one by one. For example if the teacher finds out in the class that the students are not receptive in 'phrasal verbs' classes, he or she can bring in an element of novelty through the multimedia packages. With vocabulary development gaining more and more importance these days, the students are interested in developing multimedia packages for vocabulary development. The package would enable the student learn the words and then assess his verbal ability through various objective types of exercises designed for the purpose. Though various software are available in the market for these purposes the students get a sense of accomplishment when they develop certain learning packages by themselves. Moreover, if the packages which they develop with the guidance of their teachers would be more relevant and specific to their needs. The role of English teacher is to guide them more with the matter rather than with the manner because, as the students of Science and Technology, the students are capable of using their computer skills appropriately. Of course a teacher of English with a sound knowledge in computer skills has unquestionably an edge over other teachers of ELT in taking up projects of these types. Nevertheless, they can always make conscientious efforts to acquire computer skills. Equipping themselves with these skills would enable to project themselves as effective and efficient teachers in today's technology-driven world. Though there are many countries where teachers are well versed with computer skills, there are still many other countries, which need progress in this direction.

These projects not only improve the student's English communication skills but also help him indirectly in preparing for his competitive examinations.

With the increasing globalization in almost every field of activity, the role of the teachers of English, the potential language of the world, has become extremely significant. Especially in the field of professional education because of the various professional needs of the students, their role has become pivotal in moulding the personality of the students. Despite the use of modern technologies in communication, the students of professional education need the scholarly guidance of their English language teachers. Hence ELT is very relevant in the process of professional education and it is the teachers of English who need to shoulder the responsibility of making it more meaningful, functional and fruitful.

REFERENCES

Venkateswaran S. *Principles of Teaching English.* Delhi: Vikas Publishing House Pvt. Ltd., 1995: 81.

Wright Andrew et al. *Games for Language Learning.* Cambridge: CUP, 1984: 72.

14

TEACHING THE PLAYTEXT IN THE CLASSROOM VERSUS WATCHING ITS PERFORMANCE: *MACBETH* AS A CASE STUDY

PRAKASH CHANDRA PRADHAN

I

Unlike other art forms in literature such as poetry and fiction, a dramatic text is both a literary piece and a theatrical script. In teaching such a text in our colleges and universities, we normally concentrate on analysis and interpretation of socio-cultural-ideological implications in the text and try to bring out its literary merits and aesthetic qualities with reference to *Poetics* (Aristotle) and established traditional literary criticism. In the classroom, we do not give much emphasis on audio-visual aids/any sort of performance of the text as a supplementary to its close analysis as such. Since the play-text was initially meant for theatrical performance on the stage, much remains unexplored and the text is not fully understood through such a method to the disadvantage of the student-readers. In order to enable them to understand the dramatic text better, it is necessary to bring out the living situations to the surface by some sort of performance of the text through some audio-visual effect. In the above context, this brief paper tries to throw some light on a few spectacular scenes from Shakespeare's tragic drama *Macbeth* which also need audio-visual performance rather than only critical discussions in the classroom.

II

The Macbeth universe, as we know, is replete with evil designs and actions. One needs to visualize the series of evil actions, all performed in darkness. The very opening scene (Act-I) sets the tone of evil atmosphere when the three weird sisters scheme and design the downfall of the dynamic but loyal General Macbeth. The witches, symbolic of evil forces, conspire secretly in the semi-dark, foggy atmosphere of "thunder, storm and rain" to make "fair is foul, foul is fair" (Act-I, Scene-I). The semi-dark, foggy atmosphere of "thunder, storm, and rain" (Act-I, Scene-I), is rather symbolic of subversion of the Macbeth universe which priced the moral order based on human values of integrity, sincerity and honesty. King Duncan's people in the court represented all these values even Macbeth himself at the beginning. In Act-I, the display of the witches on the stage is really terrifying. Their ugly appearances and evil designs to disrupt and invert the moral order of the Duncan court are indeed quite thrilling which need audio-visual realisation/representation. That can, of course, be done through appropriate performance with theatrical signs such as light-designs, audio-effects, costumes and make-up along with gestures and postures of the actors. Simple classroom teaching/reading the text is not much helpful to actualize the complex vision in the text. Performance of the scene should, therefore, be a necessary supplement to the classroom discussion. Let me illustrate this scene as a reference:

SCENE-I, ACT-I, A DESERT PLACE

Thunder and lightning, Enter three Witches

First Witch : When shall we three meet again
In thunder, lightning or in rain?

....

Second Witch : That will be ere the set of sun.
First Witch : Where the place?
Second Witch : Upon the heath
Third Witch : There to meet with Macbeth
First Witch : I come Graymalkin!
Second Witch : Paddock Calls
Third Witch : Anon!
All : Fair is foul and foul is fair;
Hover through the fog and filthy air.
(Exeunt)

Here, the semi-dark, stormy weather of the heath can be effectively presented through the light-designs and sound-devices. Costumes and make-up as well as the devilish gestures and postures of the actors can create the appropriate frightening but thrilling atmosphere of ghostly appearances and conversations of the witches in that desert place to capture the attention of the readers/audience. The song of the witches can be echoed through music.

Some of the subsequent events even need more audio-visual impact for comprehending the Macbeth universe. For example, let us take the scene of the first encounter of Macbeth along with his general-friend Banquo with the three witches on that "barren bushy land" (Act-I, Scene-III) on their return from the success in the battle against the rebellious Macdonald:

ACT-I, SCENE-III: A HEATH

Thunder, Enter the three Witches

....

Third Witch : A drum, a drum!

All : Macbeth doth come.
The weird sisters hand in hand,
Posters of the sea and land
Thus, do go about, about;
Thrice to thine, and thrice to mine,
And thrice again to make up nine
Peace! The charm's wound up

Enter Macbeth and Banquo

Mac : So foul and fair a day I have not seen.

Ban : How far is't call'd to Forres? What are these,
So wither'd and so wild in their attire,
That look not like th' inhabitants o' th' earth,
And get you are on 't
Live you? Or are you aught
That man may question? You seem to understand me
By each at once her choppy fingers

Upon her skinny lips. You should be women
And yet your beards forbid me to interpret
That you are not so.

So this is a situation of confusion, wonder, anxiety, excitement and chaos for the two warriors. They doubt, question and judge about semi-dark, stormy atmosphere, "foul and fair weather," "wither'd and wild attire," "skinny (thin) lips," "choppy (fairly rough) fingers," "beards of women," "earthly or unearthly creatures." The actorly gestures and postures can only bring out the confusion, excitement and wonder of the two warriors. The visual effect can make us understand the situation better. Musical effects can bring out the song better. This living situation can also be enacted in the classroom to some extent by choosing some student actors/actresses. Such a confusing situation provokes Macbeth to utter:

Macbeth	:	Speak, if you can what are you?
First Witch	:	All hail, Macbeth! Hail to thee, Thane of Glamis!
Second Witch	:	All hail, Macbeth! Hail to thee Thane of Cawdor!
Third Witch	:	All hail, Macbeth, that shalt be King hereafter
		....
First Witch		(to Banquo) Lesser than Macbeth and greater.
Second Witch	:	Not so happy, yet much happier.
Third Witch	:	Thou shalt get kings, though thou be none!

So all hail, Macbeth and Banquo!

Now "these instruments of darkness" (Act-I, Scene-III) create further confusion in Macbeth through their ambiguous language to win him with "honest trifles" (favours) to betray him "in deepest consequence" later on. To actualize the living situation in its proper perspective, the utterances of the three witches can be presented well through sound devices that can bring out a better auditory effect than the classroom teaching. The teacher's articulations of these dialogues and explaining them to student-readers will not be so much effective and satisfying. So is the case with the scenes of Lady Macbeth's determinations (Act-I, Scene-V) and persuasions to Macbeth for murdering king Duncan (Act.I, Scene-VII) and Macbeth's conflict of mind (Act-II, Scene-I).

> Is this a dagger which I see before me
> The handle towards my hand? come let me clutch thee
>
> ** ** **
>
> A dagger of the mind, a false creation
> Proceeding from the heat oppressed brain?
>
> ** ** **
>
> And on thy blade and dungeon gouts of blood.

A student may be picked up to enact this soliloquy in the classroom to bring out Macbeth's abnormality of mind before the murder. These situations can be enacted better on the stage through gestures and postures rather than monologic/ dialogic teaching process. Moreover, the visual effect of 'blood-shed' and 'murder of innocent sleep' (Act-II, Scenes-II & III) need stage performance for furthering the effect. In addition to these "the abnormal mental disorder of Macbeth" (Act-II, Scene-II), his "hallucination of mind in the Banquet Hall" (Act-II, Scene-IV) murder of Banquo (Act-III, Scene-III), Meeting of Hecate with the three witches (Act-II, Scene-V), the scene of boiling cauldron (Act-IV, Scene-I), Macbeth's last encounter with the witches and apparitions (Act-IV, Scene-I), murder of Lady Macduff and her children (Act-IV, Scene-II), somnambulism of Lady Macbeth (Act-V, Scene-I) and her death (Act-V, Scene-V), Macbeth's philosophizing life (Tomorrow, tomorrow and tomorrow/creeps in this petty pace from day today/ The last syllable of recorded time/ And all our yesterdays have lighted fools/ The way to dusty death. Out out brief candle/ Life's but a walking shadow, a poor player/ That struts and frets his hour upon the stage/ And then is heard no more, it is a tale/ Told by an idiot, full of sound and fury signifying nothing (Act-V, Scene-V), movement of Birnam Wood to Dunsinane (Act-V, Scene-V), Macbeth's final encounter with Macduff and his catastrophe (Act-V, Scene-VII) can be well brought out through audio-visual devices on the stage rather than through a discussion in the classroom. Right now, I am not illustrating all these scenes/situations due to short of space. However, I want to emphasise here that "the scene of boiling cauldron and Macbeth's final encounter with the witches, the three apparitions, Banquo's ghost followed by eight child-apparitions" (Act-IV, Scene-I) is one of the most significant and spectacular scenes in *Macbeth* which need visual effect and auditory effect as well.

III

Now, coming to a discussion of the tragic vision in this text, we know that the Macbeth world explores the superb conflict between evil and moral order and the ultimate destruction of evil being crushed by an invisible, invincible and incomprehensible moral system. As a first step, the apparently dominant evil forces disrupt the moral order by corrupting Macbeth's attitude inciting his "vaulting ambition" (Act-I, Scene-VII) to be the king. The temptation of Macbeth is the apparent beginning of subverting the moral order. A series of chaotic situations, murders and bloodshed, in once upon a time the orderly and peaceful state of Scotland, are the real designs of an encircling powerful evil system. Apparently, the evil system brings to its fold a number of victims by creating disorder in the existing moral set-up of king Duncan's court as referred to earlier. However, the incomprehensible moral system allows the evil forces work up to a peak point thereby bringing their downfall under the pressure of their own weight and re-establishes the moral order, finally. I think, it would not be irrelevant if I refer to Lord Krishna's all possible explorations to avert "the eighteen-days' long destructive War" in the great epic *Mahabharata* (Vyasdev) which the ambitious Duryodhan did not pay any attention to. Finally in the epic Duryodhan, the symbol of evil, was destroyed and *Dharma* was reestablished. Like the three witches, Lady Macbeth perhaps the fourth witch as an agent of evil plays a prominent role persuading the confused but ambitious Macbeth to choose the "nearest way" (Act-I, Scene-IV) to power by conducting a cold-blooded murder of the king Duncan in his "innocent sleep." The unnatural way of occupying the throne resulted in a series of unnatural actions in Scotland, namely "his hallucination of mind," 'his living in perpetual fear and psychological torture," "unnatural bloodshed in the kingdom," "somnambulism of Lady Macbeth, her unnatural death and the final dethronement of the usurper as well." 'His unnatural desire to have connections with witches to know more about his future made him feel that he would be invincible and supreme on the earth, which is rather an unnatural thought, an impossible proposition. He could not comprehend the ambiguous and "tricky utterances" of those "juggling fiends" to betray him in the "deepest consequences" by allowing him some "honest trifles." Hecate, the mistress of the witches instructs them to create further confusion in the mind of Macbeth by invoking artificial spirits. They precisely do that through the apparitions.

ACT-IV, SCENE-I

Thunder (an Armed Head)

First Apparition: Macbeth! Macbeth! Macbeth! Macbeth!
Beware of Macduff;

** ** **

Thunder (a Bloody Child)

Second Apparition : Macbeth! Macbeth! Macbeth!

** ** **

Be bloody, bold, and resolute: laugh to scorn
The power of man, for none of woman born
Shall harm Macbeth.

** ** **

Thunder (a child crowned with a tree in his hand)

Third Apparition : Macbeth shall never vanquish'd be until
Great Birnam wood to high Dunsinane Hill
Shall come against him.

So, these "juggling fiends" could create confusion in Macbeth that nobody could do him any harm since all men are born to women and trees do not walk. But therein lay his catastrophe because Macduff was born to his mother untimely and Birnam wood could walk to Dunsinane in the camouflage of the soldiers of England with the branches of trees on them. So till his dethronement, the design of the Moral Order remained an enigma to him. He could not understand the "tricky utterances" of the "instruments of darkness" (Act-I, Scene-IV). They deceived him in their "tricky utterances" with "double sense" in making him the "apocalypse of evil" (G. Wilson Knight) to be finally self-destructive. It would be quite appropriate here if we draw a parallel of Hiranyakasipu, from Indian mythology, who had been killed by *Nrisingh,* neither a *Nar* (Human) nor an Animal but a combination of the "intelligence of man" and "strength of a lion" although he had been blessed by Lord Siva not to be killed by any weapons/ fire/water, man or animal, day/night and so on. These great figures always forget that there is something in between these binary oppositions. Although man can have access to ample power, opportunity and freedom, he is to operate within his limitations in a System failing which his destruction is imminent and Macbeth realizes this Grand and Ultimate Truth and embraces death in a dignified manner by not surrendering in the battlefield knowing fully well by that time that "Macduff was from his mother's womb/ untimely ripp'd" (Act-V, Scene-VII) and he would be killed if he fought with him. That is where he attains his tragic grandeur like the most ambitious tragic figure, '*Abhimani* Duryodhan of the *Mahabharata* we referred to earlier. In his death he is also redeemed like Hamlet and Othello. Redemption and restoration of Moral Order are very much fundamental to any tragic drama. In Macbeth's redemption lies the grandeur of the tragic vision.

It is very difficult to bring out the complex tragic vision of the Macbeth universe fully only through the monologic/ dialogic teaching process. Since the playtext is also a performance text, the teachers in our universities must try to bring in some sort of audio-visual communication to the access of the students for better and deeper understanding of the playtext. In any case watching performance of the playtext is only a supplementary to the reading/teaching the text in its proper aesthetic, ideological and moral perspectives. It can never be a substitute to the close reading of the text. Different possibilities of the text can only be explored better by reading the text closely and combining with it "watching performance of the text in some way or the other. I think I should conclude the paper by quoting W.B. Yeats: "The falcon cannot hear the falconer" (Second Coming). The "falcon" must continue to have contact with his "falconer" for effectiveness in "falconry." In this case "close reading of the text" is the "falconer" and "performance" is the "falcon" for understanding the tragic vision of "falconry."

REFERENCES

Barthes, Roland. "The Death of the Author," "*Image-music-Text.* Ed. and Trans. Stephen Heath. New York: Farrar, Straus & Giroux, 1988, 142-48.

Belsey, Catharine. *Critical Practice*, London: Routledge, 1980.

Bradley, A.C. *Shakespearean Tragedy.* 1st Ed. 1940, London: Macmillan & Co. Ltd., 1965.

Brook, Peter. *The Shifting Point: Forty Years of Theatrical Exploration.* London: Methuen, 1987.

Bulman, James, C. ed. *Shakespeare, Theory and Performance.* London and New York: Routledge, 1996.

Butcher, S.M. ed. *Aristotle's Theory of Poetry and Fine Arts.* New York: Dover Publications, 1951.

Carlson, Marvin. *Theatre Semiotics: Signs of Life.* Bloomington: Indiana UP, 1990.

Counsell, Colin. *Signs of Performance: An Introduction to Twentieth Century Theatre.* London: Routledge, 1996.

Halio, Jay L. *Understanding Shakespeare's Plays in Performance.* Manchester: MUP, 1988.

Hattaway, Michael. *Elizabethan Popular Theatre: Plays in Performance.* London: Routledge and Kegan Paul, 1982.

Humphry, House. *Aristotle's Poetics* (London: Rupert Hart Davis) 3rd Reprint. Ludhiana: Kalyani Publishers, 1970.

Knight, G. Wilson. *The Wheel of Fire* (OUP: 1934) (First Publication). London: Methuen & Co., 1949.

Rajagopalachari, C. *Mahabharata,* Bombay: Bharatiya Vidya Bhavan, 1990

——. *Bhagavad Gita.* Bombay: Bharatiya Vidya Bhavan, 1991.

Schechner, Richard. *Performance Theory,* Revised edn. London: Routledge, 1988.

Shakespeare, W. *Macbeth.* Ed. H.J.C. Grierson. (1914 Clarendon Press); Rupa & Co.; Calcutta: Oxford University Press, 1974.

Styan, J.L. *The Shakespearean Revolution: Criticism and Performance in the Twentieth Century.* Cambridge: CUP, 1977.

Thomson, Peter. *Shakespeare's Theatre.* London: Routledge and Kegan Paul, 1983.

Viswanathan, S. *On Shakespeare's Dramaturgy.* New Delhi: Spantech Publishers, 1993.

Wells, Stanley. *Shakespeare in the Theatre: An Anthology of Criticism.* Oxford: Clarendon, 1997.

Wells, Stannley and Sarah Stanten ed. *The Cambridge Companion to Shakespeare on Stage.* Cambridge: CUP, 2002.

Yeats, W.B. "Second Coming." *W.B. Yeats: Selected Poetry.* Ed. A. Norman Jeffers, 9th imp. London: Macmillan, 1982: 99.

15

CLASSROOM EXPERIENCES OF TEACHING *PARADISE LOST I**

SHUBHA TIWARI

Classroom experiences are revelations. Once I was teaching "Imperfect Sympathies" by Charles Lamb in the class. When the explanation of the text was over, a boy got up and said, "Madam, why this fellow was not punished for writing such discriminatory, and racist pieces?" The fact that Lamb was writing at a time when the sun did not set in the British Empire did not matter to students. Traditionally we think of Lamb as an innocuous, and emotional writer of beautiful autobiographical pieces. Although I could understand the students' view, nevertheless that Lamb could evoke such a response was shocking for me. Similarly when Othello is hurt and vexed at the lost handkerchief of Desdemona, students felt, "Why such fuss over a handkerchief? He should have bought another one for her." Students see things differently. And they should.

In my more than a decade of teaching *Paradise Lost I* in the class, I have noted certain recurring patterns that I would like to share. A brief introduction of Genesis is needed to make the students comprehend the context of the book. Students are puzzled at the idea of the beginning of the human race in sin and guilt. For the last four years I have added a comparative approach in my lectures. A comparison to Indian epics, particularly *Sri Rama Charit Manas* by Tulsi Das illuminates the classroom. The students immediately

---

* All the quoted lines in the body of this paper are from the first book of *Paradise Lost.*

connect to the spirit of the epic. Their alienation with foreign sensibilities and thinking is at once dissolved.

The first portion, that of invocation of the heavenly muse is obviously very short in comparison to Tulsi's long and elaborate praying and blessing seeking. However the sentiment of deep devotion is universal. When Milton says:

> What in me is dark
> Illumine, what is low raise and support; (22-23)

we are automatically reminded of our famous Sanskrit lines, "Tam so mā jyotir gamaya; asato mā sad gamaya." The length and depth of Tulsi's invocation is much more long and profound yet the note of humility is remarkably similar. While Tulsi stresses that with the vision and blessings of the almighty a fool like him has been able to write an extraordinary book, Milton also is not ready to take the credit of authorship. Again and again he calls the muse to say and narrate the story:

> Sing heavenly muse, that on the secret top
> Of Oreb or of Sinai, didst inspire
> That shepherd, who first sought the chosen seed
> In the beginning how that Heaven and Earth Rose out of chaos [...]. (6-10)

Along with this extreme humility there is an unmistakable realization that what the poet is trying to achieve is no ordinary task:

> Invoke thy aid to my adventurous song,
> That with no middle flight intends to sour
> Above the Aonian mount, while it pursues
> Things unattempted yet in prose or rhyme. (13-16)

Similar thoughts appear in the *Bal Kand* of *Manas* (couplet 30-31) where the poet is clearly indicating the enormity and magnitude of the proposed task.

Satan continues to be the popular hero or antihero. His popularity has not diminished over the years. While studying *Paradise Lost I* some students raise the question as to who is the hero of the epic. The marvelous rising of the character of Satan in the first book remains to be its chief attraction. His dedication to his cause is openly admired in the classroom.

Whether that cause is good or evil is a different issue. The one answer to the question as to who is the hero of the epic and the answer students appreciate very much is that there will be no pleasure in watching the fight between an elephant and an ant. If Satan has to fight God his character has to be raised to a great height. To keep the interest of the readers alive and to maintain a sense of equal fight Milton has created this towering character of Satan. All of us like reading *Paradise Lost* again and again even when we know that it is futile to challenge God. Much of this attraction is due to the immense presence of Satan particularly in the first two books.

Students identify with Satan. Not that they are evil but because Satan comes to them as a strong, energetic and inspiring symbol of freedom. Satan touches the present day sentiments when he opposes the tyranny of almighty. This is the age of democracy, liberty and individual dignity. The opportunities are the same for everyone, at least in theory. No one preaches discrimination. So if Satan is powerful and deserving, why cannot he inherit the throne? Herein lies the fundamental difference in the Indian and Western approach. For us God is not almighty because He sits on throne; He is almighty because He is omniscient and omnipresent. A part of God is present in all creatures and each creature has the possibility of merging with the almighty. Between Ram and Ravana the fight is not for throne. Everyone is aware of the outcome of their fight. We have the concept of "Leela." God is playing a role for the benefit of mankind. Even Ravana is conscious of this fact. Above everything else there is no doubt that Ravana would ultimately be salvaged.

Nevertheless at the level of narrative, pride is the key sin of these two great villains of two great epics. While Satan has an inscrutable and indestructible ego, Ravana too is full of pride. In the *Lanka Kand* when his wife Mandodari tries to tell him to bow down to Lord Rama, he tells her that there is no fighter in the universe that can match him. He tells her that he has captivated gods, demons and humans and there is nothing to worry. Her pleas fall on deaf ears (*Lanka Kand* Couplet 7 to 8). Quite similarly Satan also decides to fight God and never yield to Him:

What though the field be lost?
All is not lost:
The unconquerable will,
And study of revenge, immortal hate,
And courage never be submit or yield
And what is else not to be overcome? (106-10)

The difference in their two kinds of pride is that Rayana's pride emanates from past experiences but Satan demands justice for his "injured merit." Ravana does not come out with any democratic or modern appeal. His words smell a kind of stale pride based on nothing but his immense size, and his unending "kutumb" or extended family. Satan on the other hand is more logical and to the point. What he says perhaps conveys more meaning to the modern mind.

The two concepts that I have seen as not being easily acceptable to the Indian mind are the origin of the human race in sin and secondly the unending punishment to Satan. We can say that the story of Satan begins where the story of Ravana ends. Satan has already fought a battle with God and has lost it. He has lost his former status. He is planning a different kind of war after losing his glorious state. Ravana on the other hand is fighting a battle in his full glory. The result of the fight is decisive. He dies and there ends his story. Satan is bound to be more revengeful and bitter than Ravana. His punishment is incomparably more severe than that of Ravana. In the Western concept the angels are made of imperishable stuff and therefore cannot be destroyed. This concept brings snags to the power of God, something unknown to the Indian mind. The very grace of being made of eternal material to angels becomes a curse of infinite pain to Satan and his company:

[...] he with his horrid crew
Lay vanquished, rolling in the fiery gulf,
Confounded though immortal. But his doom
Reserved him to more wrath; for now the thought
Both of lost happiness and lasting pain
Torments him [...]. (51-56)

The stress here is on unchanging and everlasting torture and damnation. The peremptory tone is:

> [...] where peace
> And rest can never dwell, hope never comes
> That comes to all [...]. (65-67)

These things are new to Indian students. Our mythology kills villains. All of them are finished by God and thus redeemed. God and His devotees bring (whether it is Ravana, Kansa, or Duryodhan) villains and evil element to complete end. At the end of *Manas* it is mentioned that leave alone living creatures, even inanimate objects like stones and dust attain salvation because of the "darshan" (sight) of Lord Rama. Some imaginative students counter the story of *Paradise Lost* by proposing that instead of sending Satan to hell God should have killed him. Such observations mark the two genres of human thinking and mind. The traditional Indian thinking and belief never doubts that even the murderer and the blasphemous can be salved by the grace of God.

Paradise Lost, particularly the first two books have a democratic undertone. The suggestions of democratic thinking appeal very much to the young generation. Without fully grasping the devotional or spiritual significance, students respond (of course if they are given a chance to respond) as to why Satan cannot inherit the throne. If he is worthy and capable he too stands a chance. As teachers we can realize that they are talking about the democratically elected successive governments. This is what they have in mind, no matter whether they are conscious of or not. Satan is liked most for championing the cause of self-respect, liberty, and individual freedom:

> Here at least
> We shall be free; the Almighty hath not built
> Here for his envy, will not drive us hence:
> Here we may reign secure, and in my choice
> To reign is worth ambition, though in Hell:
> Better to reign in Hell, that serve in heaven. (258-63)

The very tone is modern. "In my choice"—these words give a sense of liberty to the listeners. It is just like saying, "In my choice it is so; it can be something else in your opinion." This space for followers is crucial for Satan's currency. His words suggest a kind of voting between him and God:

Innumerable force of Spirits armed,
That durst dislike his reign, and, me preferring,
His utmost power with adverse power opposed
In dubious battle on the plains of Heaven,
And shook his throne. (101-05)

"Innumerable force" suggests number, "dislike" and "preferring" clearly point towards the choice of the clan, "opposed" evokes contest and finally the words "dubious" and "shook" tell that the contest was a tough one.

In a world where students face unemployment, injustice, and corruption at every level, the slogan of Satan's "injured merit" drives home. The students at once spot their own troubles when Satan roars against the power of tradition. Traditionally the authority is given to religion, administration and senior generation. Perhaps these forces have failed to justify their exalted position. The statement that God has not earned His supremacy; it is bestowed upon Him by old custom at once diminishes the worth of His supremacy in the eyes of the young:

But he who reigns
Monarch in Heaven, till then as one secure
Sat on his throne, upheld by old repute,
Consent or custom [...]. (637-40)

Satan demands justice for himself. His petition is that he wants to be weighed by his potentiality and not by his sense of slavery. The democratic spirit being the supreme God of our age, the very mention of God's monarchy draws negative reactions. Anybody opposing an authoritative and autocratic rule is seen as noble, sincere, and heroic:

[...] he opposed; and with ambitious aim
Against the throne and monarchy of God. (41-42)

Other points that endear Satan to all and young minds in particular are his establishment of the supremacy of mind, his brave and frank acceptance of the terrible change brought upon him and his followers and his indomitable spirit. He not only possesses a strong will power but also demonstrates it well. He reiterates the sovereignty of thoughts and thus infuses confidence in his folks. Physical victory is no victory. It is the victory over the mind that counts. Unless and until the psyche has not been submitted God's victory will be incomplete:

> [...] who overcomes
> By force hath overcome but half his foe. (648-49)

Similarly the valorous acceptance of his changed status is also noteworthy. Satan can call a spade a spade. He never minces his words in declaring his altered position. He does not ask for the forgiveness of the fallen angels but he definitely explains his point of view to them—why did he go to fight? Or how did he rate the strength of his side as opposed to the side of God? He takes them into confidence. These comments certainly denote that the archangel is trying to justify his decision to challenge God. He wants to convince his supporters:

> O myrids of immortal Spirits! O powers
> Matchless, but with almighty!—and that strife
> Was not inglorious, though the event was dire,
> As this place testifies, and this dire change,
> Hateful to utter. But what power of mind,
> Forseeing or presaging, from the depth
> Of knowledge past or present, could have feared
> How such united force of gods, how such
> As stood like these, could ever know repulse? (622-30)

At times the archangel does not even hesitate to pinch and assault his followers with words. He has absolute control over them. He can tackle them as he wishes:

> [...] have ye chosen this place
> After the toil of battle to repose
> Your wearied virtue, for the ease you find
> To slumber here, as in the vales of heaven? (318-21)

The process of learning more and more about this wonderful book is on for me. I have learnt so much from teaching and the reactions of students. It keeps my creativity ticking. As a teacher the trend of questioning established texts and eminent authors is welcome to me. If Shakespeare is viewed as being unjust to Caliban or Lamb is called a racist, I see a possibility of vibrant and meaningful dialogue in such statements. Every age is bound to and ought to view the classics according to its tastes. We see ourselves in literature. We try to find and understand our own thinking through literary texts. As long as this tendency lives, the liveliness and meaningfulness of classes of literature is intact.

REFERENCES

1. *The Student's Milton*, ed. Frank Allen Patterson. New York: Appleton-Century-Crofts, 1933.
2. Goswami Tulsidas, *Sri Rama Charit Manas*. Gorakhpur: Geeta Press, 1990.

16

The Importance of Learner's Perception in the Language Teaching/Learning Process

BENSON AGARWARKER

The teaching/learning of second or foreign language in a classroom is an extremely complex process. Various learner characteristics such as age, aptitude, motivation, attitude and personality play an important role in the learning process. Similarly, various teacher characteristics such as age, sex, education, experience and professional training have a significant bearing on the teaching process. Moreover, a set of environmental factors which include linguistic, socio-cultural, socio-economic and geographical factors exercise a powerful influence on language teaching/learning. Thus, a multiplicity of factors and their interaction make the whole teaching/learning activity a multidimensional phenomenon.

Our knowledge of individual learners being different from each other because of their personalities, motivations and learning styles has made our teaching more and more learner centred. Our increasing awareness that learner's own initiatives, productivity and strategies play an important part in classroom learning has led us to ask the learners themselves how they go about their learning. An investigation in learner's responses to teacher's classroom teaching is bound to indicate the extent to which there is congruency between what the teacher thinks he taught in a particular class and what the learner says he learnt. The comparison of what he has learnt in a particular class and the knowledge of the extent of mismatch if any between the two sets of perceptions and the possible causes of the same should help us make the second/foreign language classroom teaching/learning more effective.

In order to know the perceptions of the teachers and the students about a particular sample of English language class, a pair of matching questionnaires was prepared. Generally, a language lesson comprises of objectives, contents, techniques and teaching aids. The questionnaires prepared for the present study covered all these items.

A pilot project was carried out, on the basis of which the questionnaires were modified and improved. The inquiry was carried with the improved tools in five different colleges of Ahmedabad and the relevant classroom data at the level of First Year Arts 'A' stream classes were collected. In all 120 students and five teachers of different colleges were covered under the inquiry.

It is evident from the data studied that in all the major areas covered under this study, the perceptions of the teachers and the students do not show any significant degree of matching. On the contrary, in each of the areas, there is a considerable degree of mismatch between 'input' and 'uptake' as is evident from the given figure:

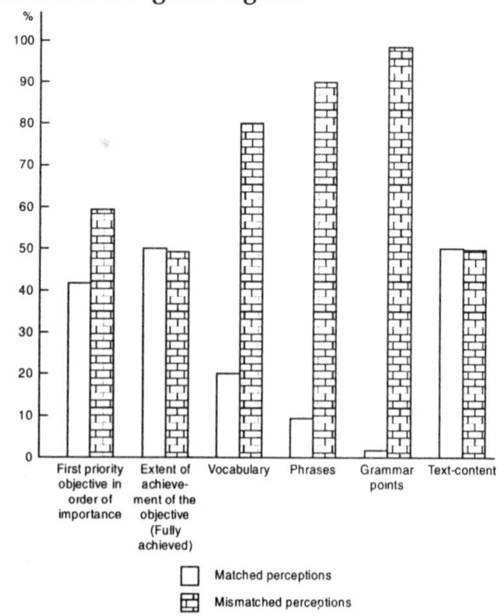

Figure : Comprehensive comparative data on matched and mismatched perceptions regarding the major areas covered under the present study.

The figure makes the overall picture very clear. The first entry in the figure shows that extent of matched perceptions even for the first priority objective in order of importance is 41.67% in aggregate. The second entry, which is regarding the extent of achievement of the objective which the teachers thought they had 'fully' achieved, the matched perceptions of the teachers and the students stand at 51.67%. The entry regarding the teaching and learning of vocabulary shows how only 20% of the students' perceptions tally with those of the teachers'. For phrases and grammar points the matched perceptions in aggregate are only 7.36% and 1.67% respectively. Regarding the last entry about the text-content, it is to be noted that even when all the five teachers claimed to have achieved fully the objective of explaining the text-content to the students, the matched perceptions for the same, in aggregate, comes to only 50%. It is evident, therefore, that there is a significant mismatch in all the important areas covered under this study.

The study clearly highlights the need to devise ways of developing a better understanding of the expectations and perceptions of the learners, so as to bring them more in harmony with the teachers' and thereby enhance the effectiveness of ELT in our midst.

What is more important, the data pertaining to the students' responses gathered in the course of the study clearly show that, contrary to some current ideas about the students in our colleges and their attitudes towards the learning of English (Compulsory), these students have fairly definite, and consistent perceptions of their teacher's classroom teaching, and that given an opportunity, they could also express their ideas and opinions in a rational balanced and responsible manner.

Other important points that emerge from this study are:

(1) Independent student-learning is taking place in the classroom even in the difficult or confused circumstances that prevailed in Gujarat. The students do learn in the classroom items which the teacher at least may not have selectively taught them. The students carry their individuality into the classroom, and different learners learn differently and different things from

the same lesson. The learner's view of the teacher's classroom teaching, then, becomes important in the process of teaching/learning. A greater knowledge on the part of the teacher about the learner's perceptions regarding classroom teaching should help him or her to improve modify and strengthen his or her use of the techniques, aids and teaching materials.

(2) The continuing use of only conventional techniques like lecturing and teaching aids like the textbook and the blackboard reduces the learning opportunities of the learners in the classroom. It limits the possibility of interaction between the teacher and the learner and among the learners themselves. Lack of interaction in a language classroom is likely to deprive the learner of encountering the language, thus reducing the scope for the learners to improve their proficiency to perform in it.

(3) As noted above this study has clearly established significant mismatch between teaching and learning. Further questionnaires could be devised on the data pertaining to matched and mismatched perceptions in order to find out, among other things, the possible reasons for matching and mismatching, the dynamics of self-learning at work ELT in Gujarat University, and the extent to which the effectiveness of the teaching English as foreign language is affected positively or negatively by the matched and mismatched perceptions.

(4) The awareness of mismatch between teaching and learning on the part of the teacher may help in the class, to deal with students with differing individualities. It would create a new role for the teacher, *viz.*, that of a learner-trainer. The knowledge of his or her own perceptions regarding teaching, when related to the students' perceptions of their learning could also make the teacher a more successful learner in the art of teaching.

(5) The awareness, on the part of the students, about the discrepancy of perceptions between teaching and learning could in turn, make them better learners.

They would learn to relate processes with purposes. The students, in the light of the knowledge of mismatch between teaching and learning, may improve, modify and strengthen their learning strategies and/or take new initiatives.

(6) This type of study may also have implications for faculty improvement. Special training programmes could be organised to bring about an awareness among the teachers about their new role of learner-trainer, inculcating in them the habit of regular self-evaluation through systematic classroom observations, possibly along the lines of the present study. The faculty could also be provided with guidelines, in the form of printed booklets, giving information on techniques and teaching aids to fulfil satisfactorily their new roles as learner-trainers. Teaching materials and the teaching aids prepared on the basis of the new experience of taking learner's view into account in the process of teaching/learning could be made available to the faculty. Thus, the implications and insights provided by the present inquiry could help evaluate and modify the teachers teaching, planning, materials and techniques in the long run.

(7) There is also ample scope for a replication of the inquiry, extending it to rural areas and different levels of undergraduate study. This type of inquiry could yield further interesting findings about the nature of teaching/learning processes if extended to other faculties like commerce, and law, science and technology. It might also be rewarding to carry out comparable research in the teaching of literature in our colleges in the light of the findings of the present research.

BIBLIOGRAPHY

Allwright, Richard L. 'Classroom Centered Research on Language Teaching and Learning: A Brief Historical Overview.' *TESOL Quarterly* 17/2 (1983): 191-204.

Allwright, Richard L. 'The Importance of Interaction in Classroom Language Learning,' *Applied Linguistics* 5/2 (1984): 156-71.

Allwright, Richard L. 'Why Don't Learners Learn What Teachers Teach?—The Inte.action Hypothesis,' *International Review of Applied Linguistics* (IRAL), 1984.

Best, John W. *Research in Education.* New Jersey: Prentice-Hall, 1970.

Byrne, Donn. Teaching Oral English. London: Longman, 1976.

——. *English Teaching Perspectives.* London: Longman, 1985.

CIEFL (Central Institute of English and Foreign Languages), Hyderabad, 1989. *Report of the Curriculum Development Centre in English.* University Grants Commission: New Delhi, 1989.

Chaudron, Craig. *Second Language Classrooms—Research on Teaching and Learning.* Cambridge: Cambridge University Press, 1988.

Ellis, R. 'The Role of Input in Language Acquisition: Some Implications for Second Language Teaching.' *Applied Linguistics* 2/1 (1981): 70-82.

Ellis, R. *Understanding Second Language Acquisition.* Oxford: OUP, 1986.

Entwistle, Noel. *Understanding Classroom Learning.* London: Hodder and Stoughton, 1987.

Gujarat State Board of School Textbooks. 'Seminar Discussions on Curricular. Programming in English,' Gandhinagar, 1983.

Krashen, Stephen. *Second Language Acquisition and Second Language Learning.* Oxford: Pergamon Press, 1981.

Krashen, Stephen. *Principles and Practice in Second Language Acquisition.* Oxford: Pergamon Press, 1982.

Littlewood, William. *Foreign and Second Language Learning.* New York: Cambridge University Press, 1984.

Lond, Michael. 'Training the Second Language Teacher as Classroom Researcher.' *Georgetown University Round Table on Language and Linguistics,* 1983: 281-97.

Pathak, R.S. 'Strategies and Processes of Language Acquisition: Implications for Teaching English as a Second Language.' *Indian Linguistics,* 47 (1986): 1-4, 59-71.

Richards, Jack, and Rodgers, Theodore. *Approaches and Methods in Language Teaching.* Cambridge: Cambridge University Press, 1986.

Roberts, J.T. 'Recent Developments in ELT' in Kinsella, V. (ed.) *Surveys 2: eight state of the art articles on key areas in language teaching.* Cambridge: Cambridge University Press, 1982.

Seliger, Herbert W., and Long, Michael H. *Classroom Oriented Research in Second Language Acquisition.* Rowley, Mass: Newbury House, 1983.

Stern, H.H. *Fundamental Concepts of Language Teaching.* Oxford: OUP, 1983.

Tarone, Elaine, and Yule, George. *Focus on the Language Learner,* Oxford: OUP, 1989.

van Lier, Leo. *The Classroom and the Language Learner,* London: Longman, 1988.

VanPatten, Bill, Dvorak, Triaha and Lee, James. *Foreign Language Learning.* New York: Newbury House, 1987.

Widdowson, H.G. "The learner in the language learning process.' In Holden, S. (ed.), *Focus on the learner: Bologna Conference 1983 organized by the British Council,* 7-12. London: Modern English Publications, 1983.

17

Second Language Acquisition: A Socio-Psychological Perspective

PRATIBHA GUPTA

When people use language they do more than just to make another person to understand their thoughts and feelings. At the same time, they are using language in subtle ways to define their relationship to each other and to identify themselves as a part of a social group, and to establish the kind of speech event they are in. These courtesy words are used to express the feelings of gratefulness. These are used to cement the social relationship and to promote solidarity. The social and psychological markers systematically differ in two cultures (British/American and Indian). Unusual manifestations in the use of expressions of gratitude and politeness (GAP) lead me to observe the phenomena of GAP in Indian speech community with reference to maithili speech community. Discussions are based on an exploratory observation in teaching English in language class, in general English class, and written texts (especially formal letters). In the last few decades, the focus of language teaching has shifted from the teacher and teaching materials to the teaching situation and learners. Hence an understanding and awareness of the intricacies of the social and psychological processes of the classroom is central to an effective teacher (Wright 1990). Learner variables (social, psychological and linguistic) have significant impact on the acquisition and usage of the second language. His age, family background, socio-economic status, ethnicity, attitude, motivation, orientation, linguistic experience, exposure to the target language are also considered to be important.

Considerable No. Researches are done in the context of socio-psychological perspective. Sridhar (1994), Verma (1994), Gardner (1985), Gardner and Lambert (1979), Sawhney (1998), Lukmani (1972), Khanna and Agnihotri (1998), Kachru (1996), Cohen and Olshlain (1981), Kellerman (1978), Olshlain (1983), Mishra (1985) and others observed that socio-psychological variables put considerable impact on the acquisition of second language. It accounts for the variance in the proficiency levels of the learners. Apte (1974) presents a comparative socio-linguistic analysis of GAP as used in Marathi Hindi speech communities and in the American society. Brown (1978) observes politeness phenomena in Goody. As regards to Maithili language, Singh and Bandyopadhyaya (1978), Singh (1976, 1979a, 1979b, and 1980, 1983, 1986), Stump and Yadav (1988), Williams's (1973a), Yadav (1980a, 1980b, 1982a, 1982b, and 1988) studied its structural aspect only. No work is reported on its socio-psychological aspect.

To study this aspect, functional approach to language is adopted. Prague school, the Firth-Halliday school and various others views expressions of feelings as a function. The expression of gratitude is considered as a feeling, a subjective expression. These are the instruments that keep the bond strong and well cemented between the members of a society. Language learning takes place in the social milieu. The learner is situated in his/her cultural beliefs, which are formed in this milieu. A second language acquisition is truly a socio-psychological phenomena (Gardner 1985), which involves feeling of self-identity, and cognitive skills reflecting language learning ability and reactions towards other cultural groups. Whenever one speaks or writes he is affected by social and linguistic conventions of one's own culture. All type of utterances (spoken/written) has some conventional rules and its users follow it habitually and are not aware of its use. In Indian speech community, the expression of gratitude is affected by a number of social psychological and linguistic variables such as age, sex, social status, nature of relationship between the speaker and hearer, his first language experience etc.

Apte (1974) observes, "the usage of gratitude expressions in American/British culture is much more extensive than South Indian communities [...]. Use of these expressions in their speech—community is so pervasive that it becomes almost mechanical. "There are situations in Indian speech community where these expressions may be considered inappropriate because role-performance of the speaker is obligatory and the acts of help are taken in the spirit of mutual cooperation and may be extended to interaction among close friends and members of a family. Hence its use is taken as the over-show of the feeling of gratitude. Therefore, ellipsis of such terms as 'Thank you,' Excuse me,' at times creates serious setback as mentioned in the essay 'On saying Please' written by A.G. Gardiner. Indian speakers are unintelligible more importantly because of their assumptions about the situations, appropriate behaviour and intentions within it. They not only differ in the choice of words and structures but in their way of giving information and in structuring an argument. Even their use of polite terms has imprint of their culture causing too much confusion on the part of the native speaker.

In certain situations, utterances produced are highly determined by cultural factors. As 'good morning' in British/ American context is a phatic communion, which requires no reciprocal statement as 'good morning' or 'good afternoon.' But when an Indian speaker says 'good morning' it evokes repeated speech act from the addressee assuming it as a mark of salutation of Indian culture as 'Namastey,' 'pranam.' Absence of repeated expression puts negative effect on the part of the hearer and considered as being rude and inappropriate, giving way to a sense of deprivation. Socio-economic hierarchy is more pronounced in Maithili culture, which is reflected through the language.

What might be unnecessarily docile or servile to a western reader is dependent on how Indian/maithili views a teacher or a superior in his culture and how the L1 provides formal choices to structure such a cultural attitude. Maithili is distinguished by the extra-ordinary exuberance of its verbal forms to use as per the person of instrument, location, social hierarchy, socio-economic stratification etc. The role-relationship and honorificity is expressed through the verbs, which have a large number of derivatives and variety of diverse forms as in:

Kata Jai chhain	for lowest order (servant)
Kata Jaichhah	for 2nd lowest order (child)
Kata Jaichhi	for equal/superior (in age/rank)
Kata Gel jait chhaik	for highest order (father in-law/VIP).

Apart from verbs, pronouns (2nd person) also show the degree of politeness. These belong to three categories on the scale of social hierarchy.

Ton	for juniors/servant
Ahan	for middle order
Apne	for highest order

On the other hand English has only 'you' to serve the purpose. There is no word to show the rank/order of the addressee. The other area which systemically differs in the two languages is 'address words.' In English, range is limited only to 'Pronoun You' and the name' of the addressee. Whereas Maithili offers six categories of words as per the degree of respect and gender.

Rau	for lowest order (male)
Hegai	for lowest order (female)
Hau	a bit superior/child (male)
Hae	a bit superior/child (female)
Yau	a bit more superior (male)
Yai	a bit more superior (female)

Even adjectives in Maithili language carry this sense, which is obvious from the following examples:

Khadhur	for lowest order (servants)
Khauak	for middle order (child)
Bhogindra	for highest order (Glutton)

Even change in stress reflects the situation and the temperament of the speaker:

Au (come)	(reception)
Aau (come)	(request)
Aaau (come)	(order)
Aaaau (come)	(command with anger)

Use of stress is a typical feature of Maithili speech community. It shows that members of Maithili speech community have a definitive place in the social stratification. Hence there is a sense of dissatisfaction in the use polite terms in English and typicality of the Maithili language creates confusion and sense of inadequacy, which is reflected in the use of the following expressions:

'Hallo, Mr Mohan

'Hallo, Mohan jee

'Hi Mohan.

The sense of politeness in Maithili is carried out by certain structural patterns that express the highest order of humbleness. In the following sentence interrogative negative pattern is used to achieve highest degree of politeness:

Kaniya sunbai nahin?
(Please listen to me.)

Here it is neither an interrogative sentence nor a negative one. It is a request to express the utter humbleness of the speaker.

To express the role-relationship and honorificity transfer of the deferential style from L1 to L2 can be illustrated from the following formal letters namely applications and invitation letters:

Our Respected and beloved sir

Looking forward to your kind presence and active participation.

Respected madam

Respected the hostel warden

Most humbly and respectfully

I will be grateful you forever

Dear sir

It gives me immense pleasure to invite along with your spouse in [...]

Honorable DRM [...] has kindly consented [...]

The above examples reflect the socio-cultural factors operating in the speech act. He/She feels that failure in these expressions may create serious setback and feels it obligatory to use such expressions wherever his sense of respect commands. In Maithili it is more extensive and strictly followed particularly on the occasion of social functions.

In English the written mode has several rhetorical prerequisites such as directness in presenting the point, very little stylistic ornamentation and emphasis on the information content. Whereas MS is characterized by extremely deferential lexical spread based on the politeness hierarchy of L1. Difference in the culture also poses difficulty in ascertaining to categorize the situation in terms of formality. It is clear from the absence of polite expressions 'would you mind,' 'may I,' 'would you prefer' in the speech act given below taken from a language class:

> O, come, come
> When did you return back from Bombay?
> Yesterday.
> How are you and how are your studies?
> That's fine.
> Well you have coffee or cold drink?

In friendship domain too many polite expressions are not taken for granted in Maithili/Indian speech community, hence ellipsis of these expressions are there. Unfamiliarity with this domain is reflected through the ellipsis of the context-dependent expression. Speech act consisting entirely of grammatically complete sentences would generally be unacceptable and it is expected that he should be able to produce incomplete but contextually appropriate and interpretable sentence fragments. His limited range of lexicon and adherence to grammatical correctness at the expense of communication shows his psychological stress in learning the target language. Social conventions are involved in determining the illocutionary force of a speech act. Cultural context provides him a way to ask directly for refreshments without using these sets of expressions. At times it is very difficult to convince them.

Overview of the politeness phenomena shows that socio-cultural factors play significant role in the acquisition of second language. Speech act has reflections of the culture. Use of too many adjectives may result from more than one underlying cause: differential style used for one's teacher, culturally different notions of what is 'grand' style, or a different concept of being learned. Deeper understanding of the working of bilingual's code repertoire and the use of such repertoires in the politeness phenomena in Maithili speech community will be helpful in determining the teaching strategy.

REFERENCES

1. Apte, M.L. *Thank you and South Asian Languages: A comparative Socio-linguistic study,* International journal of the sociology of language, 1974.
2. Brown, P.L. *Universals in language use: Politeness phenomena in Goody.* E.N. ed. Questions and politeness: strategies in social interaction, Cambridge, Cambridge University Press, 1978.
3. Cohen, A.D. and Olshlain, E. *Developing a measure of socio-cultural Competence: The case of Apology in Language Learning.* Language Learning 31, 1981.
4. Gardner, R.C. and Lambert. *Social and Psychological aspect of second acquisition.* In Giles and St. Clair, R. (eds.) *Language and Social Psychology.* Oxford Basil Blackwell, 1979.
5. Gardner, R.C. *Social psychology and second language learning: the role of Attitude and Motivation.* London: Edward Arnold, 1985.
6. Kachru, B.B. *Meaning in deviation: Towards understanding non-native English texts.* The other tongue: English Across Culture (2nd ed.), 1996.
7. Kellerman, E. *Giving learners a break: native language intuitions as a source of predictions about transferability,* working papers on bilingualism, 1978.
8. Khanna, A.L. and Agnihotri, R.K.*Some predictors of speech skills: A socio-psychological study,* 1998.
9. Lukmani, Y.M. *Motivation to learn and language proficiency,* In Language Learning, 1971.
10. Mishra, Arpita. *Language abroad: Socio-linguistic study of conversations in interethnic settings,* 1985.
11. Olshlain. *Socio-cultural competence and language transfer: The case of apology* in Gas, S. and Selinker, I. ed. *Language transfer in language learning.* Rowdy, Mass, Newbury House, 1983.
12. Sawhney, Chhya. *The role of attitude and motivation in foreign language learning,* in R.K. Agnihotri, A.L. Khanna, I. Sachdev (ed.), 1998.
13. Singh, U.N. *Maithili Kinship terminology,* 1976. Unpub. Ms.

18

Is Learning a Number of Languages a Load?*

K. BALACHANDRAN

Learning is a creative process. It begins from one's infancy. A bright infant will usually become a bright child. At first a child learns from its mother and later from other family members. At the age of three, when it is admitted in pre-kindergarten it learns its first language, its mother tongue and English, the second language. Learning is not a load for above average and bright children; it is a load to the below average and slow learning children.

Learning mother tongue: This is generally an easy task for the children. Because the child's mother speaks its mother tongue and others in the family also speak the same, the child learns the mother tongue easily. It is not a load to a child. But this may not be true in all the cases. All the children do not pass the Tamil paper *i.e.* the first language. Some children may fail in their mother tongue paper. It may be because:

(1) They may not have proper inspiration or initiation into their language.

(2) They may not have proper drilling in schools.

(3) They may not have much educated parents to coach or supervise them.

But this can be corrected if proper measures are taken. So learning one's mother tongue is not a load.

---

* Paper presented in the 'National Seminar on Language Education in India,' organised by the Centre of Advanced Study in Linguistics, Annamalai University & Southern Regional Language Centre, CIIL, Mysore, at Annamalai Nagar, Jan. 7-9, 2002.

Learning one's mother tongue in a foreign country may not be that much easy and so it may become a load. For example if one is settled in a foreign country where another language is the official language and when he marries and settles there itself, the children born to them, if they want to pursue their education in their mother tongue, it may not be possible. In that case the children have to learn everything in the foreign language only. There may be facilities to learn its mother tongue as one of the subjects. In this case, even learning one's mother tongue becomes a load.

Learning a second language (for example, English) is a load to the below average and slow learning children. It is not a load to the above average and talented children. It becomes a load because of very many factors. (1) The children should be active to learn English. If it is not so, if they fail to evince interest in it, it becomes a load. (2) Teachers are also mainly responsible. If they take much pains and interest, even an ordinary student will become bright in learning English. If the teachers are careless, it may affect a student's future.

A committed teacher is the treasure of a society. He is an asset to the institution, to the student community and in turn to the Nation. Refer to any world famous leader in India. They might have had their education from illuminating teachers and famous institutions. In this type of atmosphere, learning is a pleasure. Teaching is also pleasurable. Both the teacher and the students engage themselves in a happy learning process. The students always very eagerly wait for their teachers; the teachers also very anxiously wait to meet committed students. Here learning is considered to be a happy pastime.

Learning a third language is really an additional burden to a school-going boy or girl. For example, learning either Hindi or Sanskrit as the third language may involve extra grasping capacity on the part of the students. It is a load to the bright and above average students. It is a heavy load to the below average and slow learning students. It does not mean that they cannot learn a third language. They can, but they do with much exertion. A few do with happiness; majority students do with a feeling that they are compelled to do so, lest they may not have good job prospects later. Some fail in this process if their grasping power is less.

Once in Tamilnadu even at the school level Hindi was taught as the third language. Due to political compulsions, it was withdrawn. So students lost a good chance of learning a third language. In fact many students heaved a sigh of relief, "Ah! I need not study Hindi!" But it was a loss because it affected their job prospects—they couldn't move out of their state. Though at first it was like a burden or load, later on when they are proficient, it is a pleasurable load like that of pregnancy to a lady. As she feels immensely happy when she begets a child, one feels a conqueror if one masters a third language.

What is the present condition of students? In Matriculation schools and Navodaya schools Hindi/Sanskrit/French is offered as the third language. Since students in these institutions are above average and bright, they pick up somewhat quickly. Later they get admission in profitable courses and get good jobs. Learning a third language does not make them handicapped; on the other it opens their vistas of knowledge and also their job opportunities and later they are well placed This may not be applicable to an ordinary or a poor student. They are the special category of students who learn the third language. As one has to pay more money for a special meal, a student who wants to learn a third language has to spend more money for it.

At the student level (*i.e.* at the higher secondary level), a bright student can learn maximum three languages (i) mother tongue (ii) English (iii) Hindi/Sanskrit/French. This is not a heavy load though it is a load to learn the third language. But students of average caliber find it difficult to learn the third language and so it is a heavy load to them.

The same condition may prevail at the graduate level also. Once when they come to post-graduate level, the students will have more maturity and so they can learn the third language very effectively or they can even learn a fourth language afresh. No doubt, it is a load to them; yet they can do it sportively. Everything depends upon how they approach the learning activity. This is comparatively easy to those who join Linguistics because they have to learn a new language.

Also because they have an aptitude for learning more languages. So in their case this question—learning a number of languages—a load, does not arise. It is part of their curriculum.

How about common man? He cannot afford to learn many languages. He may be knowing his mother tongue. In addition to that, he may be knowing the National language (Hindi). Since he has to work in very many places, he may be knowing more than one language in addition to his mother tongue. But always they consider English as a tough language though in reality it is not so. For them learning many languages, is no doubt a heavy load.

About the present language education system, it is not effective and fruitful. The numbers of papers have been reduced from four to two as far as English is concerned. In the first year of the degree course students study English prose and poetry along with some grammar aspects. In the second year they study a few Shakespeare plays and a few novels or plays. Thus their reading skills have been reduced to fifty percent; their writing skills too have been reduced to fifty percent. Very rarely two hour composition classes exist. They do not practise composition work which includes comprehension, essay writing, grammar exercises, precis writing, letter writing etc. Then how can we expect standard? Standards have been falling down as the London Bridge is falling down! When there is deterioration of standards, how can we expect good and efficient students to come out of the educational institutions? Out of ten students only three or four are with appreciable standard. Because of the internal assessment system, they get good marks in assignments, which is nothing but copying from the text or notes at home and submitting it for marks.

Formerly there used to be two papers in English in the first year of the degree course (Prose and Non-detailed separately) and two papers, in the second year (Shakespeare and Poetry). There used to be one hour composition instruction and regular composition classes for two hours every week. And for correcting notebooks, there were tutors who did their work with commitment. In the next class, the students had to make all the corrections meticulously on the left hand side of the notebook. This kind of rigorous practice helped students immensely for their constant standard.

The present language education in India needs a thorough overhauling because language education is the foremost in a student's life, because students are said to be the pillars of tomorrow's India. If the language education is not a standard one, we cannot expect standard students. If we have standard in education, we will have standard teachers in future. There is more of quantity than quality in language education. Quality at all levels is a must. Maintaining the quality in learning a number of languages can be achieved through phases. Hence loading can be taken in the right perspective for the betterment of students.

19

ACQUIRING ENGLISH: MOTHER TONGUE MUST HAVE A ROLE

R.P. SINGH

The context of what follows is the issue of teaching and learning English in the setting of rural and small town of India, and the central focus is on the argument why mother tongue should have a role in the process.

Good knowledge of English distinctly occupies a prominent place in today's career calculation and job market. But the students of small towns and the rural hinterland suffer from multiple disadvantages caused by the hegemonic standards of learning English as the second language. These standards originate in England and America, are lapped up by the elite metropolitan Indians (who are very comfortable with the idea of avoiding 'mother tongue interference' in learning a foreign language because, in their case, the hiatus between the school and the home is fast decreasing) and accepted, *nolens volens*, by the vast majority of village and small town level students who need a sound knowledge of English for their real empowerment *vis-à-vis* their metro brethren.

Let us have a glance over the metro effect of teaching and learning English as a second language on small town graduates and post-graduates, many with an English medium background upto the +10 or +2 level. By way of institutional certification, they have passed, in some cases with high marks, in English, but practically their English is, of course with a few happy exceptions, simply pathetic. Their condition may be described as theoretical superiority nullified by functional mediocrity. Having failed to land employments which are secured at a competitive bidding of merit, they have become grossly ill-paid teachers in schools with signboards displaying nomenclatural obsession with English, have started computer 'centres' with 'awe-inspiring' abbreviated names, or have opened coaching 'institutions' with a highly self-conscious advertisement of pedagogical perfection. A tendentiously self-conscious advertisement is the common thread which binds all these professions joined by default. And the central belief of this self-consciousness is an obstinate self-perception that their knowledge of English is good, very good. This situation is doubly dangerous. A false self-perception is a tiresome state of mind, and it breeds a feeling of false self-sufficiency and obstructs the effort to reach out to knowledgeable persons and other sources of amelioration and advancement.

Why is this situation so common in rural and small town of India? One can answer that this is so because in teaching and learning English there is an unthinking emphasis on a uniformity of pedagogical methods and materials in all the schools and colleges of the country or in a state. The operative environment engendered by the parents, the peer and the neighbourhood playground is not taken into account. And when this mingles with the performance of incompetent teachers, the result is just intolerable.

How to ameliorate this situation? What should be the best approach behind teaching and learning English in a rural and small town setting whose hallmark is, undeniably and with nothing to regret for, the unbreakable ambience of mother tongue, the resultant context being inescapably billingual. Naturally, the approach which insists on the clinical avoidance of mother tongue interference would be unnatural, and so, bound to miserably trip behind the real target of achieving a satisfying level of linguistic competence in English. This tripping behind takes the form of 'targetitis'—an obsession with passing in the subject of English with the help of classroom spoon-feeding coupled with market-supplied help-books of substandard quality.

How to achieve the real target? By evolving a well-thought out technique in which the resources of mother tongue act as a vehicle of power which propels the process of learning English. Why a vernacular-based technique of learning a foreign language? Because both history and nature back it up. Our context is a replica of the situation in which the Europeans found themselves in India in the later years of the 18th century *vis-à-vis* the Indian languages. Their linguistic sense mingled with the pressing need to learn modern Indian languages, and they ventured upon learning these languages through their mother tongues. Out of this emerged the curious but salutary fact of Indian linguistic history that the first grammars of modern Indian languages were written by European scholars in their native languages for the benefit of their compatriots who worked in India either as Christian missionaries or administrative officials. Manoel Da Assupcam, a Portuguese missionary, wrote the first grammar of Bengali in Portuguese for the Christian missionaries in Bengal. The book, *Vocabulario em Idioma Bengalla a Portuguez,* was published from Lisbon in 1743. For the British civil servants came *A Grammar of the Bengali Language* from the pen of the famous orientalist Nathaniel Brassey Halhed in 1778. It will not be true to say that India lacked research efforts in the field of grammar. On the contrary, we had a rich tradition of grammatical learning before the advent of the Europeans. The traditional Indian education had grammar as an important component, and the corpus of grammatical literature here was very rich and copious. But the Indian scholars, though deeply engrossed with the problems of Sanskrit grammar, and to some extent that of Arabic and Persian, did not feel the need to write grammars of the languages used by the common people around them. There was no pedagogic necessity since the modern living languages were not studied at a higher level. The scholars of language and literature did not consider these languages worthy of scholarly attention and investigation. The list of writers of the first grammars of modern Indian languages is interesting in not being very short, which shows that scholars almost all over India were on the same wavelength. Father Beschi, an Italian Jesuit, wrote the first grammar of modern Tamil in Latin in the first decade of the 18th century. The credit of being the writer of the first grammar of Malayalam goes to Angelos Francis, a Portuguese, who wrote it in Latin. John Gilchrist is remembered for being the man who was behind the first grammar and dictionary of Urdu. Sindhi and Punjabi owe their first grammars to Ernest Trumpp and William Carey respectively.

This replica arches over the aspect of motivation also. The missionaries learnt Indian languages for being able to translate the Bible and to propagate it among the masses. The British administrators learnt them for the immediate practical necessity of running the administrative machinery. The overwhelming majority of Indians want and need to learn English for getting jobs. On the other hand, the possibility of going beyond the confines of immediate necessities remains alive. From among the foreigners, a prominent group of scholars and administrators with a scholarly bent of mind went beyond these confines and gave impetus to a new intellectual movement which took a concrete shape in the Asiatic society of Bengal established in 1784. India is proud of the many Indians who possess remarkable felicity in English and express native observations and experiences of nativity in a language which is not native.

Why is mother tongue so important? Because it is not just a verbal pile. It is a psychology, an environment, a source of cultural and cognitive sustenance, an emotion, a bond, and many collateral things. To attempt to guard against its 'interference' is an act of violence with a pernicious potential to damage some vital nerves of the emotional-cultural-artistic continuum of a learner's personality. The right pedagogical philosophy is that which believes in the possibility of osmosis of energy between the mother tongue and the second language. Most second language learners want and expect to operate as billinguals, rather than monolinguals. It is the natural state of participation in the learning process. What is more, insistence on the monolingual approach to learning English as a second language leads to another insistence—the insistence on treating English as a permanently foreign language with its pristine foreignness remaining intact. The manifesto of liberation penned by our renowned Raja Rao was quoted with full endorsement by Mulk Raj Anand in his presentation ('Changeling') at a CIEFL Seminar on Indian English held in July, 1972. The operative position of the manifesto—'We cannot write like the English. We should not. We can write only as Indians'—links itself seamlessly with the conviction of Gilles

Deleuze and Felix Guattari that the mother tongue is 'vernacular, maternal and territorial.'

The vital point is that English in India is to stay and should stay fruitfully, as an asset, not as a liability. An all-out effort should be made to enhance and widen its acceptability, which entails an attempt to 'deforeignise' it. The attempt at 'deforeignisation' of a language simply means a confident interface with the native language of a particular area. The context being inescapably bilingual and the command over English weak, a profuse dose of the vernacular is mixed with English in the process of teaching, but all by default, without conviction and with a sense of guilt. What should be done is to confidently tap the resources of the mother tongue and harness them in the pedagogical endeavour. This would entail learning the rules of English grammar well, and applying these rules in a constant practice of translation from the mother tongue into English. This practice must not be token and meagre. Reams and reams of paper should be spent on it. While fulfilling S. Pitt Corder's condition of exposure to 'the language data,' it would lead to the students of a bilingual context feeling their linguistic base of English getting stronger with translating complicated structures of their mother tongue into English. It would result into a liking for the target language, which would lead naturally to a love for a varied range of texts written in English.

SELECT BIBLIOGRAPHY

Corder, S. Pitt. *Error Analysis and Inter-language.* London: OUP, 1981.

Delueze, Gilles and Felix Guattari. *Kafka: For a Minor Literature.* Minneapolis: University of Minnesota Press, 1986.

Mohan, Ramesh, ed. *Indian Writing in English.* New Delhi: Orient Longman Ltd., 1978.

Singh, Rajendra, ed. *Grammar, Language and Society: Contemporary Indian Contributions.* New Delhi: Sage Publications, 1997.

Trivedi, Harish. *Colonial Transactions: English Literature and India.* Manchester: Manchester University Press, 1993.

20

TEACHING OF ENGLISH: NEED FOR A NEW AGENDA

DIPAK J. BARUAH

There is no denying the fact that both at the school and the college levels there is a fall in the standard of acquisition of the English language. Even at the undergraduate level the teaching and learning of the language is done in a restrictive sort of situation, as the learners cannot adopt the basics of it effectively well at the '+ Two' level.

In our country English was introduced as one of the important subjects to be learnt and taught in the schools and colleges with the expectation that the language would provide a window on the world to everybody who learns it. But when one takes into account 'the product,' which the contemporary India in teaching of English has achieved, one discerns on this a poor level of ability in English, particularly those at the '+ Two' and the higher levels.

The root lies nowhere but in the earlier school background of these students. The geographical and social background of the learners apart, the teachers are also handicapped by want of a methodology of teaching the language. Add to this a number of other factors including deficiencies in infrastructural facilities in and around an institution.

While there has been this growing consciousness both at the level of the educational authorities and on the part of the teachers regarding the necessity to augment the learners' proficiency over the language, it is to be realized that a learner's acquiring the basic skills in the language at the High School and '+ Two' stages can only adequately aid him towards the minimum linguistic ability.

In India majority of the students are from the ruralities. They generally fail to cope with the process of learning of English at the higher level for want of an adequate level of ability to learn for which their prior school background is to blame. In certain parts of the country including Assam the College teachers also have to impart teaching at the Higher Secondary level ('+ Two' level). What they find is that those who sit in the Higher Secondary classes do not in reality possess the basic knowledge in grammar and hence sentence construction.

The State Board holding the High School Leaving Exams are generally left with no choice but to relax the marking system considerably thus minimizing the decline in the pass percentage. Instead of such short sighed policies, the authorities would have done better if it had made a determined and continuous bid to bring changes into the conventional teaching-learning activities of these schools. For taking pragmatic corrective measures, teachers must be given occasional trainings encouraging them to do away with the conventional way of 'imparting lessons.' In fact the conventional mode in teaching is deep-rooted in the teachers themselves as they had been taught in the same way earlier when they were in schools and colleges. Communicative language teaching for their teachers then had been a misnomer.

To be precise, an English teacher in a so-called government or govt. aided school does not have the proper training for a self evaluation to measure his own performances which is a reason why he fails to alienate himself (when needs be) from the premises of his texts. For one thing, the students in a conventional class where the textbook is always at the centre, cannot participate with an active and open mind in the learning process. In absence of an interactive programme the pupils become over-conscious about having to learn a language which is not their own.

The problems relating to the teaching of English must be a part of our social concerns as English in India plays an important role in various domains (which is getting more of a recognition today in view of the changing economic priorities of the nation).

As regards to the functional remedies, we at first can say that for teaching the language in our conditions, we can adopt the respective native languages to enable the learners feel at ease in the learning process. This can be carried on upto the Higher Secondary level.

The learners generally show reluctance towards conceiving any subject as a "rule system." It is in our system that in the class the teacher is given to find out whether something told or written by a learner is right or not in grammatical terms. In such a (conventional) class the teacher is made to teach English as a body of rules, words, set answers, set questions etc. It is an approach, which puts a danger to the "skill character" of the language ability. Such a system of teaching deprives a learner of his natural learning ability. So, the teachers should be made to realize the illogicity of such a conventional method. Such a method should be replaced by the interpersonal means, which can surely enable the learners to learn the language skills. This also provides them with adequate opportunities for taking personal initiatives in playing their communicative roles effectively. Training and Orientation programmes should be arranged with such objectives in mind for the teachers. Such programmes should offer to them the appropriate functional methods. The methods should be such that the pupils can consequently possess the ability to read with understanding, and also to converse easily in English. For all this to be achieved, the syllabus must be changed or reframed with due appreciation of the reality and the entire scenario of the teaching-learning process has to be activated with training programmes of teachers *vis-à-vis* the new functional methodology of the teaching of the language.

It is generally complained by the English language teachers that they have to teach English in large classes. One perhaps cannot hope there would be any provision to scale down the largeness of the classes. The teachers therefore have no other alternative but to adjust himself with the situation in his own way. The teacher, for instance, can divide the class into certain groups (as he has to deal with a number of mixed ability groups) viewing it mentally and put every group into activities in terms of the group's individual level of learning-ability. In such a class, it needs no mention, the teacher becomes both a facilitator and a guide.

To say the least then, the teacher must allow sufficient rooms for interactions in the class involving both the taught and himself instead of simply taking the stage all by himself for transmitting of facts and informations. He has to apply his ingenuities (quite often) devising his own classroom techniques.

We can conclude then that a new kind of agenda for the improvement of the practice of teaching English in our schools and colleges has become more of a need today. Particularly the fall in standard of the teaching-learning process in the Higher Secondary stage has started to make a serious palpable effect upon the society. Even in our semi-urban societies there is a distinguishing split between those for whom English has come 'easily' and those who are being unable to learn the appropriate skills of English. The former are the students reading in the private schools. This has inevitably put a spell upon the society as after passing out from their high schools, a section of the students undergo a sense of inferiority for want of the ability for a minimum grasp over the English. In making the new agenda, these words of Prof. Mohammad Aslam may act as a guiding principle: "We need to look into the teaching and learning process in more democratic way and allow our students to share the responsibility that they have in learning English in social interactions. They must realize what it means to be a learner, an active one and as a member of the large group in the class and the society." [*English Language Teaching in India*: *Issues and Innovations*, Ed. by R.K. Agnihotri and A.L. Khanna, Sage (New Delhi), 164.]

BIBLIOGRAPHY

English in India: Theoretical and Applied Issues. Ed. by Omkar N. Koul, Creative (New Delhi), 1992.

English Language teaching in India: Issues and Innovations. Ed. by R.K. Agnihotri and A.L. Khanna, Sage (New Delhi), 1995.

Aspects of English Language Teaching: Focus and Functions. Shivendra K. Verma, T.R. Publications (Madras), 1993.

English Language Teaching: Theory and Practice. Ed. by M. Tarinayya, T.R. Publications (Madras), 1992.

21

Comprehension

V.K. JAIN

When we talk of teaching English as second language (L_2), we have in mind students who do not habitually speak that language or use it any other way besides, their own languages. Our aim is to teach such students to understand English when they hear it, to teach them to speak in such a way that people understand them, to teach them to read books rapidly and understand them, to teach them to write English accurately enough to make themselves clearly understood.

Thus in the present scheme of teaching English as L_2 our ambition is to develop the skills of reading and writing and this can be developed through exercises in the comprehension.

Comprehension is a very light exercise. The students should first grasp the sense of the passage set, fully understand the nature of questions and then answer the questions in their own words. Thus Comprehension plays a very significant part in the mental development of the students in the art of composition writing. It is one of the ultimate aims of learning English.

Comprehension is really a very complex skill. It implies a considerable knowledge of the lexicon, grammar, semantics and phonology of the language. According to the Oxford English Dictionary, comprehension is the mind's act or power of understanding and as a linguistic term it means the ability of a language learner to grasp fully and correctly the contents of a spoken or written passage in that language.

The method that we have to use for teaching comprehension through a careful study of passage is (i) partly classical and (ii) partly modern. The classical part consists of the following steps:

1. Before attempting to answer the questions the teacher first reads out the passage loudly and clearly to the class while the students follow him silently through the passage.
2. The teacher takes special care to emphasize every new word or expression and to convey the general import of the passage in the course of his reading through facial expressions and gestures.
3. The teacher may tell the class briefly about the subject matter before setting forth to read it aloud.
4. Then the students should be asked to read it aloud and the teacher must carefully observe that the students do not mispronounce any word nor do they commit any mistakes in reading. This will ward off the possibility of the students picking up wrong pronunciations.
5. Then immediately after the reading is over the teacher should ask them to point out the new or difficult words and he should clearly explain those words in his own simple and correct English, without being unnecessarily lengthy and superfluous. Allusions and figures of speech should be made quite clear in easy language. Idioms or proverbs should be fully explained in simple and direct English.
6. The next step is to write down all the dictionary meanings of words with a clear indication of their grammatical category or semantic function in the sentence.
7. Answering the questions is the main part of the comprehension. If the students are able to understand what the passage is about, study the questions thoroughly. Turn to the relevant portions of the passage, read them again and then proceed to answer the questions one by one. Take the first question first. Use complete sentences. In case the students fail to make out a general sense, they should be helped with the answer. Sometimes it may be necessary to use Grammar-Translation Method if direct method does

not work. It should be advised to answer the question by making the expression of the question, the statement of their answer. For example (i) if it is asked "What are the causes of unemployment in India." The answer should be, "The causes of unemployment in India are." This makes the answer precisely accurate. (ii) Modern method consists of framing a more searching type of questions:

(1) Besides direct questions there should be some inferential type of questions also in which the students are forced to frame their own answers by constructing their own sentences with the help of the new words and expressions which they find in the passage.
(2) The another type of questions have to be devised for testing the students' conception over the newly acquired vocabulary, structural patterns and idiomatic expressions.
(3) The students should be finally asked to write down the gist of each paragraph of the passage in their own words. The degree of success attained by them will indicate the level of their comprehension.

As comprehension is a test in language, the teacher should be very particular about his language and expression. The language should be simple and correct, while the expression forceful.

WORKS CITED

Ballard, P.B. *Thought and Language,* Longmans.

Cartledge, H.A. *Reading with Understanding,* in E.L.T. Selections 1, Oxford.

——. *Comprehension and Appreciation,* E.L.T. Selections, 2, OUP.

Frence, F.G. *The Teaching of English Abroad,* I and II, Oxford.

Palmer, H.E. *The Grading & Simplifying in Literary Material* (Tokyo, IRET).

Pink, M.A. and Thomas S.E. *English Grammar Composition and Correspondence,* Cassell.

Wren and Martin. *High School English Grammar and Composition,* S. Chand & Company.

22

Rushdie's Use of Language in *Midnight's Children*

SISIR KUMAR CHATTERJEE

Ever since it was declared the 'Booker of Bookers' (*i.e.*, the best book in 25 years of Booker history) in 1993, Rushdie's *Midnight's Children* has been at the centre of critical attention. Critics have focused their interest on various aspects of Rushdie's art in the novel. Ashutosh Banerjee, for example, has dealt with the narrative technique employed in the book; Ron Shepherd and M.L. Pandit have discussed the novelist's use of fantasy in the work; Tariq Rahman has written on the treatment of politics in it; R.S. Pathak explores Rushdie's delineation of the relation between history and the individual in the novel. Neil Ten Kortenaar discusses *Midnight's Children* as an allegory of history. Goonetileke takes up the subject of Rushdie's use of myth in the novel. Many critics have also paid attention to Rushdie's intertextual strategies in the work. Nancy E. Batty, for instance, brings out the novel's affinities with the *Tales of Arabian Nights,* while Robert Alter has done a comparative study between *Midnight's Children* and Sterne's *Tristram Shandy*. What, however, has not as yet received adequate critical attention is Rushdie's use of language in *Midnight's Children*. This article attempts to address the issue of the dynamics of Rushdie's language in the novel on the assumptions that first, what contributes, perhaps more than anything else, to the popularity, controversiality and complexity of the work is its language and, more importantly, all the important shades of the novel's perspective—which is evidently post-colonial and post-modernist—can be profitably searched for in the novelist's use of language which, it should be made clear right at the outset, is here understood as a narratorial/strategic complex that subsumes much more than what is ostensible, *i.e.*, mere vocabulary and syntax.

In a sense, the history of Indian fiction in English is a history of the evolution of the English language used by novelists, and *Midnight's Children* is a prominent milestone in this respect. The grandmasters in the field—R.K. Narayan, Raja Rao and Mulk Raj Anand—wrote their novels in what was essentially chaste or pure English which is another name for imperial English, the English of the 'centre.' Even those who succeeded the great maestros—*e.g.*, Anita Desai and Arun Joshi—did not show any fundamental departure from the basic principles that constitute the chastity of British English. As a consequence, there was a wide disparity between the novelist's subject and his/her medium of writing, the subject being Indian society and the language being English. The end result of this was that the Indian novel in English, unlike that in the Indian regional languages, only too often seemed to be a coterie-confined literary entity, studied principally by the academics of English departments and read by very few, either in India or abroad, for entertainment. There then emerged in the arena of Indian fiction in English, a group of young novelists—most of them born around 1947—who appeared to feel for the first time that it is important to indigenise the medium of writing, to project a comprehensive vision of the highly complex, multilingual and multicultural society that India is. The novelist to leave the most significant and revolutionary contribution in Indian fiction in English in this respect is Salman Rushdie who has written his novels in a language that deserves more probing critical attention than it has so far received. This article, however, will remain confined to the functionality of Rushdie's language in *Midnight's Children* only.

Rushdie believes that if he has to convey his vision of Indian culture in an original way with English as his medium of writing, he has "to break up the language and put it back together/in a different way [...] to destroy the natural rhythms of the English language [...] [and,] to dislocate the English and let other things into it" (Goonetileke, 43). Rushdie does not find the task of dislocating the English language much of a problem. In an interview he explicitly states: "The English language is, I think, less of a problem than people make it out to be." He mildly accuses the 'earlier generation of writers' "who were basically just about adult at the time of Independence, who were very heavily influenced by the English, the classical English writing." He contends that "that was their formation, and I think that their instinct was to write in that way. But I think also," he maintains, "that by now English is very domesticated in India." Rushdie desires "that Indian writers will become much freer with the English language [...] use it more and more [...] unproblematically and without that kind of echo of the colony [...] [and] use it with more verve, more confidence, more ease, and with more Indianness" (Vijay Kumar 223). And *Midnight's Children* best illustrates Rushdie's strategy or method of Indianising, revitalising and de-colonising the English language.

Rushdie's defiance of the "classical," which for him means "colonial," English is manifest at the lexical level in the following features:

(1) he inserts a considerable number of Hindi, Urdu and Hindustani lexical items into his English, *e.g.*: 'ekdum,' 'angrez,' 'phut-a-phut,' 'nasbandi,' 'dhoban,' 'feringhee,' 'baba,' 'garam masala,' 'rakshasas,' 'fauj,' 'badmaash,' 'jailkhana,' 'baap-re-baap,' 'hai hai,' 'sab kuch,' 'bas,' 'chi-chi,' 'yaar,' 'gora,' 'pyar kiya to darna kiya,' 'goondas,' 'hubshee,' 'ooper neechay,' 'sarpanch,' 'kahin,' 'bhai-bhai,' 'itr,' 'zenana,' 'buddha,' 'crorepatis,' 'ayah,' 'nibu-pani,' 'paan,' 'khichri,' 'chutney,' 'gur,' 'rasgullas,' 'gulabjamuns,' 'jalebis,' 'barfi,' 'bhel-puri,' etc.

(2) Rushdie's language at the lexical level is marked by the sudden intrusions of esoteric Latin and classical Arabic, *e.g.*: 'mucuna pruritis,' 'feronia elephanticus,' 'sunt lacrimae rerum,' 'kan ma kan,' 'fi qadim azzaman,' 'tilk al-gharaniq al,' 'ula wa inna shafa,' 'ata-hunna la-turtaja,' etc.

(3) Rushdie presses a bunch of English words belonging to a particular grammatical category occur together without either punctuating or conjugating them so that

they form a simulacrum of complex compounds. There are such compounds of nouns (*e.g.*, 'murder rape greed war,' 'animals peasants brutes,' 'mother sister lover sibyl friend,' etc.); of verbs (*e.g.*, 'yelling jabbering arguing giggling,' 'chased arrested dragged,' kick stamp trample,' etc.); of Noun Phrases having adjectives or classifiers (*e.g.*, 'rotting coconuts abandoned cigarette packets pony turds non-degradable bottles fruit peelings jellyfish'). In all these compounds the items all belong to a related set.

(4) Phrases are made to frequently run together (*e.g.*, 'overandover,' 'updownup,' 'downdowndown,' 'suchandsuch,' 'noseholes,' 'birthanddeath,' 'whatdoyoumeanhowcanyousaythat,' 'getoutofitsill-yoldmooitsthesoddingbeach,' 'blackasnight,' 'nearlynine,' 'nearlynineyearold,' 'almostseven,' 'godknowswhat,' 'dirtyfilthy,' etc.

(5) Rushdie generates the effect of onomatopoeia with sounds typically Indian (*e.g.*, 'wham bamshot,' 'doomboombadoom,' Thaii! Thaiii!,' 'khrikk-khrikk,' 'dharrraaammm,' etc.

(6) Rushdie demolishes the notion of the purity or centrality of English (i) by inventing new forms of existing English words as well as of Indian lexical items through audaciously creative hybridization (*e.g.*, 'mediocrely,' 'dislikeable,' 'alienness,' 'writery,' 'doctori,' 'suicidally,' 'unbeautiful,' 'sonship,' 'memoryless,' 'historyless,' 'dupatta-less,' 'Bombayness,' 'chutnification,' etc.); (ii) by accommodating outrageously clipped sentences that are made to function as classifiers (*e.g.*, 'long-ago-letter,' 'once-upon-a time wife,' 'long-ago desire,' 'by-now-constant itch,' 'film-poster-trolley pushers,' 'long-time-no-see-smile,' etc.); (iii) by transforming clipped sentences into nouns (*e.g.*, 'excuse-mes,' 'next-attractions,' 'coming-soons,' 'what-happened-nextism,' etc.); (iv) by forging new compound words through the remoulding of English phrasal verbs (*e.g.*, 'a looker-after'); (v) by reshaping English idioms (*e.g.*, 'to put the cart before the bullock'); (vi) by transplanting Indian concepts into

equivalent English expressions (*e.g.*, 'our little piece-of-the-moon,' 'four hundred and twenty, the number of trickery and fraud,' 'whatnextism,' etc.); (vii) by including Indian slang words (*e.g.*, 'funtoosh,' 'goo,' etc.); (viii) by creating new slang words (*e.g.*, 'other pencil' for male sex organ as in Padma's words to Saleem Sinai "Now that the writery is done, let's see if we can make your other pencil work!" (MC 39), or 'cucumber' to refer to the same object as in the phrase "the useless cucumber hidden in my pants" (MC 141), or 'soo-soos' as in "now I saw him and Cyrus behind a bush, doing such funny rubbing things with their soo-soos!" (MC 18), or 'spittoon' to refer to the female sex organ as in Saleem's candid admission "despite everything she tries, I cannot hit her spittoon" (MC, 39); (viii) by incorporating misspellings (*e.g.*, 'straaange,' 'hopeyu guessma nayym,' 'unquestionabel,' 'existance,' 'ees,' etc.); (ix) by making room for those Indian forms of English words which are traditionally looked upon as incorrect (*e.g.*, 'informations,' 'mens,' 'lifeliness,' etc.); (x) by encompassing habitual linguistic mannerisms that distinguish characters (*e.g.*, the Reverend Mother's use of the expression 'whatsitsname,') or even their stammers (*e.g.*, 'rah rah wrong,' 'hiss hiss history,' 'caw corpses,' 'ist ist istiff,' etc.) and (xi) by using nonsense back-up words which is a typically Indian language habit (*e.g.*, 'writing-shiting,' 'writery-shitery,' 'club-shub,' 'joke-shoke,' 'pumpery-shumpery,' etc.).

No critic should be so naïve as to misconstrue all this as mere gimmick(ry). It is part of a deliberate anti-colonial strategy. By using language "unproblematically" Rushdie on the one hand enhances the process of abrogating and replacing the English language and on the other hand forges a multilingual medium to capture the 'polyglossic' and multicultural reality of India. Since language is a primary means of defining the self, Rushdie, as an avowedly anti-colonial writer, seizes the language of the centre and replaces it in a discourse fully adapted to the cultural ambience of India. By re-moulding the colonial English to new, inventive, need-based usages, he gives a jolt to the notion of the illusory standard of normative or 'correct' usage. He forces the language of the centre to bear the burden of communicating the cultural experience of the periphery. It is, as Raja Rao puts it in *Kanthapura*, to "convey in a language that is not one's own the spirit that is one's own" (*EWB* 39). By conveying the syncretic and hybridized nature of his post-colonial experience, Rushdie thus refutes the privileged position of a standard code in the English language and any monocentric view of human experience. So, Rushdie's re-lexification of the English language through his innovative, imaginative use of it is a step in the process of the dismantling of the imperialist centralism as established through the privileged centrality of the English language. Thus viewed, *Midnight's Children* may be regarded as a paradigmatic demonstration of the abrogating and appropriating impetus of a post-colonial writer—his attempt at promoting the peripheral to the status of privileged centrality.

Thematically, besides reflecting an "inclusive" mode of writing of the novelist, this re-orientation of language not only enables the novelist to perceive and communicate his experience of a hybridized and complex cultural reality but also to lend it an impact of immediacy, to help capture the natural rhythms of Indian speech habits and of the basic tenor of sub-continental life manifest in its bewildering multiplicity and its non-exclusive cultural modality. This "chutnification" of language shows how Rushdie is concerned with depicting his experience with utmost honesty, exploiting all the resources he can wield. When, for example, Padma admonishes Saleem for his 'writery-shitery' and urges him to be attentive to more basic activities by saying "eat na, food is spoiling" or when the boy Saleem goes spying on his mother to a "real rutputty joint" which advertises its "Lovely Lassi, Fantabulous Faluda and Bhelpuri Bombay Fashion," Rushdie is attempting to deploy all the linguistic resources available to him for evoking the plurality of urban India for which no single language is adequate. The very texture of life in the Indian sub-continent, particularly in the urban areas, is multilingual. The young generation who speak English as a second language or a surrogate first language very often mix it up with the vocabulary items taken from many other Indian languages, particularly Hindi, Urdu and the speaker's mother tongue. In other words, they treat English as an everyday peer-group language and therefore use it in creative, though playful and impure ways. They do it constantly on college campuses, coffeehouses, playgrounds and other places where they meet. Rushdie weaves this multilingual wrap and woof of life in India into his concern in *Midnight's Children* and negotiates it at different levels—ranging from Naseem Aziz's resistance ("If God meant people to speak many tongues [...] why did he put only one in our heads?" (*MC* 48) to the Pakistani soldiers' incomprehension of the Mukti Bahini's song "Amar Sonar Bangla" which "protected [them] from the insidious subversion of the lyric, although their feet did inadvertently tap to the tune" (*MC* 424).

Interestingly enough, much more polyglossic than Rushdie's language in the rest of the novel is Saleem's treatment of the midnight's children themselves:

> The voices babbled in everything from Malayalam to Naga dialects, from the purity of Lucknow Urdu to the southern slurrings of Tamil. I understood only a fraction of the things being said within the walls of my skull. Only later, when I began to probe did I learn that below the surface transmissions [...] language faded away, and was replaced by universally intelligible thought-forms which far transcended words [...]. (*MC* 200)

Here language, as Meenakshi Mukherjee rightly observes, "may be seen as a metaphor for the rich profusion of India's multiple culture which is more an asset than a problem except when state policy decides to demarcate the differences" (Mukherjee 19). In the text Rushdie mentions the redrawing of India's map in 1956 in which the boundaries of states "were not formed by rivers, or mountains, or any natural features of the terrain; they were instead walls of words. Language divided us [...]" (*MC* 225). Judged from this point of view, Rushdie's multilingual medium in the novel may be considered a plea for resisting the artificial divisions or partitions of Indian democracy and for embracing fluidity and multiplicity, which is the ultimate reality about India.

However, Rushdie's vocabulary in *Midnight's Children* is not as strong and strategically flawless as the above discussion may tend to suggest. While he uses the technique of "selective lexical fidelity" (*EWB* 64) which is evident in his daring to leave some Hindi, Urdu and Hindustani words unglossed in the text, he cannot consistently maintain this position. There are many words and expressions taken from Indian languages which he instinctively and immediately translates or explicates in English (*e.g.*, "dugdugee drum," "dia-lamp," "hey phaelwan, hey little wrestler," "Hey, bhaenchud! Hey, little sister-sleeper," "chand-ka-tukra, [...] affectionate piece-of-the-moon," "formality [...] takalluf, "Jehad, Padma! Holy war!," "chhi-chhi! Filthy," "Ravana, the ten-headed monster," "Rama, the hero of the Ramayana," "the Devil, the Great Beast, Shaitan himself," "pagal-zagal, crazy Zagallo," "chamcha (literally a spoon, but idiomatically a flatterer)," etc. Rushdie himself once remarked: "to do footnotes or to do notes at the end was a kind of defeat. The story has to tell itself, it mustn't rely on explanations. If it needs footnotes, it's a failure" (Vijay Kumar 217). It is true that in *Midnight's Children* Rushdie has not used 'footnotes' or 'endnotes' as such. But the purpose of 'footnotes' is served by his parenthetic explications which foreground the continual reality of cultural distance. In fact, these authorial intrusions betray a two-fold weakness: first, they helplessly accord a superior status to the translated words and therefore to the language translated into over the original ones; and secondly, they expose the writer's failure to completely trust the native words as having power enough to bear the burden of effectively conveying experience. It is this tacit acknowledgment of the unreliability of words and expressions borrowed from marginal (Indian) languages which frequently leads the writer to explicate Indian concepts. This vulnerability in Rushdie's strategy of making his writing multilingual, thus, reflects his unconscious admission of and surrender to the sense of the superiority of the language of the masters. One wonders whether it does not tend to make his language more neo-colonial than anti-colonial.

This impression gains further ground when one comes to Rushdie's syntax in *Midnight's Children.* Rushdie's operation at the level of syntax is far less audacious and militant than it is at the lexical level. It is to be admitted that he does show a distinctive inventiveness and boldness in (i) the use of punctuations (particularly dots, hyphens, exclamatory signs and interrogative marks); (ii) effecting sudden changes of person (as in "Saleem Sinai came to terms with himself. I will not say he was not sad; refusing to censor my past [...] (*MC* 378) or in "After this, the boy soldiers waited for the man-dog to die; but I was stronger than the snake-poison" (*MC* 436); (iii) executing abrupt changes of tense within a single verbal group (*e.g.*, "I cannot will not say how [...]," "night is falling has fallen," "we were are shall be the gods you never had," etc.); (iv) making four or five sentences run together without separating them by stops or other punctuation marks as in "No colours except green and black the walls are green the sky is black (there is no roof) the stars are green the Widow is green but her hair is black as black" (*MC* 249); (v) abrupt switching from reported to direct speech or *vice versa*, at times doing away with the grammatical means that distinguish one from the other as the following passage illustrates:

> [...] that's my father thinking, MY FATHER, now he's looking at me all funny What's the matter son don't you feel well Yes fine Abba fine, must go now GOT TO GET AWAY homework to do, Abba, and out, run away before he sees the clue on your face (my father always said that when I was lying there was a red light flashing on my forehead) [...]. He's butting into my thoughts, hey phaelwan, hey little wrestler, what's dragging your face down, it looks longer than a bad movie, you want channa? Pakoras? what? And me shaking my head, No, nothing, Hanif mamu, so that he relaxes, turns away, starts yelling Ohé come on Dara, that's the ticket, give him hell, Dara *yara!* (*MC* 202-03)

But these have hardly anything to do with the strategy of de-colonising English language. The English stream-of-consciousness novelists, particularly Joyce and Woolf, for example, very often resorted to syntactic experimentations of this type. Indeed, Rushdie hardly effects any significant departure or deviation from the fundamental syntactic principles of British English. And since syntax is the more elemental level of a language than lexis, Rushdie cannot be said to have achieved any remarkable feat of re-placing the English language in *Midnight's Children*. Since the basic Subject-Verb-Object/

Complement syntactic pattern of British English is followed more or less uniformly throughout the novel, Rushdie's language here, all said and done, remains fundamentally classical English. The only typically Indian syntactic features that may be said to have been exploited by the novelist in the text are the plethora of relative clauses heaped upon one another and the frequent breakings off in the middle of sentences. While the former feature is related to the writer's narrational strategy of recapitulating all that was related earlier, the latter feature is exploited to create an atmosphere of gossip and fun in the telling of the tale. But, the very fact that a writer who is so blatantly defiant in his use of language at the lexical level is so disappointingly tame in his handling of syntax points to the elemental unalterability of English, or, for that matter, any language in the world. Ironically, even at the level of lexis whatever indigenisation a post-colonial writer encodes in his writing can be decoded by a native English speaker only after he/she translates the experimented items into the equivalents of his/her language. For instance, Rushdie may deliberately misspell the word 'listen' as 'lissen,' but a British reader will not understand the word before translating it back into 'listen.' This applies equally invariably to all other lexical innovations. This unavoidable reality of the process of the human act of decoding language in fact tends to thwart the very purpose behind all a post-colonial writer's effort at de-colonising a language. The greatest irony underlying the situation is that the extent of Rushdie's success in abrogating British English—his dragging of the marginal to the central—has to be examined in an English which is more or less classical and pure.

This is not to argue that Rushdie's language in *Midnight's Children* lacks in functionality. On the contrary, it operates with its own aesthetic dynamics which assumes a richly complex edge within the narratorial framework of the novel. A few examples should be enough to establish the point. Rushdie's language at the very opening of the novel functions in a self-expository manner, serving as a brilliant introduction to the work and indicating the novelist's thematic and technical preoccupations:

> I was born in the city of Bombay [...] once upon a time. No, that won't do, there's no getting away from the date: I was born in Doctor Narlikar's Nursing Home on August 15th, 1947. And the time? The time matters, too. Well men: at night. No, it's important to be more [...]. On the stroke of midnight, as a matter of fact. Clock-hands joined palms in respectful greeting as I came. Oh, spell it out, spell it out: at the precise instant of India's arrival at independence, I tumbled forth into the world. There were gasps. And, outside the window, fireworks and crowds. A few seconds later, my father broke his big toe; but his accident was a mere trifle when set beside what had befallen me in the benighted moment, because thanks to the occult tyrannies of those blandly saluting clocks I had been mysteriously handcuffed to history, my destinies indissolubly chained to those of my country. (*MC* 3)

The novel, in other words, begins in an autobiographical vein ("I was born in the city of Bombay"). This is followed by the phraseology of a fairy tale ("once upon a time," an expression that occurs repeatedly in the novel and assumes the proportion and takes on the effect of a leitmotif), suggesting the mode of fantasy. But this is rejected in favour of a recording of an actual historical year, date, and time, suggesting the novelist's sense of responsibility to history. The insertion of the image of "clock-hands joining palms" brings out Rushdie's brilliant metaphoric imagination and thinly veils his vulnerability to the thought of partition. His father breaking "his big toe" right at the fatal hour of Saleem's birth and India's attaining independence (which obviously means the birth of a nation too) foreshadows how cataclysmic the two births are going to prove. The phrases "handcuffed to history" and "my destinies indissolubly chained to those of my country" reveal the basic narrative strategy the writer is going to adopt in the novel—the synchronization of the history of an individual with that of a nation. And it is significant that the language of this passage is repeated, almost verbatim, in the passage later in the book where Saleem's description of his son's birth duplicates his description of his own:

> He was born in Old Delhi [...] once upon a time. No, that won't do, there's no getting away from the date: Aadam

> Sinai arrived at a night-shadowed slum on June 25th, 1975. And the time? The time matters, too. As I said: at night. No, it's important to be more [...]. On the stroke of midnight, as a matter of fact. Clock-hands joined palms. Oh, spell it out, spell it out: at the precise instant of India's arrival at Emergency, he emerged. There were gasps; and, across the country, silences and fears. And owing to the occult tyrannies of that benighted hour, he was mysteriously handcuffed to history, his destinies indissolubly chained to those of his country. (*MC* 500)

In fact, repetition is an unmistakable feature of Rushdie's language in *Midnight's Children*. Certain words keep on recurring throughout the novel (*e.g.*, 'recurrence,' 'form,' 'shape,' 'fragments,' 'broken,' 'cracks,' 'pieces,' 'centre-parting,' 'spittoon,' 'black,' 'white,' 'optimism,' 'nose,' 'knees,' 'snake,' 'ladder,' 'chutney,' etc.), and sometimes even a whole sentence is repeated (*e.g.*, "What can't be cured must be endured," "there is no escape from form/recurrence," etc.). These recurrent words, phrases and sentences are viscerally related to the novel's theme and technique. For example, 'spittoon' functions in the book as a receptacle of memory which holds variegated events together. 'Chutney' with its primary association with Mary Pereira seems to form the novel's thematic axis since it is her change of birth-tag which is at the centre of all that happens in the book. Also, if 'black' and 'snake' conjure up images of evil, 'white' and 'ladder' provide a potent antithesis to these by implying good; and, taken together they figure the inclusiveness which characterises the basic tenor of Indian philosophy. Again, 'centre-parting,' 'cracks,' 'fragments,' 'pieces,' 'broken'—all these form the bulk of the vocabulary descriptive of partition which is one of the major thematic concerns of the work. In sharp contrast to this group of words, however, there is another group consisting of such words as 'form,' 'shape,' and 'recurrence' which convey the idea of an attempt to define a symmetry amidst the formlessness and fragmentation all-around. Indeed, the historical forces or political events as depicted in the novel—from India's partition to Indira Gandhi's proclamation of the Emergency—as well as the different layers of the story told in it all exude a sense of disintegration, of centrifugality. Yet, throughout the novel the narrator strives to impose on these disintegrating phenomena a pattern of centripetality by using various devices, the most effectively functional of which is the recurrent iteration of certain key words, phrases, expressions and sentences which are thus made to form a complex pattern of leitmotifs that really hold the novel together. The recursive property of Rushdie's language in *Midnight's Children*, thus, may be said to be an expression of (to use Rushdie's own words in the novel) "a sort of national longing for form—or perhaps simply an expression of our deep belief that forms lie hidden within reality; that meaning reveals itself only in flashes" (*MC* 359).

Finally, the very texture of Rushdie's language in *Midnight's Children* shows an amalgamation, or, to use Rushdie's own neologism, 'chutnification' of various narrational registers which are happily assimilated. For instance, the book embodies spiralling, involved, epic interrogatives as evident in the following passage:

> [...] What weight, falling, created such an almighty crash? Whose hand wrenched a door open? In whose heel are visible two red, flowing holes, filled with venom for which there is no known antivenene, a poison which has killed stablefuls of worn-out horses? Whose body is carried out of the tower by plain-clothes men [...]? Why, when the moonlight falls upon the dead face, does Mary Pereira fall like a sack of potatoes to die floor, eyes rolling upwards in their sockets, in a sudden and dramatic faint? [...] Why are there so many bottles with rags stuffed into their necks? (*MC* 174)

If the use of these interrogatives shows Rushdie's adherence to the tradition of the comic-epic, Rushdie's work also encompasses filmy language as the following instances reveal: "zooming out slowly into long-shot [...]. Merrily it rolls along, rolls along, rolls along [...] (Fade-out)" (*MC* 283), or "I permit myself to insert a Bombay-talkie-style close-up—a calendar ruffled by a breeze, its pages flying off in rapid succession to denote the passing of the years; I superimpose turbulent long-shots of street riots, medium shots of burning buses [...]" (*MC* 414), or perhaps most effectively:

> Close-up of my grandfather's right hand: nails knuckles fingers all somehow bigger than you would expect. Clumps of red hair on the outside edges. Thumb and forefinger pressed together, separated only by a thickness of paper. In short: my grandfather was holding a pamphlet. It had been inserted into his hand (we cut to a long-shot—nobody from Bombay should be without a basic film vocabulary) as he entered the hotel foyer. (*MC* 31)

This use of film language shows up Rushdie's absorption of popular/mass culture. Correspondingly, the novel is also marked by frequent use of verbal fantasy. For instance, Boatman Tai is described as "a watery Caliban;" Naseem Aziz could even dream her daughters' dreams, just to know what they were getting up to. But the most remarkable illustration of Rushdie's use of verbal fantasy can be found in the passage describing Dr Aziz's nose:

> My grandfather's nose: nostrils flaring, curvaceous as dancers. Between them swells the nose's triumphal arch, first up and out, then down and under, sweeping in to his upper lip with a superb and at present red-tipped flick. An easy nose to hit a tussock with. I wish to place on record my gratitude to this mighty organ—if not for it, who would ever have believed me to be truly my mother's son, my grandfather's grandson? This colossal apparatus which was to be my birthright, too. Doctor Aziz's nose—comparable only to the trunk of the elephant-headed god Ganesh—established incontrovertibly his right to be a patriarch. It was Tai who taught him that, too. When young Aadam was barely past puberty the dilapidated boatman said, "That's a nose to start a family on, my princeling. There'd be no mistaking whose brood they were. Mughal Emperors would have given their right hands for noses like that one. There are dynasties waiting inside it,"—and here Tai lapsed into coarseness—"like snot." (*MC* 8)

This kind of language testifies to the fervour of Rushdie's imaginative vivre and his creative mode of fantasizing reality. It is also noticeable that at other places too Rushdie's language in *Midnight's Children* evinces a distinct journalistic flavour as in the following passage:

> It is a matter of record that the States Reorganization Committee has submitted its report to Mr Nehru as long ago as October 1955; a year later, its recommendations had been implemented. India had been divided anew, into fourteen states and six centrally-administered "territories" [...]. Kerala was for speakers of Malayalam, the only palindromically-named tongue on earth; in Karnataka you were supposed to speak Kanarese; and the amputated state of Madras—known today as Tamil Nadu—enclosed the *aficionadoes* of Tamil.
>
> Owing to some oversight, however, nothing was done with the state of Bombay; and in the city of Mumbadevi, the language marches grew, longer and noisier and finally metamorphosed into political parties, the Samyukta Maharashtra Samiti ("United Maharashtra Party") which stood for the Marathi language and demanded the creation of the Deccan state of Maharashtra, and the Maha Gujarat Parishad ("Great Gujarat Party") which marched beneath the banner of the Gujarati language and dreamed of a state to the north of Bombay City, stretching all the way to the Kathiawar peninsula and the Rann of Kutch [...]. (*MC* 225-26)

This language points to the writer's insistent fidelity to history and relates his work to the postmodernist form of the Non-fiction novel. Finally, *Midnight's Children* also incorporates a considerable amount of analytical and critical idiom which can be traced in the use of certain words, phrases and expressions scattered throughout the novel (*e.g.*, "the feasibility of the chutnification of history" (*MC* 548), "synchronistic birth," "a countdown for building suspense," etc.). But this is best illustrated in the following passages: "Reality is a question of perspective; the further you get from the past, the more concrete and plausible it seems—but as you approach the present, it inevitably seems more and more incredible" (*MC* 197), and

> How, in what terms, may the career of a single individual be said to impinge on the fate of a nation? I must answer in adverbs and hyphens: I was linked to history both literally and metaphorically, both actively and passively, in what our (admirably modern) scientists might term "modes of connection" composed of

> "dualistically-combined configurations" of the two pairs of opposed adverbs given above. This is why hyphens are necessary: actively-literally, passively-metaphorically, actively-metaphorically and passively-literally, I was inextricably entwined with my world. (*MC* 285-86)

If this is a type of language that uses a typically critical idiom, it also displays a fundamental self-reflexive, even self-parodying quality. In other words, Rushdie's critical-analytical phraseology serves as a vehicle of a self-conscious, self-reflexive, metafictional method of writing. And ultimately, it is these multidimensional aspects of Rushdie's language in *Midnight's Children* that make the novel a protean and inexhaustibly attractive post-modernist text.

NOTE

The authors of *The Empire Writes Back* opine that India is a 'diglossic society' (*EWB* 39). But, it seems more appropriate to categorize India as a 'polyglossic' society because here a multitude of languages "interweave to form a generally comprehensible linguistic continuum" (*EWB* 39).

REFERENCES

Ashcroft, Bill, et al. *The Empire Writes Back: Theory and Practice in Post-colonial Literatures*. London: Routledge, 1989, Rpt. 1993. Cited as *EWB*.

Banerjee, Ashutosh. "Narrative Technique in *Midnight's Children*." *The Novels of Salman Rushdie*. Eds. G.R. Taneja and R.K. Dhawan. New Delhi: Indian Society for Commonwealth Studies, 1992: 23-32.

E. Rege, Josna. "Victim into Protagonist? Midnight's Children and the Post-Rushdie National Narratives of the Eighties." *Rushdie's Midnight's Children: A Book of Readings*. Ed. Meenakshi Mukherjee. Delhi: Pencraft International, 1999: 182-211.

Goonetileke, D.C.R.A. *Salman Rushdie*, Macmillan Modern Novelists Series. Houndmills: Macmillan, 1998, Rpt. 1999. Cited as Goonetileke.

Kortenaar, Neil Ten. "Midnight's Children and the Allegory of History." *Rushdie's Midnight's Children: A Book of Readings*. Ed. Meenakshi Mukherjee. Delhi: Pencraft International, 1999: 28-48.

Mukherjee, Meenakshi, ed. *Rushdie's Midnight's Children: A Book of Readings*. Delhi: Pencraft International, 1999. Cited as Mukherjee.

Nair, Rukmini Bhaya. "History as Gossip in Midnight's Children." *Rushdie's Midnight's Children: A Book of Readings*. Ed. Meenakshi Mukherjee. Delhi: Pencraft International, 1999: 49-68.

Natarajan, Nalini. "Woman, Nation and Narration in Midnight's Children." *Rushdie's Midnight's Children: A Book of Readings*. Ed. Meenakshi Mukherjee. Delhi: Pencraft International, 1999: 165-81.

Page, Norman, ed. *The Language of Literature,* Casebook Series. Houndmills: Macmillan, 1984.

Pandit, M.L. *New Commonwealth Writing,* New Delhi: Prestige, 1996.

Rushdie, Salman. *Midnight's Children.* New York: Avon Books, 1982. Cited as *MC.*

Shepherd, Ron. "Midnight's Children as Fantasy." *The Novels of Salman Rushdie.* Eds. G.R. Taneja and R.K. Dhawan. New Delhi: Indian Society for Commonwealth Studies, 1992: 33-43.

Taneja, G.R. and R.K. Dhawan, eds. *The Novels of Salman Rushdie.* New Delhi: Indian Society for Commonwealth Studies, 1992.

Vijay Kumar, T. "'Doing the Dangerous Thing': An Interview with Salman Rushdie." *Rushdie's Midnight's Children: A Book of Readings.* Ed. Meenakshi Mukherjee. Delhi: Pencraft International, 1999: 212-27. Cited as Vijay Kumar.

23

THE LINGUISTIC DEVIATIONS IN *THE GOD OF SMALL THINGS* AND THE LEGACY OF JOYCE

SANTOSH CHAKRABARTI

The colonial discourse of power envisages the twin processes of subversion of the culture of the colonised and imposition of the coloniser's language upon the latter. A section of writers of the erstwhile colonies wants to subvert these twin processes by a post-colonial discourse of language which has an abrogative stance. It is debatable whether such a 'decolorizing' project is 'false' and 'ultimately contradictory,'[1] but the fact remains that post-colonial writers in many diglossic societies like Africa and India forge a language in cross-cultural texts which not only seeks to assert a new power of creativity, but to give the language a distinctive look.

This is achieved mainly by creating a language variance from the 'imperialist'/'metropolitan' variety by interweaving indigenous/native/local terms with the standard/conventional English, or by using hybridized words, unglossed terms and syntactical variations. In other words, the post-colonial texts of the diglossic societies mentioned above use a language which is different from the language of power and give the writer an amplitude of freedom which conformity to the metropolitan/standard variety so far denied. Distinguishing between 'English' as is the norm for the metropolitan centre and 'English' as is the now-devised post-colonial variety, Bill Ashcroft *et al.* in *The Empire Writes Back* quote Terdiman to show how English has established itself as distinct and separate: "In this process of 'becoming,' English, by asserting its opposition to the centre and constantly interrogating the dominance of the 'standard,' establishes itself as a contrastive or counter-discourse (Terdiman[2] 1985 [...]). At the same time, that is, as an English, 'emerges' from English it establishes itself as distinct and separate. A considerable range of linguistic variance is generated, even though such variance is always attacked from centre by the dismissive terms 'colloquialism' or 'idiom.'"[3]

The scope for this language variance however is embedded in the inherent flexibility and in-built absorptive liberality of the English language. The post-colonial cross-cultural texts take advantage of this essential liberality of the tongue and make extensive use of hybrid and unglossed local terms. The post-colonial writers go through the process of abrogation and appropriation to make it possible.

The question is whether this adoption of language variance as a technique for literary discourses undermines the homogenous character of English and make it a distinct entity creating a linguistic distance from English. Critics of the post-colonial language use suggest that the creativity of the post-colonial writers does not make a thrust for cultural difference but rather for a cultural compromise effected through the alchemy of 'colonial structures and indigenous processes.' 'The language used by these writers sets upto, albeit inadvertently, an implicit hierarchy between imperial structure/language/culture on the one hand and indigenous process/practice/experience on the other.'[4]

The concrete reality about the Indo-English, especially post-colonial, literature is that it has successfully stormed the bastion of the Anglo-American literary establishment. The expressive medium of this literature—the Indo-English language—has come a long way from the mimicry that the early stages of the colonial situation in India encouraged in literacy discourses. Even before Macaulay advocating percolation of Western education from the English-educated elite to the *hot polloi* through a filtration process, the early Indian practitioners of English mimicked the English authors (for example, Derozio and Kashiprasad Ghosh in Bengal writing poetry in the first half of the 19th century in imitation of the English masters). The language that Arundhati Roy uses in

The God of Small Things evinces a penchant for forging innovative English, which is a big leap from the early days of lisping English terms to earn fame. R.K. Narayan once observed that 'the time has come for us to consider seriously the question of a Bharat brand of English. So far English has had a comparatively confined existence in our country chiefly in the halls of learning, justice, or administration. Now the time is ripe for it to come to the dusty street, market place, and under the banyan tree.'[5] What Roy seeks to do is just that—to forge 'a Bharat brand of English or a brand of English that very often deviates from the standard conventions." The variance in lexis is the result of a conscious hybridization of standard English by the use of unglossed culture-specific linguistic counters, misspelt and telescoped words and adjective clusters without verbal conjuncts, reverse sentence orders etc. Indeed Roy is unconventional and deliberately iconoclastic at every step of her writing—in lexico-syntactical as well as punctuational appearances. This deviationist strategy gives her novel a bold new look, which, in a major way, has contributed to her being catapulted to fame. Yet, even as the language that Roy has forged gives it an innovative new appearance, it at the same time opens up the problematics of its relationship with standard English. At the primary level, a distanced lexis with local and hybrid terms abrogates the power of metropolitan English, but it may also enlarge the scope for a comprehension gap in the cross-cultural text. Roy seeks to circumvent this difficulty by intentionally citing the contextual homogeneity of identical linguistic terms. When Muralidharan, the level-crossing lunatic, says, '*Onner/Runder/Mooner*,' the contextual referrality of the terms makes them self-evident: 'Muralidharan moved his mouth when he *counted*, and made well-formed words' (63, emphasis mine). The following extract shows how contextual affinity with cognate words closes the comprehension gap:

> Their families had come to meet them. From all over Kerala. On long bus journeys. From Ranni, from Kumili, from Vizhinjam, from Uzhavoor. Some of them had camped at the airport overnight, and had brought their food with them. And tapioca chips and chakka velaichathu for the way back. (138)

The keyword in the comprehension process of 'tapioca chips' and 'chakka velaichathu' is 'food' which is used in the right context.

Roy uses unglossed works like '*keto*' (meaning 'do you hear'), '*Valarey*' (meaning 'quite') in the sentence, "'Thanks, *keto*!' he said, '*Valarey* thanks!'" (70), '*Poda Patti*' (meaning 'go dog') in the sentence, "Hup! Hup! *Poda Patti*" (90) etc. to give the novel its distinctive cultural identity and an indigenous look. Though such corrupted vernacular hybrids as '*Porketmunny*,' a patois term used by the Orangedrink Lemondrink Man (102) do not hamper comprehension, there are other hybridized constructs like juxtaposition of unglossed native words/sentences and English words/sentences which do, for example,

(i) "He kept dropping his packages and saying, '*Ende Deivomay*! *Eee sadhanangal*!'" (meaning 'My God, these things!') (143).

(ii) "'*Aiyyo kashtam*,' Velutha said" (the Malayalam phrase meaning 'how sad') (177), etc.

The latter varieties of hybridized constructs are subversive of the hegemony of the metropolitan variety of English, but they also initiate a distancing process which is difficult to bridge. Roy also gives English equivalents to native words/ sentences, for example, the English equivalent of the Malayalam term 'Modalali' is given in a explicatory sentence: 'Modalali means landlord' (80). Meanings of Malayalam sentences are given in brackets, for example,

Avaney kadalamma kondu poyi.
(So Mother Ocean rose and took him away.) (220)

This mixed variety of language adumbrates a fundamental linguistic compromise on Roy's part. As a post-colonial writer and a member of a small group of English-speaking (and writing) Indians, catering to an international community of English-speaking (and writing) people, she clearly adopts linguistic and syntactical variance which has an innovative stance, but which is not so avant-garde as to incite incomprehension. Roy's linguistic mode is thus one of compromise, a careful balancing act on the edge between a traditional ethics of language and a wholly different register.

Certainly this act of compromise is not without its occasional flashes of brilliance. One may notice her use of telescoped words—two or three words dovetailed into each other: 'lefrightlef' 141, 'Pleasetomeetyou' (212), 'Bluegreyblue' (238), 'mydearjudges' (271) etc. Apparently these compressions are among the many subversive licences taken by the post-colonial writer to break away from the standard English, but in some cases they also relate to the mood of the speaker or the tone of the context in which they are used. Roy takes liberty with syntactical formations. To give an example:

> Margaret Kochamma told her to Stoppit.
> So she Stoppited. (141)

The compressed formation 'Stoppit' shows the speaker's strong disgust at the behaviour of Rahel at the homecoming of Sophie Mol. For thereafter 'She (Ammu) turned around to find her crisp knickered daughter communing with cement marsupials. She went and fetched her, scoldingly' (141)

Other licences include:

(i) subjectless and verbless sentences:

> 'Collapsed fountains.
>
> Flattened puffs.
>
> Crumpled yellow bellbottoms and a go-go bag that was loved. Jet-lagged and barely awake. Then the swollen-ankled adults. Slow from too much sitting.' (172)

(ii) expressive phrasal compounds used as adjectives:
'There was a short, Sad-About-Joe silence.' (173)

Linguistic device as a tool for social discourse is best illustrated by the reverse order in which Estha and Rahel read aloud the mottoes inscribed on a board on the wall of the Kottayam police station:

> 'ssenetilo**P**', he said, 'ssenetilo**P**, ecneideb**O**,'
> 'ytlayo**L**, ecnegilletn**I**,' Rahel said.
> 'ysetruo**C**.'
> 'yeneiciff**E**.' (313)

The reverse ordering of the value-laden words—'Politeness,' 'Obedience,' 'Loyalty,' 'Intelligence,' 'Courtesy' and 'Efficiency' —is a telling commentary on the state of things in the police administration. Velutha's death in police custody is an eye-opener to the malpractices and rank injustice lurking behind the facade of high ideals set by the custodians of the law in Roy's home state.

A common favourite practice of Roy is to use short, crisp sentences in simple parataxis which heightens the tonality of a given situation. The following extract describes the sexual union of Ammu and Velutha in the concluding chapter of the novel:

> She could hear the wild hammering of his heart.
> She held him till it calmed down. Some what.
> She unbuttoned her shirt. They stood there.
>
> Skin to skin. Her brownness against his blackness. Her softness against his hardness. (334-35)

Talking of sexual encounters it may be mentioned that Roy demonstrates and exploits the multivalent potency of the language she uses. While the pedophiliac exploitation of Estha by the Orangedrink Lemondrink Man in Abhilash Talkies is described in a raucous and crude language:

> Then the gristly-bristly face contorted, and Estha's hand was wet and hot and sticky. It had egg white on it. White egg white. Quarter-boiled. (104)

the language of the sexual union between Ammu and Velutha has a suggestive yet evocative configuration:

> Biology designed the dance. Terror timed it. Dictated the rhythm with which their bodies answered each other. (335)

The tonal difference of the two sets of language may be explained by the fact that while in one instance it is forced and the partner (Estha) has an unconscious and reluctant involvement, in another it is a willing involvement for sexual satisfaction and fulfilment.

Thus the language of Roy registers a deliberate and calculated shift from the norm and standard of conventional English. Critics have acclaimed Roy's 'verbal wizardy'[6] and innovative language,[7] but a close look at the post-colonial use of English reveals Roy's imitation of a mixed lexis in her text.[8] Most importantly, Roy emerges as a close follower of the language wizard of modern English. James Joyce, whose techniques of telescoped lexis and subjectless and verbless syntactical structures form the very basis of his linguistic magic. Listed below is a comparative study of the uses of language by Joyce and Roy:

Cluster I

Roy	Joyce
Then she sat up and put her arms around him. Drew him down beside her. (*The God of Small Things* 327)	He had his grand manner on. I supple and suave. Attacked me on the score of love for one's mother. Tried to imagine his mother: cannot. (*A Portrait of the Artist as a Young Man* 363)

Cluster II

Roy	Joyce
bluegreyblue eyes (*GOST* 146)	hitherandthithering waters (*Finnegans Wake* 216)

Nearer home there is also Kamala Das who before Roy evinced an impulsion against following the syntactical norms of the English language, which may be construed as her penchant for 'forging another variety of English,'[9] for example:

> A faded beggar maid. But later he said, we are in love. I believed him His dark skin reminded me of Krishna. The libertine. The inconstant lover. The monarch. (*The Sign of the Lion* included in *A Doll for the Child Prostitute.*)

It emerges from these considerations that Roy's much acclaimed innovativeness is part of a longer tradition of Western and Indian English writing. Even the visual display of an architectural design as evidenced in Roy's prosaic equivalence to 'pattern poetry'/'pruning (pruned) poetry' goes back to the ancient form of *technopaignia* (pattern poem). Practitioners of the art included the 16th century English poets, Stephen Hawes and Richard Willes, though a more accessible and familiar figure is that of George Herbert's famous poem, *Easter-wings.* That Roy has clearly drawn upon this tradition is made clear if we compare the two architectural patterns:

GOST	*Easter-wings*
Nictitating	Lord, who createdst man in wealth and store,
ictitating	Though foolishly he lost the same,
titating	Decaying more and more,
itating	Till he became
tating	Most poore:
ating	With thee
ting	O let me rise
ing	As larks, harmoniously,
(189)	And sing this day thy victories:
	Then shall the fall further the flight in me.[10]

In these terms, the myth of Arundhati Roy's innovativeness is largely uncovered by the reality of her Eurocentric vision in the compositional architectonics of written language. We may draw from this case study of her novel the conclusion that Roy's case is symptomatic of the post-colonial writer's predicament of location in the problematic of contestation between the need to forge a new linguistic register and the inability to do so without falling back on many of the resources of entrenched English linguistic practices. The larger shadow cast on the screen of our consciousness as readers and critics is that of a bi-lingually enabled writer who seeks to build her post-colonial identity on the superstructure of the monolithic edifice that is the English language and culture.

NOTES AND REFERENCES

1. Bill Ashcroft, Gareth Griffiths and Helen Tiffin. *The Empire Writes Back* (Routledge, 1989, rpt. 1999) 53: 'It is false because it confuses usage with property in its view of meaning, and it is ultimately contradictory, since, if it is asserted that words do have some essential cultural essence not subject to changing usage, then post-colonial literatures in English, predicated upon this very changing usage, could not have come into being.'
2. Richard Terdiman. *Discourse/Counter-Discourse: The Theory and Practice of Symbolic Resistance in Nineteenth-Century France* (Cornell Univ. Press, 1985).
3. *The Empire Writes Back* 56.
4. Leela Gandhi. *Postcolonial Theory, A Critical Introduction* (OUP, 1999) 175.
5. Cited by K.V. Surendran in *The God of Small Things: A Saga of Lost Dreams* (New Delhi: Atlantic Publishers, 2000) 192.

6. Beth Yahp in her review, 'Larger than Life,' admires Roy's 'verbal wizardy.' vide C.V. Driesen's paper entitled 'When Language Dances: The Subversive Power of Roy's Text in *The God of Small Things*' in *Arundhati Roy: The Novelist Extraordinary*. Ed. R.K. Dhawan (Prestige, 1999) 375, Note 1.
7. Vide *The God of Small Things: A Saga of Lost Dreams* 192.
8. *The Empire Writes Back* 53-54. Bill Ashcroft *et al.* refer to the use of such local terms as '*obi*' (hut), '*kurta*' (shirt) etc. in post-colonial texts. Moreover, they also show how in an extract from *The Cord*, a play by the Malaysian writer K.S. Maniam "the English variant establishes itself in clear contradistinction to the 'Standard' within the dialogue itself."
9. *Encyclopedia of Post-colonial Literatures in English*, Vol. I (Routledge, 1994) 333.
10. Ist stanza of the two-stanza poem included in *The Metaphysical Poets*. Ed. Helen Gardner (Penguin Books, rpt. 1975) 121.

N.B.: Flamingo's (London) 1997 edn. of *The God of Small Things* is used for reference and extracts.

WORKS CITED

Ashcroft, Bill, Gareth Griffiths and Helen Tiffin. *The Empire Writes Back*. Routledge, 1989, rpt. 1999.

Gandhi, Leela. *Postcolonial Theory*. OUP, 1999.

Dhawan, R.K. ed. *Arundhati Roy: The Novelist Extraordinary*. Prestige, 1999.

Surendran, K.V. *The God of Small Things: A Saga of Lost Dreams*. New Delhi: Atlantic Publishers, 2000.

24

Linguistic Deviations in Translation

MUKTA MAHAJAN

Translation is a vital aspect of all those fields that are using language as medium of expression. Translation and language are actually characterized by each other in the sense, translation uses languages to express itself and language is nothing but the translation of the prior mode of expression, thought, idea, imagination etc. In a way, the very primary idea can be that, each skill of language travels through the process of translation.

If the above mentioned statement contains an element of truth then it can be extended further that translation is a multiplied process which is continuous and linguistic and cultural as well as paradoxical, in the sense the medium of translation is language, the content of its content is cultural but it is at a time paradoxical because it preserves and changes one at the same time. It is conservative as well as innovative. It is twofold process which is intended to be unidirectional.

Translation is another sort of creative activity because here the exercise is double edged. Translator must be basically a creative person who has better eye for imagination and interpretation. Translation is a twofold process, even though the outward medium is language, it is like a vein filled by the blood of culture. Thus translation is culturally determined linguistic process. It is a sort of bypass to the heart of another culture. Translation is more a process than an activity because once the script is translated that cannot be called the full and final translation. Even then, there is scope for better and different translation especially in creative writing. In this sense, literature is itself a translation and *vice versa*. Translation is within literature. Of course this statement can be restricted by the bracket of 'Scope of Liberty' for translation as well as translator.

Translation is subjected by the given material for translation, unlike the writer who enjoys fullest and absolute liberty of material selection, the translator may enjoy the liberty of choosing the source language and target language but not the text. Thus, the process of translation is characterized by decodification and recodification. The translator very painstakingly decodifies the source text and recodifies it with balance. Translation is not merely changing the language only, but also shifting to another culture. Translation is not linguistic imitation but linguistic as well as cultural transmission. It thus becomes a cross cultural idea.

J.C. Catford calls it the replacement of textual material in another language. *R.L. Varshney* interprets it as substitution of meaning. *Sujit Mukherjee* finds it the most useful method of training the reader of literary text. *Heidigger* views translation as action of an interpretation of thought. *Derrida* sees translation as a continuing process which aims at modifying the original meaning and simultaneously reveals a network of text both enabling and prohibiting inter lingual communication. *Jose Lanmbert* argues that translation is an on-going process of an endless semiotic chain. According to *G.N. Devy* translation is a replication of an ordered subsystem of signs within a language to another correspondingly ordered subsystem of signs within a related language. *Henry Mechonnic* expresses his view in regard of translation that the theory of translation is not an applied linguistics. It is a new field in the theory and in the practice of literature. Its epistemological importance lies in its contribution to the theoretical practice of the homogeneity is proper to that social enterprise which we call writing.

Heidigger views translation as an action of an interpretation of thought, a translation of ourselves into the thought of the other language and not a linguistic, scientific transfer from something into the present.

Mary-Snell Hornby considers translation not as an activity that takes place between two languages but as an interaction between culture and culture.

Above views about translation bring out the following factors about the process of translation that translation is the replacement of textual material with equivalence, it is also the process of substitution, analysis and restricting. It is mode of discovery to enjoy the total effect created by literature.

In such a process there may be possibility of leading to everywhere than to translation. It may lead to explanation, commentary, summarizing or creating altogether new text that shows some resemblance with SLT. In order to avoid it, according to Alexander Frazer Tytler in his 'The Principles of Translation,' the translation should provide a complete transcript of the idea of SL text. The style and the translation should be of the same character as that of SL text. The translation should have all the smoothness and grace of the SL text.

Consideration of it, confirms the idea that translation is skill, an art, and science also. Translation is a process that leads to replacement of a set of linguistic contextual and cultural equivalence from the same set from source language through the stages of analysis, interpretation and creation. Even after it, some theorists are of the view that no translation is possible. Of course, this statement requires a lot of non-optimistic understanding of the term translation. Rather it can be said that translation is not possible in its totality.

Translation, according to me, thus can be defined as possible approximate redelivering of the socio-cultural linguistic set up of a context from SLT to TLT.

The history of Translation brings forth various elements of translation emphasized by noted practitioners of translation of various periods as method of translation.

In Greek period, they accepted the idea of imitation along with moderation in translation. Renaissance period prefers word for word translation as well as liberal translation. 17th and 18th century provided three sets of ideas of translation—Strict literalism, more freedom to translation and totally free hand to the translation as in the words of Dryden—Metaphors, paraphrase and imitation.

The introduction of automatic or machine translation

brought a considerable change in the process of translation. It is mostly a word to word translation.

During the period of 60s, translation studies are found greatly influence by Richardsian Criticism, Chomsky's ideas about grammar, Formalistic approach and introduction to the theory of deconstruction.

After this period, Translation theory came with linguistic dimension which was added by Chomsky, Nida Wolfram Wils. 70's translation research focuses on literary concerns or linguistics and grammar theories. J.C. Catford, James Holmes, Lefevere Popvic, Jury Tynjanov, Gideon Toury, Zohar contributed their efforts in this regard. Michel Foucault, Heidigger and Derrida proposed their deconstructionist practice of translation.

During the decade of 90's translation of theories also covered the element of subjectivity as well as also accepted translation becoming more a multiplied network of variety disciplines. This much discussion automatically creates the background for the reasons for linguistic deviations in translation. Let us deal with few examples of it from Marathi into English.

Drama form, like poetry, is highly precise form that uses flowy language. Translation of dialogues from Marathi into English frequently suffers from skipping the dialogues that are mocking, ironical or satiric in tone. Certain social personal expressions also are omitted Vijay Tendulkar's 'Silence! The court is in session' translated by Priya Adarkar illustrates it very well. The protagonist Benare is a teacher. English translation of her Marathi dialogues many times prove incomplete to catch the covert meaning. Such as sarcasm in her words—बाळू बोल रे अ आ ई, or the cutting edge in her words or the intensity in her words. The translator has to omit the words like अतृप्त वासना, हुकलेली आत्महत्या, प्राण अलौकीक अपुर्वाई or certain typical Marathi feminine expressions like इश्य, अगबाई काहीतरीच काय? are missing in translation. The sound in various tones or some typical habits of Marathi couple—where the wife all the time needs her husband's confirmations to emphasis her points—हो किनई हो and the husband's oppressive response गप्प बस, सारखी पुढे पुढे करायची सवय are absolutely omitted.

Vilas Sarang has translated some Marathi poems 'Song.' Here is the line—Hey Kishnya, let'shave a first rate lavani—the translator has used the word 'first rate' for Marathi word, फक्कड which is not suitable replacement nor could he find another term for lavani.

Many times the translator carries the words as it is such as for instance 'Some would cook bajari bhakris and barbaat.'

cultural expressions like शिमगा करणे, दिवाळं वाजणे, संक्रांत येणे
social expressions like बांगड्या वाढविणे
Historical expressions like पानिपत झाले, खिंड लढविली, दोर कापले
Religious expressions like तांडव केले, झारीतील शुक्राचार्य
Political expressions like घराणेशाही, तुघलक

cannot be translated with the contextual meaning properly.

What could be done to avoid these linguistic deviations? Are these deviations avoidable at all? It is a fact that linguistic deviations are inevitable. No translator can avoid these for the simple reason that he has to coin a new term for the terms and concepts from source language. As we have already sighted examples from various texts, it is impossible to translate almost all words from source language, nor is the possibility of recreation of equal words. Consequently same word is carried out in target language or an expression of explanation is added with the term from source language, both these ways add to the difficulty and confusion of readability for the reader. It affects the aesthetics of the text. Of course, it maintains the cultural flavor of source language even in target language and enriches TL. In a way linguistic deviations in translation leads to the cosmopolitan language in nature and texture.

Another solution possible is to introduce a sub language only for the sake of translation. Language used for every communication proves different from the use of language in literature, Gerard Genet calls it metalanguage but the language used for translation claims to be different from language and metalanguage, because it cannot fulfil the requirement of translation process. The ways left are allowing the assimilation of source language and target language or introducing a sub language having a new grammar as well as new vocabulary. When I say new grammar, I mean to say suitable structures, because linguistic deviations also create structural and style deviations. Translation of texts like 'Bharatiya Sanskriti' by Sane Guruji requires first of all making a new dictionary so that translation could be possible as well as new structures. It may also be proposed that the use of cosmopolitan language, to some extent, can satisfy the need of language required for translation. To end with the words of Renate Poggioli—It may be an error to believe that the translator has nothing to offer but an empty vessel which he fills with a liquor he could not distill by himself. One should play, at least tentatively, with the constancy hypothesis One should even suppose, using a related, if opposite image, that the translator himself is living vessel saturated with a formless fluid or sparking spirit, which he cannot hold anywhere in check. To accept such a hypothesis one must believe, with the protagonist of Dr Zhivago, the recent novel by the great Russian poet Boris Pasternak, that art is not "an object or aspect of form, but rather a mysterious and hidden component of content."

According to such a view, the translator is a literary artist looking outside himself for the form suited to the experience he wishes to express.

REFERENCES

1. J.C. Cattford, The art of Translation; Pranati Pattanaik—Herman Publishing House, New Delhi.
2. R.L. Varshney, *Ibid.*
3. Heidigger, Translation Studies—P.K. Kalyani. Creative Books, New Delhi.
4. Derrida, *Ibid.*
5. Jose Lanmbert, *Ibid.*
6. G.N. Devy, *Ibid.*
7. Renate Poggioli, Translation Studies Susan Bassnett-McGuire, London Roultedge.
8. Susan Bassnett, Translation Studies (London, Routledge).
9. The art of Translation, Pranati Pattanaik—Herman Publishing House, New Delhi.
10. Translation Studies, P.K. Kalyani. Creative Books, New Delhi.
11. Poisoned Bread, Ed. Arjun Dhangle, Orient Longman.
12. Silence! The Court is in Session—Vijay Tendulkar.
13. Ghashiram Kotwal, Tran. Priya Adarkar.

25

Rasa, *Dhvani* and *Auchitya* in the Indian and the Western Poetics

NANDINI SAHU

The object of this paper is to clarify the interpretations of literature by the application of Indian criteria in judgment and analysis of both Indian and Western works of art. My interest does not remain confined to only the anthropological understanding of the Indian poetics, rather a comparative criticism of both Eastern and Western poetics is aimed at. The Indian world views, the metaphysical as well as the practical requirements of the Indians, *Alankara Sastra* of Sanskrit literature, the study of the modern Indian literature with the help of both Western and Eastern tools are some of the points that I wish upon emphasizing. We must interpret literature through a proper creative medium—through language, rhythm, image, symbol, metaphor, myth—which are Indian, and the critical terminology should not be thoroughly Aristotelian. Bharata's *Rasa*, Anandavardhana's *Dhvani*, Kshemendra's *Auchitya* should be employed profitably by assimilating the two worlds together.

In Indian literary scene we scarcely see any effort made to demand a new poetics with a critical awareness of Indian cultural heritage. The interpreters, readers like to take two safe and separate lines to show the growth of Indian and Western poetics. The two streams are hardly merged or interacted to build up a new critical terminology. Indian scholars like Rabindranath Tagore, Buddhadev Bose, Sudhindra Nath Dutta, Hazari Prasad Dwivedi, Mardhekar etc. had tried to develop a modern Indian poetics taking the cue from ancient India with the passage of time. Now Indian poetics is facing a most unfortunate situation due to our schizophrenia in the national psyche. We evaluate current literature from Aristotle, Eliot, I.A. Richard's points of view. The Western critical apparatus has a stronghold over us. Whereas the Western critics have extended their hands to us before more than a century by interpreting Indian poetics in their terms. Paul Regnaud in his *La Rhetorique Sanskrite* (Paris, 1884) has written about the concepts of *visranti*, repose, *savilkapa* and *nirvikalpa*, ideational and non-ideational meditation in Sanskrit literature. In his book *La Absolce Selon Vedanta* (Paris, 1937). Oliver Locombe clarifies about the poetic contexts in Indian literature critically examining *vibhava, anubhava, sanchari.* Herbert Read in his *Collected Essays in Literary Criticism* (Faber, 1950), writes about the functionalism of figures in Indian theory, identifying the poetic figures like simile, upama, and the mother of all figures, *anupamaya-garbha.* Louis Renou finds Indian poetics very powerful, saying "Of all branches of learning which stem from the genius of Indian few are as profoundly Indian as aesthetics."[1] Leaving out such profound theories of our own that are far more comprehensive and psychological, we have always interpreted literature with the western theoretical backgrounds. This paper is an attempt to critically examine these less explored theories in Indian poetics. The three cardinal concepts, *Rasa, Dhvani, Auchitya,* are my main concerns.

The supreme end of a work of art is the realization of its *rasa*, the sap, juice, and this is the chief feature of Indian aesthetics. We must look for *aahlada*, delight, in a work of art by *rasa-swadana*, understanding, without which literature is a mere verbal art. *Rasa* helps literature communicate itself before it is understood. But without understanding the *rasa* theory, the structuralists, post-structuralists, the deconstructionists are re-writing the texts of classical, ancient origin. W.B. Yeats has observed, "out of our quarrels with others we make rhetoric; out of our quarrels with ourselves we make poetry." It could be compared with the theory of the ancient Indians who believed that *Kavyapurusa*, the poet, should wed *Sahitya Vidya*, literature, as the wife can only set fire to her man's incentives leading to new creation. This is what T.S. Eliot felt when he compared two poems by the same poet. When one is better than the other, it is obvious that during the creative process the *Kavyapurusa* was sufficiently stimulated by *rasa* during the former, and less so during the later. *Rasa* is that aesthetically relished feeling that is aroused in the reader, audience, by the expressive behaviour, *satvikabhava*, of the writer, actor. *Rasa* communicates a *varta*, intense feeling, nor a *varnana*, description, *darsana*, vision. For *rasanubhava*, poetic experience, one must perceive the miraculous power of sound that is in harmony with the temper of the meaning of the poem. The end of art is to leave the mind of the reader in a positive state of joy and fulfilment, and not to simply empty it out of all tensions, worries, as per Aristotle's theory of catharsis. *Rasa* has that power to enlighten the mind. The Upanishads have described *Rasa* as God, as the highest goal of attainment for the Brahma, the Soul. *Rasa* must be sought out in terms of sight, hearing, meditation, union, as it is the common quest of all human faculties leading towards the perfection of the soul. Thus, Indian philosophy and religion intend to remove the wrong concept that aesthetic pleasure is inferior to that of religious, philosophical or yogic experience. The highest attainment on the part of the soul is *rasa-siddhi.*

There is no Western equivalent for this concept of *rasa*. *Rasa* is the flavour that appeals to the taste or savour that is inherent in it. It is evocatively and keenly associated with delight. The highest delight is reached when the poet by the incantation of his verse can make the reader attain supreme bliss, *anandam*. That is when Wordsworth says, "with an eye made quiet by the harmony and the deep power of joy we can see in the life of things." In poetry the word must suggest the meaning immediately, the language of poetry must have the immediacy of communication the relish of which is *rasa*. The outstanding difference between the western and the Indian poetics is that the former describes aesthetic emotion to be one and invisible, something akin to delight or joy which may differ in degree and contexts. But Indian poetics analyses the different types of aesthetic emotions. *Sringara rasa,* heroic: *Veera,* humorous: *Hasya,* furious: *Bhayankara,* piteous: *Karuna* fearful: *Bhaya,* terrible: *Vibhatsa,* marvellous: *Ascharya,* peaceful: *Santa.*

Sound, word and poetic figure, *sabda, artha, alamkara,* should not violate *Auchitya* as they emerge from a world experience, they serve delight, link up ethics with aesthetics. *Purusartha,* manliness, *Kaama,* impulses, are the parts of *rasanubhaba,* but they should oblige *dharma,* self-discipline. For both Indian and Western theories imitation, *anukarana,* is an ideal for art. The Indian *Acharya* is the western voracious reader, the *Pandita* the learned. *Bhakta* is the unsuspect, blind follower of literature, *Sadharanjana* is the common learner, *Alpabuddhijana* is the poor reader who lacks understanding. Walter Pater defines Romanticism as "Strangeness added to beauty." G.K. Bhat defines *rasa* as an emotion of wonder and joy that culminates in beautiful peace, *santi,* the elements of art construction, *vibhava,* and *anubhava* build the emotional experience of wonder and joy, from which *adbhuta rasa* takes birth. Bharata lays down his *rasasutra* in these words: "The *rasa* is born of the union of *vibhava, anubhavas* and *vyabhicari-bhabas*: *Vibhavanubhavavyabhicarisamyogad rasanispattih.*"[2] If we do a comparative study of *Shakuntala* of Kalidasa and *The Tempest* by Shakespeare, the heroines in both the works suffer in love, the *Sringara rasa,* watching the ultimate suffering of both Mirinda and Shakuntala the reader may attain catharsis. The only important point is *rasanubhuti,* the deep understanding. Dowden has commented that all the plays of Shakespeare are like different acts of but one great play, and the classifications as Tragedy and Comedy are irrelevant in his context. If we examine his plays with the *rasa* theory, each one of his plays would satisfy one or other *rasa* out of the *navarasas.* Similarly, the epics like *The Iliad, The Odyssey, The Ramayana, The Mahabharata* satisfy. Aristotle's theory of tragedy as an imitation of an action that is 'serious and complete,' that can arouse the emotions of 'pity and fear' in the audience, and through such emotions would lead their minds to a proper purgation, the 'Catharsis.' Again, the standards of the Indian poetics, the *navarasas,* can be more relevantly applied to all these epics. The Ramayana has overwhelming *Karuna-rasa* as its origin goes to Valmiki's famous Krauncha episode of the two love-birds separated by the hunter, as Sita is separated from Rama by Ravana. There is separation, death, grief, treachery, cruelty of destiny in the Ramayana, all of which lead to sorrow, *karuna*. Mahabharata has a more complex, serious, subtle plot about a disastrous family war among brothers for the throne of Hastinapur. There is jealousy, hatred among kins, somewhat encouraged by the elders, the gambling, humiliation of women, the final revenge, leading towards the effect of horror, pity, fear, finally the tragic relief, the poetic justice, the catharsis. Homer's 'Iliad' and 'Odyssey' are epics based on the legends of the Trojan War. In 'Iliad' Homer presents the tragic fall of Achilles and in Odyssey, the achievements of Odysseus. *Veera rasa* is the theme in both the epics. *Santa-rasa* is the tone of Bhagavad Gita. *Karuna rasa* being the central motif of the 'Ramayana' we may quote four lines of Valmiki. The autumn night makes Rama melancholic when Sita is away:

Panduram gaganam drvstvaa
Vimalam chandramandalam
Saaradeem rajaneem chaiva
Drshtvaa jyotsnaanulepanam.

The similar miraculous power of *karuna rasa* is evoked in one of Byron's poems though setting is different.

Had we never loved sae kindly,
Had we never loved sae blindly,
Never met, or never parted,
We had ne'er been broken-hearted.

(Byron's 'The Bride of Alaydos')

Here we have a depth of poetic quality which resides in no verse of Byron's own. The Western critics blame Byron for a lack of artistic finish. Eliot writes in On Poetry and Poets that Lord Byron added nothing to the English literary world. But considered from the rasa theory, Byron is a much appreciated poet. As a contrary to Aristotle's theory of tragedy being purgatorial of our sorrows, Anandavardhana cautioned against excessive pathos, *Karunarasa*, as it may leave the heart dejected.

Sringara and *Veera* are the principal *rasas* as love and war are the principal interests in poetry, both Eastern and Western. *Sringara* with its phases of *vipralamba* and *sambhoga*, separation and union, was the chief concern of the Sanskrit court poets.

In Mahabharata, in the battlefield Gandhari wails looking at the dead body of Bhurisrava, whose hand is cut off by Arjuna. Gandhari says "Look on this hand, O Krishna, the hand that Arjuna cut off was not this the hand that used to loosen the girdle, that caressed the breasts, the hand that tenderly exploited the waist?" ('Mahabharata,' Stree Parvan, Ch. 24). Here Sringara, eroticism, gives birth to *Karuna rasa*. The same erotic feeling is aroused by the lines of the Metaphysical poets of Elizabetham literature, even if there is no touch of *Karuna rasa*. Andrew Marvell invites his coy mistress for conjugal love in these words:

> [...] while the youthful hue
> sits on they skin like morning dew,
> And while thy willing soul transpires
> At every pore with instant fires,
> Now let us sport us while we may,
> And now, like am'rous birds of prey,
> Rather at once our time devour,
> Than languish in his slow-chapt power.
> Let us roll all our strength, and all
> Our sweetness, up into one ball:
> And tear our pleasures with rough strife
> Through the iron gates of life.
>
> ('To His Coy Mistress')

Poetry has a philosophy *darshana*, that accepts the authenticity of life and death in the same vein. All these love poems only confirm this theory.

Bharata's foremost disciple Anadavardhana narrated the theory of *Dhvani* which penetrates the meaning that is suggested by the word, the sense that lies beyond the sound and reaches the reader through sound. Its implications are profound as it transfers a attention from the sensous basis, the *rasa* theory, to the deeper cells of the mind. Sound itself is meaningless unless it is expressive. Hence the expressive word with the momentary effect and the phenomenon of suggestiveness together constitute the essence of what Anandavardhana means by *Dhvani*. By this the meaning is conveyed by the language. It sounds almost similar to Onomatopoeia, which is weaker than *Dhvani*. Onomatopoeia is a figure of speech in which the sound echoes the sense like in Coleridge's 'Ancient Mariner':

> Alone, alone, all, all alone,
> Alone in a wide, wide sea.

Anandavardhana has expressed *Dhvani* through the imagery of the lamp and its flame of life. The suggestion is the flame that eliminates the meaning of words. The poet has to see that his use of words has this light giving property, the means must reveal the end. Anandavardhana says that mere co-existence of sound and sense will not produce great poetry unless each is adopted to the other. This theory of poetry as a linguistic discourse, the theory of *dhvaṇi*, is analysed in Europe by Mallarme, theoretician and important poet of French symbolism, and a millenium earlier in India by Anandavardhana in *Dhvanyalika* and by Abhinava Gupta in *Lochana*. The dhvani theorists insisted that the power of language on the poetic context is nothing but a derivative from its own intrinsic semantic structure. But Visvanatha, another important critic in Indian poetics, says that in order to know the real meaning of an uttered word we must not only know the sense of utterance but also the addresser, the addressee, their relationship, the location, time, contest. Some words may sound reproachful when said to a person of our hatred, but the very words change their tone when said to a loved one.

Auchitya refers to ideally appropriate relationship between the written words in the poetic organism. "*Rasa* is the soul and *Achitya* the life [...]. *Auchitya* is the life of *rasa*-ensouled poem,"[3] says Kshemendra. *Auchitya* is the decorum, congruity in a work of art. It is the proper arrangement of the poetic figures, poetic diction, verbal tissue that the Indian critics name *Auchitya.*

T.S. Eliot defines a poem as the objective correlative of a state of feeling: "a set of objects, a situation, a chain of events which shall be a formula of the particular emotion; such that, when the external facts, which must terminate in sensory experience, are given, the emotion is immediately evoked."[4] The same formula can be compared with Bharata's *Rasa Sutra* in *Natya Sastra* where he says when the poet creates any aesthetic context, he both represents and re-presents life. The *sthayi bhava,* instinct, of man is further shaped by *prakriti.* Nature, and *seela,* culture, so that he corresponds to the emotions intended by the poet. The *alambana vibhava* and *uddeepana vibhava* are able to create that 'particular' emotion intended by the poet. The poet awakens the *bhavayitri prativa* of the reader, listener, with his *kavayitri prativa* with the touch of *sadharanikarana* which is equivalent with Eliot's theory of the Objective Correlative. One can suspect Eliot's sources to be Indian as elsewhere he has admitted his acquaintance with the author of '*Vibhava.*' In the creative process, *bhavakatva vyapara,* the artist's emotional ecstasy, *bhavanvesa,* takes him first to the world, loka, and then beyond, *lokattara,* and reaches the readers through *sadharanikarana,* the objective correlative. This process is the product of the *karmasu kausala,* workmanship, *ananda chinmaya,* supreme state of bliss, *visranti,* reader's response—in both the artist's and the reader's parts. For the author, it is the state of *paranirvitti,* total release from the self, and for the reader, it is *nishkama dharma,* momentary release from the outside world, because of his *samskara,* cultivated sensibility. In this context, one may agree with A.K. Coomaraswamy that a poet is not a special kind of man, rather every man is a special kind of poet.

In Indian context, '*Neti*' means not questioning, and reaching a stage when the author reaches the soul of the poetic personae. This is an attitude which Keats called Negative Capability, to negate the self with humility. The chief message of 'Bhagavad Upanishad 'Charaivetic Charaiveti' can be best compared with Eliot's 'Theory of Impersonality in Art' when he says, "Poetry is not a turning loose of emotion but an escape from emotion; it is not the expression of personality, but an escape from personality [...]. The emotion of art is impersonal. And the poet cannot reach this impersonality without surrendering himself wholly to the work to be done."[5] In the *Mahabharata,* Lord Krishna teaches Arjuna to make the mind objective and impersonal when necessary. "The progress of an artist is a continual self-sacrifice, a continual extinction of personality"[6]—says Eliot. The *nishkama karma,* the Indian virtue of detachment, is similar to a heightened awareness, fine sense of aestheticism, self-discipline, introspection and practice in the interpretation of a work of art.

After a thorough analysis of the Eastern and the Western poetics, one may safely comment that a critic must be a *rasika*, a lover of art, as *arasikata*, lack of sensibility, leads to wrong aesthetic appreciation. But one must be careful that like the *sthitaprajna* of the *Gita* the evaluation of literature should be indifferent, formed, mature, free of any bias, to recognize the gifts given and received by each tradition, Eastern and Western, to enrich the total heritage of man. The universal aesthetic ideas need not remain confined within the geographical boundaries of their origin. We should adopt the discipline of testing literature with the touchstones of both the worlds as the universality of the scientific laws of poetics make our interpretations homogenous. About the closeness of the Indian and the Western poetics Krishna Rayan says, "*Dhavani* cannot be defined or described except in relation to the Romantic-Symbolist concept of suggestion and the post-Saussurean concept of loose signification. Nor can rasa be elucidated except in terms of Reader Response. Such cross-illumination only enhances the accuracy of our perception. [...] Even if the Sanskrit poetic were to insulate itself from all that is Western and modern, it would still have to respond to the extensive and vigorous innovation and experiment in literary practice within the Indian system, much of which is inspired by Western and modernist writing and theory."[7] All this is nothing but a give-and-take, an interaction between the two cultures. Because "the essential human experience that literature communicates is not historically or culturally conditioned but appeals to what is most basic and elemental in human nature."[8] To achieve this end, Indian poetics, that may have a universal application, should build up its own literary tradition. G.K. Bhat points out this fact when he says, "Unfortunately, Sanskrit poetics seems to be preoccupied with theoretical speculations on the nature of poetry itself, and did not do much to develop an independent science of literary criticism."[9] Indian poetics which is a treasure house of insights about the creation, analysis, and evaluation of works of literature should be properly recognized by the West, so that it may become part of international scholarship. Comparative criticism should be followed by both the Orientalists and the Occidentalists. With a view to absorbing the best and distinct sensibility of all, Aurobindo, Coomaraswamy, Kshemendra and Anandavardhana should be read with equal justice like Bradley, Mason, Saintsbury, Elton, Richards, Eliot Leavis and others.

NOTES

1. Louis Renou, *Diogense,* 1, 1953: 130.
2. *Natyasastram.* Delhi: Bharatiya Vidya Prakashna, 1983: VI. 32.
3. Kshemendra, *Auchitya Vichara Charcha.* Nirmaya Sagara Press, 1950: 63.
4. Abrahams, M.H. *A Clossary of Literary Terms.* Madras: Macmillan India Ltd., 1971.
5. Enright and Chickera, eds. *English Critical Texts.* Delhi: OUP, 1962: 300-01.
6. *Ibid.,* 269.
7. *Indian Literature.* No. 160, March-April, 1994: 14-17.
8. V.K. Chari, *Sanskrit Criticism.* Honolulu: Hawaii University Press, 1990: 247.
9. *Rasa Theory and Allied Problems.* Baroda: M.S. University, 1984: 65.

26

'INSCAPE' AND THE THEORY OF *DHVANI*

RAMA KUNDU

Gerard Manley Hopkins, the renowned priest-poet of nineteenth century England found critical acceptance after forty years of his death, and still enjoys only a controversial reputation[1] in spite of his unmistakable power as a poet; this is largely owing to his highly distinctive individuality as an aesthetician. Indeed, Hopkins's startlingly original concept of beauty made him isolated in his own time and unique for all times in a way. In this context it may be interesting for an Indian scholar to note how Hopkins's theory of 'inscape-instress' corresponds to the aesthetic principle of Anandavardhana as expounded in his theory of *dhvani.*

It is true that there is no evidence of Hopkins ever coming across the findings of Anandavardhana from whom he was separated by ten centuries and global hemispheres. One can at best conjecture about the remote possibility of his attending Max Muller's lectures,[2] and thus gathering some hints. However, the correspondence in certain aspects of their respective approaches to the subject appear remarkable. Among these various points of resemblance are: originality of both as aestheticians who had found earlier attitudes to poetry inadequate as they formulated their own principles on the subject[3]; shifting of emphasis from outer to inner, from sheer melodious/pictorial description of the outer form of an object to the suggestion or evocation of the 'essence' of something profounder, and more transcending; anticipation of certain perceptions which are being shared by recent schools of criticism since the 1960s; a number of other related ideas regarding the function of poetry as perception and expression.

However, Hopkins and Anandavardhana seem to converge in a most interesting manner at three points which again, appear to be of continuing significance for both modern poetry and criticism. These are: the revelatory or suggestive power of poetry; the function of word as played in the process of this revelation; the reader-poet nexus that operates to make effective the suggestion/*dhvani* of a poem.

Before going ahead in this matter it may be useful to have a look (however simplistically) at the comparative meanings of *dhvani* and 'inscape-instress.' The historical-critical importance of the *dhvani* school as expounded by Anandavardhana is generally acknowledged by Sanskrit scholars. Anandavardhana's is a very carefully explored, analysed, and systematically developed theory exemplifying various kinds of poetic effect. But at the core there is the idea of *vyāñjanā* or suggestion that carries the essence of the theory of *dhvani.* "The several expressed parts of a poem [...] reveal the unexpressed deeper sense; which is something singular and different from the denotative and indicative elements both in order and in essence, and which is termed the *dhvani* [...] *or Vyāñjanaārtha* (suggested sense) in poetry" (De 143). The school of *dhvani* seems to assume a process by which the poet's revelation of meanings through words and the perceptive reader's affective response to that suggestion are made to converge and coalesce, after going through three successive stages. A word (in a poem) firstly makes an *Abhidhā/ Vācyārtha* (denotation/literal meaning), secondly *Lakṣhanā rtha* (figurative meaning); then these two meanings may further lead to and be finally transcended by a third one, *i.e. vyāñjyaārtha/dhvanyārtha* (suggested meaning). Thus *vyāñjana/ dhvani* has got the connotation of sudden revelation. Not that it says something new; but rather reveals "almost in a lightning flash, what is already there" (Roy 28). This *vyāñjyaārtha* or *dhvani* is supposed to constitute the soul of poetry. S.K. De defines "the special doctrine of the system" as follows: "the unexpressed or the suggested sense (*vyāñjyaārtha)* to which the name *dhvani* is applied when it is predominant, is definitely posed as the 'soul' or essence of poetry" (De 157).[4]

In contrast to Anandavardhana's *dhvani,* Hopkins's *inscape-instress* was not a systematically developed theory but rather a growing and continued conviction till the end of his brief life and poetic career. Hopkins's aestheticism was less concerned with the exact object in its overall totality, than with the 'essential' beauty that inhered in the object. What makes an object distinct and individual? How to define that unified complex of characteristics which constitute the outward reflection of the inner nature of a 'thing,' its individual essence? These were the questions Hopkins had been asking himself since his Oxford days. As an object revealed its 'essence' to him Hopkins would often be thrown into ecstasies of delight. It is possible that in course of his attempt at discovering the law or principle which gave an object its delightful and surprising uniqueness that he came across his new aesthetic. Since 1866 the poet was preoccupied with the problem of capturing this essential beauty; he had tried, excitedly sometimes and ecstatically on occasions, to define and redefine, clarify and explore his theory of the revelation of beauty which he had finally clinched as 'inscape-instress.' By the term 'inscape' Hopkins implied the revelation in a flash of what is already there, but is perceived only by the activated poetic imagination. He said "All the world is full of inscape" (*Notebooks* 210); but "unless you refresh the mind from time to time you cannot always believe how deep the inscape in things is" *(Notebooks* 140). This seems to echo the idea of *"vyāñjana* (which) does not consist in the utterance of something new, but in the manifestation of something already existing" (De 144). Thus at the basis of both the theories there operated the delight of discovering a revelation. And for Hopkins too, like Anandavardhana's *dhvani,* "inscape was the very soul of art" (quoted by Gardner xxii).

Since 1868 the term begins to appear frequently and in various contexts[5] to designate the principle of beauty suggested by an object, to signify the rich and revealing oneness of an object. The very prefix indicates, as Austin Warren explains, the shift from the outer to the inner by implying the contrary—an outer scape,

> [...] that is, an inscape is not mechanically or inertly present, but requires personal action, an attention, a seeing and a seeing into. (171)

One of the chief assumptions of the *dhvani* school, on the other hand, is that "the most necessary and fundamental principle of all higher poetry" is "the art of suggestion, which should lead the reader through diverse routes from that which is distinctly expressed to that which is left unexpressed" (De 174). Thus the two concepts *(i.e.* 'Inscape' and *dhvani)* are finally related to the perception of an epiphanic revelation.

Dhvani does not, however, make room for vague, elusive mysticism. "Anandavardhana takes care to point out that this *dhvani* is not [...] mystical but it is something that can be properly defined and grasped" (De 144). And like *dhvani* "inscape" too is defined, divined and grasped. At the same time, like *dhvani,* it rests on that basic quality of poetry—the emotive-suggestive-evocative quality which distinguishes it from the descriptive and narrative quality of prose. It is true, as John Wain, notes, that a certain fluidity is there about Hopkins's use of 'inscape' and its companion term 'instress' (64). But the basic emphasis remains the same: the ecstasy of suddenly discovering the revelation of essential beauty. The poet could have this flash while looking at a row of elms after a heavy fall of snow (*Poems & Prose* 120), or in observing the wind-tossed chestnuts as they plunged and crossed one another, to show how "motion multiplies inscape [...] when inscape is discovered" (*P&P* 120), or the blooming bluebell whose "inscape is mixed of strength and grace" (*P&P* 120); the spring-time spraying of trees could bring him "a new world of inscape" (*P&P* 122); even the duck, as lifting its head, could carry the "fascinating instress of the straight white stroke" (*P&P* 123); from the shut bud to the full blowing of the flower he could trace "successive sidings of one inscape"; again, "even in withering the flower ran through beautiful inscapes by the screwing up of the petals into straight little barrels or tubes" (*P&P* 124); it could also be seen spread over the huge backdrop of the tree-tops against the vast moonlit semi-clouded sky, "a broad careless inscape flowing throughout" (*P&P* 125). Hopkins would be equally delighted at discovering the "scape" of the break flooding of the wave (*P&P* 126), the "inscape" of the green-white tufts of long-bleached grass (*P&P* 127), of the snow-waves on the hill-tops, as well as the snow-heap on the road broken by a broom" (*P&P* 128).

'Inscape' was simultaneously an aesthetic-cum-ascetic principle of perception, though this may sound paradoxical. After a period of conflict between his innate sensuousness and serious asceticism which prompted rejection of the senses, Hopkins finally arrived at the idea of 'inscape-instress'—the suggestion of the inner essence which was also the expression of God's bounty and the hence permissible ecstasy associated with it—which helped him out of the crisis, by shifting the focus from the outer to the inner beauty and thus achieving a kind of ascetic aestheticism.

II

As a poet Hopkins held that poetry was to be the inscape of an inscape, that is, all the other elements were to subserve this purpose of making the suggested sense. Here, again, it seems interesting, to recall what S.K. De says in the other context: Since, according to Anandavardhana, good poetry must suggest, and not simply describe "The learned call that particular kind of poetry *dhvani* in which the expressed word and sense, subordinating themselves, manifest that (other suggested) sense" (De 169). Similarly Hopkins also believed:

> Poetry is in fact speech employed to carry the inscape of speech for the inscape's sake—and therefore the inscape must be dwelt on. ('Poetry and Verse' [1874], Gardner xxii)

Thus 'speech' or words played an important part in this process of poetic revelation which needed a perfect orchestration of all its parts. Every poem was considered by Hopkins as a *new* inscape which just have "down to the least separable part an individualizing touch" (Gardner xxii). The chief instrument in this orchestration was necessarily constituted by words.

In this respect Hopkins was a conscious technician. He was, self-declaredly, after an unattainable perfection of language. This ideal of 'perfection' does not imply photographic accuracy, but the accurate expression that would create the exact suggestion of the inner essence. Similarly, "starting with a theory of expression, the *dhvani* school concerns itself, first of all, with the grammatico-philosophical problem about the function of words and their meaning or, in other words, about the relation of a word to that which is expressed by it" (De 145). The special role of words in this process is particularly underscored in *dhvani*: "The unexpressed [...] which is directly inexpressible, but which can only be suggested by an expressive word or its sense" (De 161).[6] Hopkins's inspired yet careful use of 'speech'/'language'/'word' in his poems may be considered from this perspective. In a poem Hopkins would usually employ a word to radiate all its associated connotations; all the semantic meanings and sonic evocations of a word, considered together, helped to create the essential suggestion or inscape in a Hopkins's poem.[7] By putting into practice his conviction that "every word (in a poem) may be considered as, the contraction and coinciding point of its definitions" (*Notebooks*; Wain 67) Hopkins had anticipated the multi-dimensionality and plural significance which was the pre-occupation of a later age. Similarly, as M.K. Ray observes, "the main thrust of the theory of *dhvani* (also) is that the language of good poetry is emotive/ambiguous, non-logical and open to multiple interpretations" (229).

Hopkins's bold experiment and ecstatic delight in finding the right word corresponds to Anandavardhana's insistence on the suggestive power or *Vyāñjanā Vṛtti* (instead of mere description) as the real power/function of words. In Hopkins one finds a reaffirmation of the idea of *dhvani* that the suggestive meaning of the words and of poetry itself arises out of the language of poetry:

> The *vyāñjanā* or power of suggestion is generally defined as that function of a word or its sense by which a further meaning comes into being when the other functions, viz., *abhidhā* and *lakṣanā,* are exhausted in their scope. Ideas and notions are what are conveyed by words through their powers of Denotation and Indication [...]. Now another power is postulated by which a deeper sense, the *vyāñjya ārtha,* is revealed, consequent upon but distinct from the simple thought. All good poetry called *par excellence* the *dhvani-Kāvya,* must have such a sense implicit in it, a sense which can only be realized by the *Vyāñjanā-vṛtti* or power of suggestion. (De 150)

Northorp Frye, well-known Canadian critic of our times also holds the same idea: "a poem meaning is literally its pattern or integrity as a verbal structure. Its words cannot be separated and attached to sign-values of a word are absorbed into a complexity of verbal relationship" (77-78). Words in Hopkins's poetry are not used as invariably defined logical counters to ideas, but as interacting elements in a complex of sense.

Hopkins was ready to wrench a word to exploit all its potentials in the particular poetic context; he would harness all the combined phonetic-semantic effects of an expression simultaneously even when they might appear to work at cross-purposes; he would accumulate around a word all its possible denotations and connotations. This was his way to reveal inscape/inner suggestion, or *Vyāñjyaārtha/Dhvanyārtha* in other words.

Though language of poetry was the essential thing for both the thinkers it was not a language divorced from daily life to create vague, mystic meaning. For Hopkins, it was 'current language heightened' (Letter to Bridges), enlivened, quickened, sensitized into a living, solid, multidimensional, radiant thing. Anthony Thwaite offers a remarkable insight into Hopkins's language when he says: "Hopkins's poetry is written in a language of excitement"[8] (Thwaite 25). This excitement spurred him to exploit and innovate words in a way unknown to his British contemporaries and their predecessors.

As Wain exclaims in admiration: "Alone among the English poets, he (Hopkins) is willing to try anything, to desert logic, to wrench language, to treat the individual words as a mystery and challenge" (61). Indeed, as Thwaite too observes, Hopkins was "one of the very few linguistic innovators in the English language [...]; he used the full resources of the language—and, when those resources seemed to be inadequate, he invented [...] with the energy of man whose mind enjoyed all the cognate and sound-linked shades of language" (25).

It was owing to his special way of treating language that Hopkins had later emerged, without knowing it himself as an early exponent of the theory of simultaneity and multidimensionality which were central to much of early twentieth century poetry and an yet untrod ground in the nineteenth,—one of the reasons of Hopkins's non-acceptance by his contemporaries.[9]

III

Revelation is made through words. But ultimately it involves a process of communication and therefore needs a receptive reader. This need is underscored by both the schools. The Dhvani school assumes a *Sahṛdaya* reader and Hopkins a 'perceiver' who is, indispensable as the receiving end. As M.K. Ray points out "starting with a theory of expression, the Dhvani school is mainly concerned with the semantic problem, of the function of words and their meanings. But the theory, nevertheless, reaches out to a phenomenological problem of discerning the affective response of a perceptive reader."

Again, the concept of *Rasa* which Anandavardhana had revived and extended to the domain of poetry has its basis on the response of the reader. The *rasa* can be given a name: love, sorrow, anger. "But the mere naming of the Rasa in poetry is not capable of awakening the mood itself in the reader which, consists of a self-manifested state of the mind. Therefore [...] the poet can only *suggest* the Rasa; in other words, he can call up a reflection of the mood which the reader realises as a particular condition of his own mind" (De 161). Anandavardhana contends that it is only for a *Sahṛdaya* reader to get at the *rasa* which is manifested through *Vyāñjanas* (suggestors). Because it is only such a reader who could be instrumental in getting the link established between the expressed and the unexpressed and thus having achieved what is called *arthāntar sankrāmita.*

Hopkins spoke of a 'perceiver' who reminds one of this *Sahṛdaya.* The discovery of an 'inscape' usually meant an intense excitement for the poet who used the word 'instress' to describe the intensity of feeling and associations so stirred. Instress was defined by Hopkins as "the impulse *from* the 'inscape' which acts on senses and, through them, actualizes the inscape in the mind of beholder on rather 'perceiver,' for inscape may be perceived through all the senses *at once* (Gardner xxi). Similarly, according to *dhvani* this perception could be a sudden, intense and instantaneous process; for "the perception of the suggested *rasa* [...] involves a process, but from its quickness the process is not perceived, like the process [...] of the apparently simultaneous piercing or a hundred lotus-leaves placed one upon another" (De 162). Without the 'perceiver' inscape falls flat just as *dhvani,* to be effective, needs the *Sahṛdaya.* Since the poem is 'an inscape of an inscape' both the poet and the reader become 'perceivers' at two successive stages; only then the 'instress' (or *dhvānyartha?*) is evoked—thus, leading to "a sudden perception of deeper pattern, order and unity which gives meaning to external forms" (Gardner xxi).

This recognition of the role of *Sahṛdaya* 'perceiver'[10] to seen in relation to 'reader-response' school of modern criticism helps one to realize the continuing relevance of the two theories. The following observations could be taken as a leaf from any modern discourse on hermeneutics or reader-response criticism.

> The unexpressed is bound up by means of definite links with the expressed; but [...] it is not understood by those who know grammar and lexicon, but only by men of taste and literary instinct who know the province or the *sahṛdaya,* the connoisseur, who is expert in discerning through the intricate meshes of veiled word and sense into the aesthetic relish of deeper significance, in which the pleasure of the beautiful is mixed up with the pleasure arising from the fineness of the problem itself. (De 174)

IV

Anandavardhana had assimilated the prevalent theoretical canons of his time including *Rasa Śāstra* and *Alaṅkaraśāstra* and went further ahead to give his new direction to this tra‹‹ition. On the other hand Hopkins's acknowledged debt to Dun Scotus and Ruskin—Pater is common knowledge. But curiously enough, Hopkins seems, imaginatively and intuitively, much closer to the Indian theorist than to his acknowledged Western masters. And indeed Hopkins may be considered in a way the nineteenth century British exponent of the Indian theory of suggestion, and his theory of 'inscape-instress' a modern Western counterpart of the ancient Indian system of *dhvani* which Anandavardhana had upheld some eleven centuries ago.

Again, both the thinkers anticipate three strands of modern criticism: *New Criticism* with its emphasis on words, reader-response criticism with its focus on the reader's percipience, and post-structuralism with its emphasis on the multiple interpretations of a text, *i.e.* Derrida's theory of indeterminate text and infinite plurality of meanings.

This brief discourse is intended to indicate, once again, how great minds, even when cut off by centuries and oceans, and working independently, could yet arrive at certain common insights of continuing importance and relevance across time and space.

NOTES

1. "He is likely to prove, for our time and for the future, the only influential poet of the Victorian age, and he seems to be the greatest" (Leavis, 36).

   "After almost fifty years of close reading and superb editing, Hopkins's verse remains something of a scandal" (Hartman 1).
2. Max Muller, the German Indologist, had settled in Oxford in 1848, and delivered his two remarkable courses of lectures on 'The Science of Languages' in 1861-64, and Hopkins joined Balliol College as a student in 1863.
3. "The effect of studying masterpieces is to make me admire and do otherwise" (Letter to Bridges, 1888, Gardner xxiv).
4. "Jatrārthaḥ śabdo bā tamarthamupasarjanikṛtaswārthau.
   Vyanjaḥ kābyaviśeṣaḥ sa dhvaniriti suribhiḥ kathita."
   —(*Dhvanyaloka* 1/13)
5. From 1868 to 1875 the word occurs nearly 50 times in his journal.
6. "Ālokārthī jathā dīpśikhayam yatnabān janaḥ
   Tadupāyata tadvadarthe vācye tadādṛtaḥ" —(*Dhvanyaloka* 1/9).
7. One may recall Hopkins's stress on the auditory effect of a poem: "Poetry is speech framed to be heard for its own sake and interest even over and above its interest in meaning" (*Notebooks*); also "read it with the ears, as I always wish to be read, and my verse becomes all right" (Leavis 24).

   Seamus Heaney, the Irish poet and Nobel Laureate of the year (1995), confesses his admiration for "the way words strike off one another [...] are drilled, marched and countermarched [...] that constitutes his (Hopkins's) proper music" (*Preoccupations* 87).
8. Hopkins rejected casual/inadequate/unenergetic expression by coining the term 'Parnassian' poetry, which, he found, "not in the highest sense poetry, (since) it does not require the mood of the mind in which the poetry of inspiration is written" (*P&P* 154).

9. John Wain: Hopkins, in trying to explain 'inscape' to Bridges "was in reality pouring into that monumentally deaf eardrum the doctrines of irreducibility and simultaneity" (64).

10. Rabindranath Tagore voices a similar idea in his poem 'Ganbhaṅga' (The Ruining of a Song):

    Ekākī gāyaker nahe to gān, milite habe duijane —
    Gāhiba ekjan khuliā galā, ārekjan gābe mane.
    Taṭer buke lāge jaler dheu tabe se kalatān uṭhe—
    Bātāse banasabhā śihari kāpe, tabe se marmar phuṭe.
    Jagate jethā jata raeche *dhvani,* jugal miliāche āge—
    Jekhāne prem nāi, bobār sabhā, sekhāne gān nāhi jāge.

    The singer can't sing alone, the twain have to meet
    One will sing aloud, the other silently repeat—
    As the river laps the bank, laughing ripples leap,
    As forest bends shivering to the wind's kiss,
    murmuring music is released.
    Twains had to meet first before any *dhvani* was stirred
    in this world—
    Music can't soar in a gathering of the dumb
    with no loving listener to respond.

WORKS CITED

De, S.K. *Sanskrit Poetics.* Calcutta: Firma K.L., 1976.

Frye, Northrop. *Anatomy of Criticism.* Princeton: Princeton Univ. Press.

Gardner, W.H. 'Introduction,' *Poems and Prose of Gerard Manley Hopkins.* Ed. W.H. Gardner. (1953), London: Penguin, 1963.

Hartman, G.H. 'Introduction,' *Hopkins.* Ed. G.H. Hartman. New Delhi: Prentice Hall of India, 1980. Subsequently referred to as Hopkins.

Heany, S. *Preoccupations,* quoted by R.J.C. Watt, 'Seamus Heany : Voices on Helicon, *Essays in Criticism,* Vol. XLIV, No. 3.

Hopkins, G.M. *Notebooks and Papers of Gerard Manley Hopkins.* Ed. Humphery House, London: OUP, 1937.

——. *Poems and Prose of Gerard Manley Hopkins.* Ed. W.H. Gardner (1953), London, Penguin Books, 1963.

Leavis, F.R. 'Gerard Manley Hopkins,' *Hopkins.*

Ray, Mohit K. 'Mallarmé and the Indian Theory of *dhvani,*' *Historical and Cultural Contexts of Linguistic and Literary Phenomenon.* Ed. D. Killiam. Guelph: University of Guelph, Canada, 1989.

Tagore, R.N. 'Ganbhanga,' "Sonār Tarī," *Rachanabali,* Vol. 1, Calcutta, Government of West Bengal, 1986.

Thwaite, A. *Contemporary English Poetry.* Melbourne : Heinemann, 1961.

Wain, John. 'Idiom of Desperation,' *Hopkins.*

Warren, A. 'Instress of an Inscape,' *Hopkins.*

27

Sanskrit Grammar and Linguistics

AMAR NATH JHA

Of the various systems of Sanskrit grammar, the best known is Pāṇini's *Aṣṭādhyāyī* or *Aṣṭaka*; it is so titled because it has eight chapters. This is his central work which has at its periphery four other constituent units. These together make *pañcāṅgam vyākaranam*, of five-organ grammar. The four constituent units are *ganapāṭha* (a list of word groups), *dhātupāṭha* (a reading of verbal roots), *uṇādipāṭha* (a list of uṇ-etc. affixes) and *liṅgānusāśanam* (a treatise on gender). Besides these five units, Pāṇini has also been credited with writing *sikśā* (Phonetics), available both in verse and *sūtra* forms, the former, rendered into verse supposedly by his younger brother, Piṅgala, being more popular. Pāṇinian grammar is corpus-based, and for this reason, it is a scientific and linguistic grammar.

The *Aṣṭaka* is in the form of *sūtras* stitching together a particular *prakaraṇa* or topic. The topic is stated in the *adhikāra* or heading *sūtras* followed by subordinate ones. Each subsequent *sūtra* may have the influence (or *anuvritti*) of the terms used in the previous *sūtras*. By rearranging the key words differing in case affixes except adjectives the *vritti* or meaning of the *sūtra* gets established in a verbless sentence.

The *Aṣṭādhyāyī* begins with an exposition of technical terms. These have been described and rarely defined. Many of the technical terms are algebraic codes, such as *ṭi* for the ultimate vowel. The names given to some of the suffixes are codes or algebraic symbols, such as *ph* of *āyan*; *ḍh>ey*; *kh>in*; *ch>īy*; *gh>iy*; *—h>ik*; *yu>an*; *vu>ak* etc. Moreover, certain indicatory letters, in the initial or final positions, which disappear on application, are devices to signal vowel transformations known technically as *vriddhi, guṇa* and *samprasāraṇa* and also give clues to stress patterns, etc. In the case of the *dhātupāṭha,* the initial or the final constituents of a verbal root indicate the various conjugational forms and transformations. Everyone of the chapters has four *pādas* or quarters each. The number of *sūtras* including the fourteen preliminary *śiva-sūtras* come round to about four thousand *sūtras* that could be printed within forty pages in a book of normal size. The three subsequent numerals after a *sūtra* refer respectively to chapter, quarter and serial number.

S.K. Balvekar draws our attention to "nearly a dozen different schools of Sanskrit grammar and more than a thousand separate treatises, original as well as explanatory."[1] "Beside such a concourse, the thousand manuscripts of Priscian's grammar, the pride of our Western tradition," as W.S. Allen writes, "are but a drop in the grammatical ocean."[2]

The grammar of Panini is comprehensive and embraces the entire corpus of the language. It deals with phonemes, allophones, morphemes, allomorphs, morphophonemic changes, syntactical patterns, stress, rhythm and intonation of the Vedic language, considerations of meaning, intralingual comparison and so on. R.H. Robins acknowledges the debt of Pāṇini in the morphological studies as follows:

> Recognition of the status of the morpheme in linguistic analysis was one of the achievements of the ancient Indian linguistics, of whom Panini is the most famous, and this is one of the debts Western linguistic scholarship owes to Indian work, which became known in Europe during the course of the nineteenth century.[3]

It is, as J.B. Carroll says, "a purely descriptive, non-philosophical account of the Sanskrit language [...] (which) [...] is still regarded as one of the most comprehensive descriptive grammars of any language."[4] Pāṇini's *sūtras* were supplemented by Kātyāyana and commented upon by Patañjali. Incorporating all three, many others wrote commentaries and also rearranged the *sūtras.* All these are grammar in the Pāṇinian tradition.

It is difficult to determine how much Pāṇini borrowed

from the long tradition of grammar before him and how much he created with his individual talent. So perfect a model of human intelligence could not have been the produce of one mind. Based on sufficient reasons, Leonard Bloomfield considers Pāṇini's grammar to be "one of the greatest monuments of human intelligence."[5]

The *Aṣṭādhyāyī* is a grammar of the current language which Pāṇini calls simply *bhāṣā*, as against the *chāndas*, the Vedic language. It is mainly a synchronic grammar which occasionally enters into diachronic differentiation, thus paving way for synchronic and diachronic linguistics. Dr Mahabir, following an observation made by Patañjali, is rightly aware of "the generative capacity"[6] of Pāṇini's grammar, but to pass a judgment that it is "prescriptive and normative" is not justified. To Chomsky also Pāṇinian grammar can be interpreted as a fragment of such a 'generative grammar' in essentially the contemporary sense of this term.'[7] R.H. Robins illustrates the transformational-generative nature of Pāṇini's grammar as follows:

The generation of the word form *abhavat* (he, she, it was) from the root *bhū-*, to be, passes through the following stages (the numbers refer to some of the relevant sūtras):

bhū-a	3.1.2,	3.1.68.			
bhū-a-t	1.4.99,	3.1.2,	3.2.111,	3.4.78,	3.4.100.
a-bhūa-t	6.4.71,	6.1.158.			
a-bho-a-t	7.3.84.				
a-bhav-a-t	6.1.78				
abhavat.					

Only the final representation is the form of a real word as pronounced in isolation; those preceding it illustrate the ordered application of rules, covering, of course, the formation of large numbers of words other than this one. The whole descriptive procedure may be compared with the stages by which the transformational-generative grammarians, more than two thousand years later, arrive at an actual form through successive representations of elements combined with each other in accordance with ordered rules.[8]

It is common knowledge that Pāṇini records usage. He catalogues regional variations and registral variables of different trades on the basis of which Dr Vāsudeva Śarana Agrawāla[9] has built up his findings on the different aspects of the life of the time. Kātyāyana takes into consideration the importance of *lokatah,* that is, the usage by people, as a standard of acceptability and Patañjali that of *sarve desāntare,* that is the acceptability of regional variations. The latter also refers to social variations, called by him *bhāṣā* (standard language), *vibhāṣā* (dialect) and *apabhāṣā* (slang).

Pāṇini admits the importance of changing usage in the aphorism, *tadaśiṣyam sa¤jnāpramānatvāt/* 1.2.53/, that is, the rule regarding the concord of gender and number etc. need not be taught as these depend upon the varying usage.

Pāṇini's grammar is systematic, objective and explicit. The economy of expression has not been excelled in other *sūtra* literature. A sentence, to Pāṇini, is the real unit of analysis. Apart from it neither the sound unit nor the word has any autonomous existence. *Avasāna* or pause is the indication of a sentence boundary, which Pāṇini states in virāmo 'vasānam/ 1.4.110. Vidyā Nawās Miśra traces in Pāṇini a perfection of "mathematical model." He elaborates:

> Pāṇini intuitionally without the modern equipment of mathematical modelling evolved a system of description which is (1) independent of consideration of meaning as a factor in description of forms, (2) based on sets and subsets and (3) binary.[10]

Dr Misra is of the opinion that

> If a genuine reconstruction of the *Aṣṭādhyāyī* in terms of modern symbology for visual purposes is attempted, it would be worth-while.[11]

No wonder, nearly two and a half thousand years before the invention of computer, as Dr R.V. Joshi writes, Pāṇini had a "computerized brain"[12] that could produce perhaps the best linguistic computer 'software.' No wonder, Akhshar Bharati *et al.* consider it to be the most computer-friendly.[13]

Pāṇinian grammar influenced the grammar of Tamil in *Tolkappiam.* Buddhist monks carried the linguistic scholarship based on this system to China. The grammar of Arabic titled *Al-kitab* by Sibawaih of Basra at the end of the eighth century has also been said to have been influenced by the Pāṇinian phonetic description.[14]

Jesuit missionaries were the first to take Sanskrit to the West. Heinrich Roth, German missionary, was the first to write Sanskrit Grammar; but it could not be published as he died at Agra in 1668. Sir William Jones's lecture delivered at the Asiatic Society in 1786 made Sanskrit learning popular in the West. Though to him Pāṇini's sÊtras were "dark as the darkest oracle,"[15] he introduced and recommended the Indian grammarians and phoneticians to the West. As J.R. Firth says, "it is difficult to imagine our nineteenth century school of phonetics"[16] without the insight of the Indian grammarian, Pāṇini who became known to the West through translations in all the major languages including Latin.

The rise of philosophy grew out of the dissemination of Sanskrit learning in Europe. It reached America somewhat later. Some of the Sanskritists did not only write books on language in general, but also English grammar. W.D. Whitney in America, for example, wrote both Sanskrit and English grammar. His *Essentials of English Grammar* (1877) did not follow the Latinate model and was, therefore, not popular. He writes that "the whole more modern literature has been Pāṇinized, so to speak."[17]

The historically-oriented comparison in the nineteenth century led to the typological and genealogical classification. These studies, as R.H. Robins says, were "partly as a result of the stimulus derived from the study of Sanskrit [...] by Western scholars, and the demonstration at the end of the eighteenth century of the indispensable historical connection of this language with Latin, Greek and German."[18] Max Muller has rightly pointed out that "a comparative philologist without a knowledge of Sanskrit is like an astronomer without a knowledge of mathematics."[19]

There were language studies in the West even before the Indian impact. The Greek grammarian, Dionasius Thrax, was imitated by the Latin grammarians, Donatus and Priscian. Traditional English grammarians have been mostly 'Latinate' for their model.

The native English tradition of scientific language studies before the nineteenth century was meagre. The linguists of the 19th century such as Henry Sweet, A.J. Ellis, Alexander Melville Bell had no great predecessors. Whatever little tradition existed in the field "was enriched by the Indian tradition."[20] Being aware of the inadequacies of the Roman alphabet, the British phoneticians, led by Henry Sweet, tried to evolve a phonetic alphabet, which has now been standardized as the International Phonetic Alphabet (I.P.A.). Daniel Jones, Sweet's successor in the twentieth century, did a lot to the field of the phonetic research on sophisticated laboratory equipment. Even Sweet and Daniel Jones have been influenced by the Indian system. Bernard Shaw refers in *Pygmalion* to the phonetic anarchy caused by the Roman alphabet. He has given a portrait of Sweet in the character of Higgins, who could, though to the amazement of his friend, Pickering, pronounce a "hundred and thirty"[21] vowel sounds, only two short of the list enumerated in *Siddhānta Kaumudi* as a gloss to *anuditsavarnasya cāpratyayah* 1.1.69.

Contemporary linguistics has branched off into several scientific disciplines, many of which are interdisciplinary. Many of the branches of linguistics have taken up seminal ideas from Pāṇini and elaborated them as their theories. Pāṇini has given them a model of analysis and description. It is not that his aphorisms could directly be applied to any other language than Sanskrit.

A few of the linguists have themselves admitted to having derived inspiration from Pāṇini; in some of the cases there are certain striking analogues to Pāṇini. These might be accidental analogues. One cannot be certain of the influence without the statement made to this effect by the theorists of linguistics. Ferdinand de Saussure was Professor of Sanskrit. His theories have affinities with some of the Indian ones. His *langue* and *parole* distinction has perhaps been suggested by Bhartṛihari's distinction between *Prākritadhvani* and *Vaikritadhvani*.

"The link between the ancient Indian and modern Western schools of linguistics," writer W.S. Allen, "is considerably closer in phonetics than in grammar. For whilst Pāṇinian techniques are only just beginning to banish the incubus of Latin grammar, our phonetic categories and terminology owe more than is commonly realized to the influence of the Sanskrit phoneticians."[22]

The concept of *lopa* (unseen presence) in *adarśanam lopah*/ 1.1.6, *pratyayasya luk-ślu-lupah* 1.1.61/ and elsewhere has been an important linguistic contribution of Pāṇini. This is illustrated in *avyayādāpsupah*/2.4.82, that is the feminine termination *āp* and the case affixes *sup* are unseen presence in *avyayas* or indeclinables, which are *padas* or terms called *subanta* or ending in *sup* case affixes. The concept of zero in linguistics is a serviceable borrowing.

It is evident that in descriptive linguistics and grammar, Pāṇinian ideas and terms have been freely used. The descriptive analysis of some of the categories of English shows the impact of Pāṇinian technique. As Bloomfield says, Pāṇini's concept of *lopa* (zero) has been "in practice eminently serviceable device"[23] of linguistic explanation of irregular forms. The forms such as singular *sheep* and plural *sheep, deer* (sing.)—*deer* (pl.) etc; past and past participle forms like *cut—cut—cut* etc. are explained as zero-alterants. Bloomfield and others use it with reference to phonology, morphology and even syntax. An infinitive without to is termed a zero-infinitive; an article omitted is called a zero-article.

At the level of word-formation Pāṇinian techniques have yielded a rich harvest. Sanskrit terms such as *samasa, dvigu, dvandva, avyayibhava, bahuvrihi* etc. have been freely used. Randolph Quirk and Sidney Greenbaum explain *bahuvrihi* as follows:

"A 'bahuvrihi' compound names an entire thing by specifying some feature."[24] 'Compounds of this type have also been called exocentric.'[25] 'Co-ordinating compounds are sometimes referred to by the Sanskrit term *dvandva.*'[26] Explaining the meaning of compounds and their syntactical relations is like the *vigraha* (paraphrase relation) of a *samasa* (compound). The processes of *sandhi* forms have also been freely used and applied to the case of English. They talk of internal and external *sandhi*. Terms like *sandhi* juncture and explanations of changing word-shapes in suprasegmentals are evidences of the Pāṇinian impact.

George Cardona in *Pāṇini: A Survey of Reseach*[27] has critically examined the opinions of several linguists who find in Pāṇini striking parallels or analogues to the grammatical and linguistic insights present in the *Aṣṭādhyāyī*. These could not be chance similarities, since the Pāṇinian system of grammatical studies had been introduced to the West during the nineteenth century itself. Moreover, in the linguistic circles, Pāṇinian ideas must have been in the air. Though a few of the linguists have admitted to being influenced, lots of others, perhaps, fight shy of doing so, even when their theories are applications of Pāṇinian techniques to the cases of European languages.

Paul Kiparsky and J.F. Staal, both jointly and also individually, have pointed out many of the Pāṇinian techniques that have been taken over by modern linguistics. According to them, there are evidences in Pāṇini of the considerations of deep structure as well as surface structure.[28] Staal, in particular, draws our attention to "an array of transformational techniques" and also to the concepts of performance and competence in Pāṇini.[29] Cardona also considers the opinions of some other linguists, such as Jan Gonda, Toporov and Ivan A. Sag who have compared Pāṇinian contributions with those of modern linguistics.[30]

Among the Indian linguists, Vidyā Niwās Miśra, P.S. Subrahmanyam, H.S. Anathanārāyana, and Anil C. Sinha have all studied Pāṇini's contributions with those of modern linguistic trends. Ananthanārāyana[31] compares Fillmore's *Case Grammar* with the Pāṇinian *Kāraka* theory *vis-à-vis* the *vibhakti* (case ending). *Kāraka* and *Vibhakti* play on "logical subject and object versus grammatical subject and object."[32] Moreover, *Kārakas* belong to deep structure, while *vibhaktis* to surface structure. These two concepts of Chomskyan Transformational-generative grammar had been used much earlier in *A Course in Modern Linguistics* by C.F. Hockett, a linguist in the tradition of Leonard Bloomfield, a renowned admirer of Pāṇini. It would be no exaggeration to say that Hockett could have got the idea of surface structure and deep structure from Sanskrit Grammar, which relies so much upon *Vigraha* or paraphrase relation to explain ambiguous expressions especially those in *Samāsa* and *Kāraka*. It is common knowledge how the surface structure of a *samāsa* can belong after its *vigraha* or paraphrase relation to *tatpuruṣa, karmadhāraya* or *bahuvrihi* and so on. Fillmore's *Case Grammar* does not mention Pāṇini as an influence. But despite the differences in details in the context of English as an analytical language, the general framework is on all fours with the Pāṇinian *Kāraka* theory. Anil C. Sinha considers Pāṇini's *Kāraka* theory "a semantic category"[33] and criticizes Cardona, who regards it to be a syntactic category though he admits to the role of semantics in Pāṇini. Pāṇini's *Kārakas,* as Sinha says, constitute "generative semantics."[34]

P.S. Subrahmanyam and Vidyā Niwās Miśra trace in Pāṇini linguistic theories analogous to the theory of modern transformational-generative grammar. Subrahmanyam discusses this in an article "Deep Structure and Surface Structure in Pāṇini."[35] Vidyā Niwās Miśra traces in Pāṇini "a combination of process and item arrangement grammar."[36] To him "Pāṇini's syntactic analysis seems to be a combination of transformational and stratificational techniques."[37] Sydney Lamb's stratificational grammar can also be traced back to Pāṇini.

Thus many of the trends of modern linguistics have been traced back to Pāṇini. Cardona, however, cautions us against looking "only at parts of Pāṇini's system in isolation"[38] like the legendary blind men who had their wrong analogical pronouncements on what an elephant looked like "None of these views is without some foundation," as Cardona says, "yet none of them is fully acceptable either."[39] Cardona seems to blow hot and cold in the same breath. It cannot, nevertheless, be denied that modern linguistics harks back to Pāṇini for seminal ideas.

Firthian school has been greatly influenced by Pāṇini. In his system of prosodic phonology, as F.P. Dineen points out, "Firth claimed to have inspiration in the work of Pāṇini [...] whose description of Sanskrit revolutionized Western linguistics in the nineteenth century."[40]

English linguistics has a recent history; but it has taken a giant leap forward. It has reached its height, as R.H. Robins says, "not attained in antiquity, nor in the middle ages, nor despite the excellence of their work, among the linguistic scholars of Pāṇinian India."[41] Mr Robins ignores the fact that Pāṇini gave a model of computer software before they could even dream of it, and despite the computer modelling, English language has not yet been completely described. However, Mr Robins admits that the 'profound' influence of Pāṇini upon Western linguistics "is by no means over,"[42] and as pointed out by David Crystal, Pāṇinian principles are "still used in modern linguistics."[43]

REFERENCES

1. S.K. Belvekar, *Systems of Sanskrit Grammar* (Delhi: Bhartiya Vidya Bhavan, 1976), 1.
2. W.S. Allen, *Phonetics in Ancient India* (London: OUP, 1953), 2.
3. R.H. Robins, *General Linguistics: An Introduction* (London: Longman), 193.
4. J.B. Carrol, *The Study of Language* (Harvard: HUP, 1953), 16.
5. L. Bloomfield, *Language* (London: George Allen & Unwin, 1953), 11.
6. Dr Mahabir, *Pāṇini as Grammarian* (Delhi: Bharatiya Vidya Prakashan, 1978), 46.
7. Chomsky, Noam, *Aspects of the Theory of Syntax* (MIT Press, 1964), v.
8. R.H. Robins, *A Short History of Linguistics* (London, 1967), 146.
9. Vāsudeva Śarana Agrawāla, *Pāṇinikālina Bhāratavarṣa* (Varanasi: Chowkhamba, 1969).
10. Vidyā Niwās Miśra, "Pāṇini's Grammar as a Mathematical Model," *Indian Linguistics*, Vol. 25, 1964, 158.
11. *Ibid.*, 178.
12. R.V. Joshi, Foreword to Mahabir, *op. cit.*, vii.
13. Akshar Bharati, Vineet Chaitanya & Rajeeb Sangal (I.I.T., Kanpur), *Natural Language Processing: A Pāṇinian Perspective* (New Delhi: PHI, 1999).
14. R.H. Robines, *A Short History of Linguistics* (London: Longman, 1967), 98.
15. Quoted in J.R. Ballantyne (trans.), *Laghu Siddhānta Kaumudi* (rptd. Delhi: MBD, 1961), ii.
16. Quoted in W.S. Allen, *op. cit.*, 3.
17. W.D. Whitney, *Sanskrit Grammar* (rptd. Delhi: MBD, 1962), xiii.
18. R.H. Robins, *General Linguistics: An Introduction* (London: Longman, 1967), 295.
19. Quoted in David Crystal, *Linguistics* (Harmondsworth: Penguin, 1980), 153.
20. R.H. Robins, *General Linguistics: An Introduction* (London: Longman), 378.

21. G.B. Shaw, *Pygmalion*. Ed. A.C. Ward (Bombay: D.L., 1976), 17.
22. W.S. Allen, *Phonetics in Ancient India* (London: OUP), 3.
23. L. Bloomfield, *op. cit.*, 209.
24. Randolph Quirk & Sidney Greenbaum, *A University Grammar of English* (London: Longman, 1973), 447.
25. Randolph Quirk *et al.*, *A Comprehensive Grammar of the English Language* (London, 1985), 1576 (Note).
26. *Ibid.*, 1578 (Note).
27. George Cardona, Pāṇini: *A Survey of Research* (rptd. Delhi: M.B.D., 1980).
28. *Ibid.*, 232.
29. *Ibid.*
30. *Ibid.*, 344.
31. H.S. Ananthanārayan, "Kāraka Theory and the Case Grammar," *Indian Linguistics*, Vol. 31, 1970, 14-27.
32. *Ibid.*, 16.
33. Anil C. Sinha, "Generative Semantics and Pāṇini's Kārakas," *Journal of the Oriental Institute*, Vol. XXIII, 1973, 27.
34. *Ibid.*, 28.
35. P.S. Subrahmanyam, "Deep Structure and Surface Structure in Pāṇini," *Indian Linguistics*, Vol. 36, 1975, 346-66.
36. Vidyā Niwās Miśra, "Pāṇini's Grammar as a Mathematical Model," *Indian Linguistics*, Vol. 25, 1984, 177.
37. *Ibid.*, 160.
38. George Cardona, *op. cit.*, 236.
39. *Ibid.*
40. F.P. Dineen, *An Introduction to General Linguistics* (New York: Holt, Rinehart and Winston, 1967), 189.
41. R.H. Robins, *General Linguistics: An Introduction* (London: Longman, 1967), 379.
42. *Ibid.*, 377.
43. David Crystal, *Linguistics* (Harmondsworth: Penguin, 1980), 45.

28

Structuralism and Structuralist Literary Theory

MADAN M. SARMA

I

Structuralism can be defined as a movement of thought that emerged in the 1950s and 1960s in Europe. This movement affected a number of intellectual disciplines such as anthropology, cultural studies, history, literary criticism and philosophy. Structuralism studies all social and cultural phenomena including folk or fairy tales, myths, literary texts, advertisements, films, fashions in clothes, patterns of social decorum and so on. It tries to explain how these phenomena have achieved their cultural significance. In order to do so it tries to refer to the systems underlying these phenomena.

The term 'structuralism' is derived from the word 'structure.' 'Structure' is used frequently in linguistics and many other disciplines. Some linguists use the term 'structure' in two senses:

(a) Structure is taken to be synonymous with system. From this perspective the structure of a language is the language system.

(b) In another sense the abstract category that indicates syntagmatic or sequential (or horizontal) relationships of the elements of language is structure. (Halliday 5)

However, some linguists would like to use the term 'system' with reference to classes of paradigmatically (or vertically) related elements. Structure can be observed in the systematic arrangement of entities. The constituent parts of the structure have no independent existence outside it.

In case of language we talk of phonological, morphological, syntactic and semantic structures. Different sound units (phonemes) combine to form words, words combine together to form phrases and clauses, phrases and clauses combine to form sentences. When we talk of the 'sentence structure' we mean *the way the sentences are formed by the interrelation of their constituent parts or elements* (sounds, words etc.). An element, for example, a sound of a language, has no significance by itself; its significance is determined by the relationship to all other elements involved in a word or a sentence. A sentence can be analysed or broken into clauses, phrases, words, morphemes and phonemes, which are its constituent elements.

Structuralism derived its initial impetus from linguistics and especially the writings of the Swiss linguist, Ferdinand de Saussure (1857-1913). Certain key concepts of structuralism have been borrowed from Saussure. Saussure's lecture notes were collected and edited by his students who later got them published as a book, *Cours de Linguistique Générale* in 1915. Its English translation *Course in General Linguistics* was published in 1959.

Unlike earlier linguists who were primarily concerned with the history and characteristics of particular languages Saussure considered the structures that underlie all languages the proper study of linguistics. Saussure distinguished between two fundamental dimensions of linguistic study: *synchronic* and *diachronic* study. Synchronic study means the study of a language at a particular point of time, taking it as a complete or self-contained system of communication. A language can be studied synchronically, apart from its historical existence. Diachronic study means the study of a language over a period of time, taking into account the changes that had occurred over time. Synchronic is also called descriptive while diachronic is also known as historical.

Saussure also coined the terms 'langue' and 'parole' to designate the underlying system of rules or principles and the language in performance or use or concrete manifestations of the system respectively. In fact, Saussure distinguished between 'language' and 'speech.' By 'language' he meant the abstract system or 'langue'; by 'speech' he meant the utterances spoken (or written) by the individual or 'parole.' Saussure showed that *langue* must be described synchronically as a system of interrelated elements. An utterance is a manifestation or an instance of the langue. Langue is social and communal (belonging to a speech community); parole is individual, dependent on the individual. According to Saussure the proper object of linguistics is the langue of a speech community.

According to Saussure language is a system of 'signs' that should be studied synchronically. A sign has two aspects: a *signifier* ('signifiant' in French), and a *signified* ('signifié' in French). In other words, a sign is constituted with a signifier and a signified; both are inseparable, interrelated, just like the two sides of a paper:

$$\text{Sign} = \frac{\text{Signified (concept-the concept of a tree)}}{\text{signifier (sound-image-the word 'tree')}}$$

A signifier can be an audible sound-image or a visible written symbol (a word); signified is the thought, idea or meaning behind what is said or written. Apparently, there is unity between signifier and signified. But Saussure pointed out that the relation between a signifier and its signified (a word and its meaning or sense) is *arbitrary,* not natural or inherent. The word 'hot' is a sign or a combination of signs. The concept or feeling (of hotness) it indicates has no direct connection with the written or spoken word 'hot'; there is no sensation of hotness in the word 'hot.' Any other word could have conveyed the same sensation. Another example will make it clear. The traffic light 'red' is also a sign; it means 'stop.' There is no natural or inherent relation between the red light and the direction 'stop.' It gets its meaning from the system of traffic lights to which it belongs. Before Saussure it was more or less accepted that the relationship between the 'words' of a language and the 'things' or 'entity' in the world was natural. That relationship was taken to be the basis of 'meaning.' Saussure showed that the society and its conventions give the values or meanings of the signs of a language. A sign becomes meaningful within the system of which it is a part or constituent.

Saussure spoke of two types of relationships between the

signs or elements of a language: (a) syntagmatic or sequential; and (b) paradigmatic or selectional. Syntagmatic means horizontal or sequential arrangement of the elements in a sentence. In the sentence 'She is a teacher' the relationships between 'she' and 'is,' 'is' and 'a' and 'a' and 'teacher' are syntagmatic. On the other hand, the paradigmatic relationship is vertical arrangement of the elements, which is obtained by replacing one element by another. For example, in the sentence quoted above 'she' and 'teacher' may be replaced by other words to get totally different sentences:

> She is a teacher.
> Mr Singh is a businessman.
> They are students.

The relationships between 'she,' 'Mr Singh' and 'they' and those between 'teacher,' 'businessman' and 'students' are paradigmatic.

The four concepts discussed above pertain to Saussure's views on language. However, he spoke of a yet unborn science of signs, Semiology (now replaced by the more familiar term 'Semiotics') for carrying out scientific study of all signs and sign systems.

The Structuralists felt that Saussure's concepts and the model offered by linguistics could be applied in fields of study other than language too. They made an attempt to do so. Later, however, they appropriated some ideas from other linguists such as Emile Benveniste, Roman Jakobson and even Noam Chomsky.

II

The Russian Formalists were the first to apply Saussure's linguistic thoughts in the discussion and analysis of literature. The Moscow linguistic circle came into existence in 1915 at the initiative of Bogatirev, Jakobson and others. Eikhenbaum, Shklovsky, Tynyanov and others took the lead in setting up OPOYAZ, that is, the Society for Studying Poetic Language. The members of the two groups were collectively known as the Formalists.

Jakobson wrote on various functions of language. In poetry the aesthetic function of language becomes dominant. He did not negate the social base of the forms of art. Nor did he reject the notion of historical evolution. On the other hand, the members of the Opoyaz considered any art form to be autonomous. The Formalists aimed at developing what they called the 'science of literature.' For Jakobson the aim of the science of literature was to study 'literariness,' that is the qualities or characteristics that make a literary work 'literary.' According to the Formalists the literary devices are basically linguistic. They gave more importance to the form rather than the content of literature and talked of a literary system. The essence of the formalist poetics was 'ostranenie' or defamiliarization. Literature makes those sensations strange or fresh which become mechanical as a result of over use. This is done with the help of the form of literature. A critic's function is to study the interrelationships within a particular work or among different literary works, in other words, their formal relationships. They accepted Saussure's concept of syntagmatic relations.

Vladimir Propp (1968) studied Russian fairy tales as structural units. He proposed that there are a limited number of characters and functions in these fairy tales. Functions, that is the role of acts (of the characters) in a story, play the determining role in the nature and formation of fairy tales. A particular act may have a number of functions. Propp shows that the narrative structure of all Russian fairy tales can be explained with the help of 31 functions distributed among seven spheres of action. He also spoke of seven 'spheres of action' (hero, villain, false hero, donor, helper, despatcher and the person sought after) which are combined in specific ways in a fairy tale. A limited number of functions recur in a specific order in the fairy tales. Thus they form the grammar or the system of rules of all fairy tales. The totality of the functions is the langue; a fairy tale is parole. In other words, there is the same structure underlying different fairy tales. The structuralists in their discussion of the narrative later utilized Propp's concepts, particularly his view that narrative is basically syntagmatic.

A few years after the revolution in Russia Jakobson left for Prague and joined Mukarovsky and other Czech linguists in setting up the Prague Linguistic Circle. The members of the Circle internalized the influence of Saussure and Russian Formalism. In 1929 Jakobson used the term 'structuralism' in a paper (written in Czech) and said that a concept can be explained by its position in the system of concepts. He treated literary text as message. Literary works have special poetic or aesthetic structure. He also elaborated the concepts of binary opposites present in the linguistic system.

Czech structuralism developed by the Circle had some influence on literary structuralism. French linguist Benveniste (1971) stressed that for the language user the relations between signifier and signified is not arbitrary; it is necessary. Arbitrariness is present between a sign and the reality to which it refers. Structuralism utilized this idea.

After the Second World War Jakobson settled in the U.S.A. and continued his research in linguistics and poetics. He treated poetics as a part of linguistics. In the USA he came in contact with Claude Levi-Strauss and influenced the latter. In 1945 Levi-Strauss studied 'kinship relations' prevalent in different societies. In his analysis he utilized Jakobson's concept of binary distinctive features. It may be mentioned here that the lowest or the most basic elements in the linguistic system are phonemes (distinctive speech sounds). In English /p/ and /b/ are two distinctive (consonant) phonemes. A distinctive phoneme is understood by its difference from another phoneme. 'Pin' and 'bin' are different words as their meanings indicate. But /p/ in 'pin' cannot be understood or perceived unless it is contrasted with and differentiated from /b/ in 'bin.' This is the essence of binary distinctive features. Structuralists have adopted the concept of binary contrast or opposition from this. Hot/cold, black/white, good/bad, male/female are some examples of binary opposites.

Levi-Strauss regarded all cultural phenomena as signs. They are part of a cultural system. All human activities, behaviours are 'parole;' underneath them is the langue, a system of differential relationships. These phenomena are perceived or understood by their opposition to or contrast with others. As a cultural anthropologist Levi-Strauss was interested in the system underlying the cultural organizations and artifacts of different societies. He analyzed myths and showed that various myths prevalent in different societies are really different forms of certain basic content. Underlying the myths that appear to be totally different from each other is a universal structure. Myth too is structured like a language. Myths can be broken into mythemes. Mythemes combine to form meaningful units as phonemes combine to form words. The rules for combining these are the grammar of myths. According to Levi-Strauss myths are created by universal psychic activities; they are the indicators of how all men think. Levi-Strauss applied structuralist concepts in studying social customs and kinship relations.

French theorist Roland Barthes was influenced by the thoughts of Claude Levi-Strauss. He studied contemporary myths on the basis of Saussure's theory. Barthes's work on this was published in 1957, a year before Levi-Strauss published his famous *Anthropologie Structurale* (Structural Anthropology).

III

Saussure's linguistic theory and Levi-Strauss's thoughts and practice inspired and influenced the French intellectuals of the 1950s and 1960s. Especially those intellectuals who were associated with French New Criticism and analysis of narrative started applying structuralist thought and ideas in studying literature and literary theory. Among the intellectuals who played significant roles in the emergence of literary structuralism were Roland Barthes, Gerard Genette, Jacques Lacan, A.J. Greimas, Tzvetan Todorov and Umberto Eco.

Roland Barthes who was associated with Existentialism and Marxism till the 1960s made useful contribution to structuralism and semiotics. He took the lead in developing literary structuralism. However in his later (post 1960s) writings Barthes moved towards post-structuralism. In fact, in some writings Barthes seems to have taken a position that is between structuralism and post-structuralism.

The models provided by linguistics and the linguistic thoughts of Saussure and Jakobson were applied by structuralists with a view to carrying out systematic investigation into and study of literature.

Structuralism does not treat literature as something mysterious, inexplicable, something that can only be felt. The structuralists are opposed to imposing the critic's subjective opinion or view on literary works. Literature is a creation of language. Literature too is a construct. Literary works can be analysed in detail and can be categorized. In analyzing thus the aesthetic beauty or other qualities of the literary works do not get destroyed. Literature is not something unique.

According to Jonathan Culler the aim of structuralism is to create such a poetics that stands to literature as linguistics stands to language. Obviously then, structuralism does not want to say what a literary text means or, what a text signifies. Rather it wants to spell out the system of rules that make the forms and meanings of literary texts possible. A literary work is 'parole.' Structuralism aims at uncovering the 'langue' of literature. Usually while understanding or searching for meaning of a literary text we go out of the text and relate it to reality, life and the world. Structuralism does not consider it necessary to do so. For structuralists a text is an autonomous system. Structuralism aims at discovering the grammar of text, in finding a set of general principles or a system of rules about how texts function.

It has already been pointed out that Levi-Strauss's structuralist applications influenced the study of narratives. Under the influence of structuralism and as a result of the efforts of Greimas, Todorov, Genette, Bremond and Barthes emerged a new field/discipline, *Narratology.* Narratology is the study of the poetics of narrative texts. As Barthes says, Narrative is found in myths, folktales, epics, history, comic and fiction—everywhere. Narratology concentrates on the functions of narrative, not its medium. It explains how the sequence of events that constitute a story is described or narrated. Narratologists seek to propose a grammatical analysis of a story or a work of fiction. In their attempt to do so they treat a story in such a manner as if it is a sentence. As a linguist shows how different constituents make up the sentence, so narratologists try to show how the story is constituted by various elements or units within it. On the analogy of the syntactic rules, that is the rules for sentence formation, the structuralists propose the principles of narrative. A sentence can be divided into subject and predicate. In a story character is subject; action is predicate.

According to Barthes deductive methods should be adopted for analyzing narratives. At first a model or a theory of description/narration has to be constructed. Narratives of different types can be analyzed with its help. In his analysis of texts Barthes's avowed aim was to identify or locate the forms and codes that make the meaning of a text possible and then to classify them. He used a series of procedures for analysis. He divided a text into small parts or sections called lexia. Lexia is textual signifier. It may be a sentence, a part of a sentence or a group of three or four sentences. The rationale and the basis for such divisions are not clear. Apparently, lexia is modelled on phoneme; but it is not as objective as a phoneme. It is intuitive. Barthes mentions five 'codes' associated with reading. With the help of these codes the reader can identify the elements in literary texts and relate them to specific functions. The five codes are—(a) proairetic code (code of action); (b) hermeneutic code; (c) cultural code; (d) code of semes or connotative code; and (e) symbolic code. The proairetic code enables the reader to determine the result of an action. The hermeneutic code raises questions, creates suspense and finally resolves these. It can be described as the story telling code. The cultural code refers to established and authoritative cultural forms and accepted knowledge. The code of semes utilizes hints of meaning generated by certain signifiers. The symbolic code refers to the groupings by various means to create a pattern in the text. While reading a text the reader may not use all five codes at a time.

Another narratologist, Greimas aimed at a kind of universal grammar of narrative. He proposed a structural unit of narrative called the *actant*. In place of Propp's seven 'spheres of action' he proposed six actants that are organised in three pairs of binary opposites: subject/object; sender/receiver; helper/opponent. These three pairs, he believed, could easily account for three basic patterns found in narrative: (a) desire, search or aim (subject/object); (b) communication (sender/receiver); (c) auxiliary support or hindrance (helper/opponent).

Gerard Genette extended the Russian Formalist concepts of plot and story to posit three levels of narrative: *recit, histoire* and *narration*. Recit means the actual, chronological order of events in a narrative. Histoire refers to the sequence in which those events occurred in a narrative. Narration is the act of narrating. Genette also discussed narrator's 'voice' and 'viewpoints.'

Todorov believed that individual stories are derived from a grammar of narrative.

Jacques Lacan added another dimension to structuralism by applying structuralist theories in psychoanalysis. He believed that human mind or human consciousness is structured like language. The unconscious is a product of language. Suppressed desire, will, memory-everything is signifier; everything is interrelated.

Structuralist theorist Jonathan Culler feels that structuralist literary theories are relevant to the study of practical criticism and literature teaching. For him teaching (and studying) literature is concerned with the development of certain special rules and procedures and also with certain degree of expertise in applying those. Culler points out that structuralism is not a new method of interpreting literary texts: it is rather an attempt to understand how a literary text acquires meaning. In analogy of Noam Chomsky's notion of *competence* Culler proposed the notion *of literary competence.* Chomsky's (linguistic) 'competence' means the intuitive knowledge of the linguistic system that enables a native speaker to understand and produce grammatically correct sentences.

Culler wants to assert that literary competence is essential for understanding or appreciating literature. Literary competence means the knowledge of the system of rules, codes and conventions used in literature. Structuralist poetics examines the nature of that knowledge. Literary competence can be acquired through training in reading literary texts. Literature teaching makes the acquisition of this competence possible. Culler's competence refers only to the understanding or reception of literary texts, not to the production of literature. Chomsky's competence, on the other hand, covers both language comprehension and production. Chomsky's competence is communal; it is not unique to a particular native speaker. Culler's competence is individual.

Some of the Marxist theorists turned structuralists in the 1960s. Louis Althusser who advocated a really 'scientific'

Marxism in place of 'humanist' Marxism and some other Marxist intellectuals developed a structuralist version of Marxism. Althusser wanted to define society on the basis of the concept of structure. He viewed society as a combination of interrelated activities at different levels, each activity with its own contradiction.

IV

Some critics of structuralism do not see it as radically different from American New Criticism. New Criticism regarded a literary text as autonomous. New Critics did not consider it necessary to relate the text to any biological, social, psychological, political or cultural context.

Structuralism does not consider a literary work as the creation of an individual or of a conscious, free, thinking subject. The subject or the author is not the creator of meaning. As Eagleton remarks, structuralism wants to place structure in the position of the human subject. By denying human role in the creation of meaning structuralism has taken an anti-humanist position.

Apparently, structuralism aims at doing away with subjectivity in its practice and at ensuring scientific objectivity. Like the Russian Formalists the structuralists wanted to create a science of literature. According to Barthes the approach of looking at texts to discover/develop general rules and theory of literature is what a science of literature implies. Structuralism emphasizes structure or system that is unconscious and anti-humanist and that is based on difference and contrast. It does not want to relate structure to any system outside it. It can, however, be argued that if a thing or a phenomenon becomes meaningful only when it is associated with a structure, then the structure as proposed by the structuralists has no meaning other than itself unless it is related to something outside it.

Structuralism accepts a fixed meaning of the text. For Structuralists difference is the basis of meaning. A sign refers to another sign different from the first one. If meaning of a word is another word, then the second word will have a third word as its meaning. Thus one sign will lead to another. As a result, as Derrida points out, meaning gets perpetually deferred; it will not be possible to arrive at a fixed or final meaning.

By subordinating the parole of individual texts to langue the structuralists neglect the specificity of actual texts. Structuralists often select texts for illustrating or applying their theories according to their convenience. Moreover, while taking up an analysis of a text they do not make the basis or rationale of the units of division of the texts transparent. Neither do they think it necessary to justify why these and not any other kind of divisions are acceptable. For example, Barthes does not care to tell us why he calls the units of texts 'lexia' and what exactly a 'lexia' means.

Although the structuralists have utilized Saussure's concept of signifier and signified in their theory, they give more importance to the analysis of the relations between the signifiers rather than between signifiers and signifieds. For example, as the various parts of a text (say, lexia) are signifiers and as the structuralist critic is concerned with the relations between these parts (that is, between the signifiers), not with what they mean or signify, they ignore the signifieds. It needs to be pointed out that analysing the structure of a language and that of a work of literature is not the same thing. Structuralism has not been able to describe objectively the procedures for identifying the structure of a literary text. 'This is the structure'—this kind of statements seems to be entirely dependent upon the analyst's intuition.

Structuralist literary critics give importance to description and analysis of the text, not on its interpretation or evaluation. They do not want to relate the text to the world or to the reality. At the same time they relate their description and analysis to something outside the text—to their own structuralist theories.

Perhaps the most positive contribution of structuralism is to free literature and the process of literary creation from mystification. Structuralism questions the privileged status of literature. At the same time it lays special emphasis on the role played by language in a literary text. It does not see meaning as the creation of an individual. The question, however, is—how can one get at the meaning without relating a text to reality, society and to the context of its reception? Structuralism does not accept any reality outside the text. Reality is seen as a construct of language. This is really an idealist attitude.

Jacques Derrida and other post-structuralist theorists do not accept structuralism as a theory based on any radical thinking. They want to refute some of the central tenets of structuralism such as the notions of structure, text and meaning.

REFERENCES

Asher, R.E., ed. *The Encyclopedia of Language and Linguistics*, Vol. 8. Oxford: Pergamon Press, 1994.

Barthes, Roland. *Image-Music-Text.* Trans. S. Heath. London: Fontana, 1977.

Benveniste, Emile. *Problems in General Linguistics.* Trans. Mary E. Meek. Coral Gables, 1971.

Coyle, M., Garside, P., Kelsale, M. & Peck, J. eds. *Encyclopaedia of Literature and Criticism.* London: Routledge, 1990.

Cuddon, J.A., ed. *The Penguin Dictionary of Literary Terms and Literary Theory*, 4th edition. London: Penguin Books, 1998.

Culler, J. *Structuralist Poetics: Structuralism, Linguistics and the Study of Literature.* London: Routledge & Kegan Paul, 1975.

Derrida, *Jacques of Grammatology.* Trans. Gayatri Chakravorty Spivak. Baltimore and London.

Eagleton, Terry. *Literary Theory: an Introduction.* Oxford: Basil Blackwell, 1983.

Halliday, M.A.K. *Language as Social Semiotic.* London: Edward Arnold, 1978.

Hawkes, T. *Structuralism and Semiotics*, London: Routledge, 1991.

Lodge, David, ed. *Modern Criticism and Theory: A Reader.* London, New York: Routledge, 1988.

Propp, Vladimir. *Morphology of Folktale.* Trans. Laurence Scott. Austin: University of Texas Press, 1968.

Rice, P. & Waugh, P, eds. *Modern Literary Theory: A Reader.* London: Edward Arnold, 1989.

Selden, R., Widdowson, P. & Brooke, P., eds. *A Reader's Guide to Contemporary Theory.* London: Prentice Hall & Harvester Wheatsheaf, 1985.

Selden, Raman, ed. *The Theory of Criticism, From Plato to the Present: A Reader.* London: Longman, 1988.

——, ed. *The Cambridge History of Literary Criticism, Vol. 8: From Formalism to Post-structuralism.* Cambridge: Cambridge University Press, 1995.

29

Teaching of Language and Literature in Ancient India

R.S. PATHAK

All literate civilizations made appropriate provision for teaching and learning of language and literature. Very few of them, however, have surpassed India in this respect; learned persons here have always been accorded unqualified praise and recognition. Their remarkable virtues and strength of intellect have been recognized variously. Max Muller, for example, remarked: "Whatever sphere of the human mind you may select for your special study, whether it be language, or religion, or mythology, or philosophy, whether it be laws or customs, primitive art or primitive science, everywhere you have to go to India, whether you like it or not, because some of the most valuable and instructive materials in the history of man are treasured up in India and in India only."

In fact, in no other tradition grammar, grammarians and grammar teaching were regarded with the same sense of respect as in India. Very often elsewhere grammarians, not unlike philosophers, were made the butt of ridicule. A grammarian has been compared by Michael West, for instance, to "an unskilled camper who does not know where he is going or what he is going to do there" and has therefore "tumbled into the bag all sorts of useless articles like the White Knight in *Alice through the Looking-glass.*" In India, on the contrary, grammarians were designated as the foremost scholars and originators of several sciences. In his great work, *Dhvanyāloka,* Anandavardhana declared from the house top as it were: "*Adye vidvansah hi vaiyakaranah, vyakarana-mulatvat sarva-vidyāpnām*" (*i.e.*, Grammarians were the earliest scholars, and all branches of learning owe their origin to grammar). Even creative writers, who generally do not like to see the grammarian eye to eye, have borrowed from and referred to the views of the early grammarians gratefully.

The common people also generally cared for grammatical 'correctness,' as would be clear from the following cases. One of the popular verses in Sanskrit reads as follows:

Yadyapi vahunādhite
Tathapi putra patha vyakāranam/
Svajanah svajano mābhūta
Sakalah sakalah sakrcchakrta

(Although you have studied a lot, my son, -you must study grammar lest you should confuse between *svajana* and *svajāna, sakala* and *sakala,* and *sakrt* and *sakrt.*) One of my uncles who was a scholar of considerable merit, would emphasise the significance of Sanskrit studies, particularly its grammar, and conclude his arguments with the following verse:

Ajarghā yo na jānāti yo na jānāti barbarī/
Acīkamat naiva jānāti tasmai kanyā na dīyate/

(He who does not know the import and application of the three Pāṇinian rules, *i.e.* Ajarghā, Barbarī and Acīkamat, should never be chosen as a son-in-law.) Lastly, a Malayali young woman is said to have turned down the matrimonial proposal simply because the young man chosen by her father did not know even the basics of grammar:

Aham katham dvitīyā syāt
Dvitīyā syāmyaham katham/
Vasya sasthī caturthī ca
Vihasya ca vihāya ca/

(How can I be the Second to one who considers aham to be an accusative case form, and to whom the verbal forms *Vihasya* and vihāya are the examples of genitive and dative cases respectively.) The three cases cited above will clearly 'reveal the, high position of grammar and grammar teachers in the society.

According to Indian tradition, there are six subjects (vedāngas) the study of which was necessary for proper reading of the Vedas and for their sacrificial employment. These are:

Śiksā (phonetics), Chhandas (prosody), vyākarana (grammar), Nirukta (etymology), Jyotisha (astronomy), and Kalpa (ceremonial practice). The first two are necessary for reading the Vedas, the next two for their understanding, and the last two for their sacrificial employment. Grammar, which was given a pride of place, attained dizzy heights with Pāṇini's *Astādhyāyī*. Grammar was called in India the uttara vidya (of Māhabhāsya 1.2.32: *Vyākaranam nāmeyam uttāra vidyā; pradhānam ca satsu angesu vyākaranam*). Some Western scholars tried to denigrate Pāṇini's grammar calling it "both inaccurate and ill-conceived." Whitney wondered "whether any one in his right mind would have chosen to compose a grammar as Pāṇini did." But its qualities were recognised more than once even by scholars in the Western world.

To Bloomfield, the Astādhyāyī is "one of the greatest monuments of human intelligence." He regarded it as "an indispensable model for the description of languages." It is not surprising that Bloomfield modelled his classic Algonquian grammar and his *Postulates* on Pāṇini's grammar. He found the traditional grammars of Greek and Latin "woefully incomplete and unsystematic." As compared to Pāṇini's grammar, says W.S. Allen in his excellent book *Phonetics in Ancient India,* the thousand manuscripts of Priscian's *Latin Grammar,* "the pride of our western tradition, are but a drop in the grammatical ocean." Concentrating on Pāṇini's and his predecessors' views on issues in phonetics and phonology, Allen adds: "These early [Indian] phoneticians speak in fact to the twentieth century rather than to the Middle Ages or even the mid-nineteenth century, and many a statement which the commentators and even Whitney or Max Muller have failed to comprehend makes immediate sense to the phonetician today." It may also be remembered that even before Pāṇini there had been a long tradition of grammarians in India. Pāṇini himself mentions ten of his predecessors: Āpiśali, Kaśyapa, Gārgya, Gālava, Cakravarman, Bhāradvaja, Śākatāyana, Sākalya, Senaka, and Sphotāyana. Burnell has listed by name no less than sixty-eight of these pre-Paninian grammarians. Unfortunately, but for fragmentary citations, their work has been lost to us, but, as the medieval philosopher Kumarila remarks in his Tantravartika, "We cannot think of any point of time totally devoid of some work or other dealing with the grammatical rules treating of the different kinds of roots and affixes." The magnitude of Indian grammarians' achievement—particularly that of Pāṇini, the "linguistic Homer," as Goldstucker would call him and later "grammatical saints." Katyayana and Patanjali, would be evident if we place their great works alongside of the first Greek grammar by Dionysius Thrax which is a short practical manual of some fifteen pages and concentrates on Greek morphology and phonology.

Born in the fifth century (?) B.C. at Salatura on the Upper Indus, Pāṇini took up the challenge of writing a complete grammar of Sanskrit with reverential piety and humility. In a passage in the *Mahābhāsya,* Pāṇini is said to have sat in a pure place facing East, with a ring of the Kusa grass around his fourth finger. His monumental work, says John Lyons, is in respect of exhaustiveness, consistency and economy "far superior to any grammar of any language yet written." The Astādhyāyi is formulated in a morphologically, syntactically and lexically comprehensive manner. It is based on the spoken language (bhasa) of Pāṇini's time, although rules have also been given on Vedic usages and on regional variants. We have separate forms for calling from distance (Durāddhūte ca, 8.2.84), phatic communion (pratyabhivāde sūdre, 8.2.83), counter questioning (prastaprativacane, 8.2.93), snubbing (bhartsne, 8.2.95) and so on. Rules are organised into hierarchies of generality between the points of maximally general applicability rules (samanya and special rules [Visesa]). A special rule is said to block a general rule. The optional forms distinguish between preferable and marginal forms. Some rules, as Vasudeo Sharan Agrawal shows, take cognizance of even socio-linguistic conditions. Moreover, the difference between the virtual or permanent element and ephemeral elements suffering modifications at the level of actualisation have been mentioned, which was known to Katyayana also. Commenting on Panini's rule *Taparah tatkalasya* (1.1.70), he points out that the sounds (varnas) are fixed while styles of diction (Vrtti) depend upon the speech habits of the speaker.

The significance of Pāṇinian techniques was recognised by Western linguists in due course. Sir William Jones was acquainted with his statements of the sound system and based on Indian models the order of treatment and descriptive technique in his "Dissertation on the Orthography of Asiatic Words in Roman Letters." The English School linguists also were influenced by Pāṇini's technique, as J.R. Firth, the leader of the group admits in his paper on "The English School of Phonetics": "Without the Indian grammarians and phoneticians whom he [Jones] introduced and recommended to us, it is difficult to imagine our nineteenth century school of phonetics." Many of Pāṇini's grammatical generalisations would bring to mind some important 'rules' postulated by Chomsky and later grammarians. Significantly, contrary to general impression, Pāṇini's rules are systematically related to semantic categories. His Karakas correspond to several semantic relations, and a sentence is seen as a little drama played out by an Agent and other actors, which may include Goal, Recipient, Instrument, Location and Source. The grammatical tradition of Pāṇini was maintained and furthered in different versions of his work and in various commentaries.

It is not possible to specify even the basic features of education in language and literature obtaining in ancient India. Some very important points, however, deserve to be highlighted here. The students had to study at the initial stage a few verses from the Vedas—specially hymns from the Rgveda—necessary for their religious duties and a good deal of grammar which would enable them to obtain facility for understanding works of an advanced nature. The period could extend for about twelve years, if the study of subsidiary branches is also taken into account. The full grammar courses alone took at least ten years in the seventh century. Paper and printing being unknown and books fragile, costly and beyond the means of average students, Vedic learning was transmitted orally. Moreover, the preservation of sacred literature was tabooed for a long time. The *Mahābhārata* would condemn to hell a person who commits the Vedas to writing. Understandably, great importance was attached to the proper accent and pronunciation in Vedic recitations, which could be learned only from the lips of duly qualified teacher. The *Taittirīya Prātisakhya* (24.4.6) says that young boys and girls were trained to realise the difference between short and long vowels, to familiarise themselves with varieties of accents, and to master the rules of conjuration and coalescence of vowels and consonants:

Gurutvan laghutā śamyam hrasvadīrghaplutani ca/
Lopāgamavikārasca prakrtir vikrtin kramah/
Svaritodāttanīcastvam svāso nārdo gameva ca/
Etat sarvam tu vijnēyam chandabhasam adhīyāta/
Padakramaviseasajnō varnakramavicaksanah/
Svarama trāvibhagajno gacched a cāryasamasadam/

Thus, it was enjoined that "he who knows the distinctions of tone and length may go and sit with the teachers." On the contrary, direct penalties were threatened for mispronunciation, including descent to the Kumbhipaka hell (Parasarti Siksa, 65). The prerequisites of good enunciation as mentioned by the Vajnavalkya Siksa include the following factors: good health, peaceful nature, absence of nervousness, delivery free from elision, speaking without undue emphasis, sing-song way of speech and unusual tremor, articulation of initial and final sounds clearly, absence of cacaphony, speaking without vibrating lips or indistinctness and without nasal twang, and delivery without intermittent breaks in the speech flow and tightening of the tongue:

Svasthah prasānto nirbhīto varnān uccared vudhah/
Nābhyāhanyanna nirhanyān na gāyenna ca kampayet
Yathādavuccared varnān tathaivētan samapayet/ [...]

Na karālo na lambostho navyakto nānunasikah/
Gadgado baddhajihvaśca na varnan vaktumarhati
Prakrtir vasya kalyāni dantosthau vasya sobhanu/
Pragalbhasca vīnitaàca sa varnān vaktumarhati/

Besides, the teeth and lips should be kept in the proper shape and condition. According to the *Naradiva Siksa*, clarity of the throat is also essential for effective articulation.

The ancient Indian system of education banked heavily on rote learning. But meaningless cramming of rules and verses was not encouraged. The *Rgveda* contains flings at parrot-like or frog-like reciters, and highlights the distinction between one man "firmly established in the friendship of speech" and another who "bears speech without fruit, without flowers" (10.71.5). The *Nirukta* recommends the learners' reading and ruminating over the text among themselves and reflecting on the meaning of what they had learnt (1.18). Yaska warns of the tendency of being satisfied with merely committing the Vedas to memory. Patanjali also denigrates meaningless recitation and cites an old verse in this support:

Yadadhitamavijntam nigadenaiva sa bdyata/
Anagnaviva suskaidho na tajjvalati karhicit/

Pāṇini mentions different kinds of mistake in oral presentation such as the use of incorrect word (Padam mithya karayate), error in the articulation of vowels, etc. (Svaradi dustam), recurrence of the same mistake (Asakrd uccarayati) and so on. He also refers to terms like *aikanyika, dvaiyanyika, traiyanyika* and so on which pointed out the number of mistakes up to ten during revision or examinations (*Karmadhyayane vrttam*, 4.2.63-64). During their course, the students were required to note how precisely their teachers used to pronounce and intonate the Vedic verses when teaching them to their students. Several time during the course the students were called upon to pass through the fiery ordeal of learned discourses (*sastrarthas*).

The courses at the secondary level were relatively broad-based but specialisation began rather too early and an undue emphasis was laid on grammar, Vedic literature and logic. Subjects of aesthetic value like music and painting and useful courses like mathematics, history and geography generally did not exist. Another interesting point worth mentioning in this context is the introduction of writing. There are ample evidences to show that the art of writing was known to Indians at least from 1000 B.C. whereas it was introduced in Greek schools in 6000 B.C. From the early centuries of the Christian era, writing and arithmetic came to be regarded in India, in the words of the Tamil thinker Tiruvalluvar, as the two eyes of the soul. Talking about the system of education in the Nalanda monastery, the Chinese traveller I-Tsing observes: "After having studied this commentary [Kasikavritti on Pāṇini's grammar], students began to learn composition in prose and verse and devote themselves to logic and metaphysics, in learning [...] logic they rightly draw inference; and by studying Jatakamala their powers of comprehension increase. "The *Lalita-vistara* (Ch. 10) pertinently refers to primary schools and their teachers as *lipisalas* (alphabet schools) and *darakacaryas* respectively. There is a sculpture in the Peshawar Museum representing the Buddha in his primary school as holding a rectangular board in his hand and engaged in writing upon it. This must have been the first introduction to writing for a rich person's wards.

Some other aspects of ancient Indian education pertinent to our discussion may also be briefly mentioned. The teaching of grammar, as said earlier, received top priority in most cases. Besides several schools imparting education in grammar in different parts, there was a big grammar college at Tiruvorriyur in Chingleput district in the thirteenth century which was established in the memory of Pāṇini. According to the local tradition, Lord Siva had appeared in the adjoining temple before Pāṇini for fourteen days in order to teach him the first fourteen aphorisms. There were also special schools right from the fifth century B.C. run by teachers who admitted to their family as many students as they could manage. We find references to various kinds of teachers in the thirty-second and ninety-fourth sargas of the *Ramayana.* As the *Taittiriya Upanisad* (1.4.3) points out, to such teachers students came from all sides "as water runs downwards, as months go to the year." A hymn in the *Rgveda* compares the meeting of the teachers and the taught with the gathering of the frogs in the rainy season:

When one of these repeats the other's language,
as he who learns the lesson of the teacher,
Your every limb seems to be growing larger,
as ye converse with eloquence on the waters. (7.1.30)

Such seats of learning continued at least till the time of Harsa. Bana, on his return from Harsa's court and greeted by his relatives makes the following equiries: "Do the boys pursue their studies at the proper time? Is there the same unbroken daily application to the Veda? The old earnestness in the practice of the art of sacrifice? Are there the same classes in grammar exposition, showing respect by days not idly spent in series of emulous discussion? Is there the old logic society, regardless of all other occupation? The same excessive delight in the Mimamsa, dulling all pleasure in other authoritative books?" (*Harsacarita* 71).

As for the method of imparting education, during the initial teaching only the broad hints were furnished by the preceptor and the student was asked to work them out fully. An example of this practice is found in the *Taittiriya Upanisad* (Ch. 3) where Varuna, while teaching his son Bhrgu, indicates only in general terms the features of the Absolute, repeating four times; the fifth effort on the part of Bhrgu enables him to decipher His exact content. This use of the method of reinforcement and problem solving is also noticed by I-Tsing: "He [the student] reads a portion of the scripture and reflects on what he has learnt. He acquires new knowledge day by day, and searches into old subjects month after month without losing a minute." The progress from the general to the specific will get approval of methodologists of various shades and hues.

What is even more remarkable is the high rate of literacy in ancient India. Both boys and girls were given the same opportunity of education. An Upanisadic king, in the *Chandogya Upanisad* (5.2.5), proudly claims that there was no illiterate in his kingdom (*Na me steno janapade* [...] *nannahitagnir naviddvan*). According to one estimate even in the days of Asoka literacy was as high as sixty per cent (Altekar, 259). Scholars who had completed their education were held as the greatest force in society (*Mahad vai etad bhūtam yah snātakas*). According to the *Bharadvāja Grhya Sutra* (2.1.8), the sun can shine only with the lustre he borrows from the graduates (*Etadahah snātānām ha va esa etat tejasa tapati tasmadenam etadaharnaphitapet*).

During the period 200 B.C. to 1200 A.D. female education in general received a great setback, but it continued to be given adequate attention in rich, cultured families. Rajasekhara writes: "*Purusavad yosito'pi kavibhaveyuh* [...] *sruyante drsyante ca rajaputrayo'mahamatraduhitaro ganikah kautumbika bharyasoa sastraprahitayvuddhayah kavayasca* (*Kāvyamīmamsā*, 53). By the end of the eighth century, however, women as a class ceased to be literate, although Vātsyāyana, in his *Kāmasūtra* (1.3.16) laid down that girls should be trained in sixty-four arts, some of which are directly related to reading and writing: *prahelikā, pustakavācanam, nātakākhyayikādarsanam, kāvyasamasyapuranam, aksaramustikakathana, desabhasavijnana, manasikāvyakriyah, abhidhanakosah, candojnana,* and so on. It is a pity that the clock of female education came to a standstill amongst common people for which the society has already paid a very high price.

It would be interesting to have an idea about the people's attitude to languages other than Sanskrit. The Indo-Baktrian rulers of Taxila (2nd c. B.C.) were the inheritors of the rich Greek civilization. Their rule in Taxila extended over a century and quarter, which must have made some impression on the education system of the place. It is quite possible that a few renowned teachers of Taxila may have learnt and opened classes in Greek, Epigraphical testimony conclusively evidences the replacement of the Brahmi script by the Kharostri consequent upon the Persian occupation (6th c. B.C.). These must have been Indians' first encounters with foreign languages. During the period 250 B.C. to c. 250 A.D. Prākṛtas were in ascendancy. The use of vernaculars by Mahāvīra and the Buddha and the patronage of Aśoka must have given impetus to their cultivation. Public documents during this period were composed in Pali or Prākṛtas, Sanskrit appearing in inscriptions very rarely. The Satavahana kings of the Deccan had decreed that all their public documents be in Prākṛta alone (*Kāvyamīmamsā* 50). After about 250 A.D., however, Sanskrit regained its position. The Guptas were great champions of Sanskrit and had ordered the use of Sanskrit even in their harems. It was in the thirteenth century that provision was made first for the teaching of Telugu, Marathi and Kannada in some schools and colleges in South India. From about the eighth century A.D. Prākṛtas and vernaculars became widely differentiated from Sanskrit. But the society at large was not alive to the importance of languages other than Sanskrit. Alberuni observes: "The language in India is divided into a neglected vernacular one, only in use among the common people, and a classical one, only in use among the upper and educated classes, which is much cultivated." This was the beginning of linguistic elitism and the politics of language in India.

WORKS CITED

Agarwal, V.S. *Paninikaleen Bharatavarsha* (in Hindi). Banaras: Motilal Banarasidass, 1955.

Allen, W.S. *Phonetics in Ancient India.* London: OUP, 1938.

Altekar, A.S. *Education in Ancient India.* Banaras: Nand Kishore & Bros, 1944.

Das, S.K. *The Educational System of the Ancient Hindus.* Delhi: Gian Publishing House, 1986.

Marrou, H.I. *A History of Education in Antiquity.* Trans. G. Lamb. London: Sheed & Ward, 1956.

Varma, Siddheshwar. *Critical Studies in the Phonetic Observations of Indian Grammarians.* London: Royal Asiatic Society of London, 1929.

30

Philosophy of Language

BHASKAR ROY BARMAN

To begin with, I must admit that I am dealing in this Paper with such a topic as is well-nigh difficult to grapple with. In discussing philosophy of language I shall lay a particular emphasis on theories of meaning.

Many of the philosophical problems can be applied to human concerns, relevant as they are to them, and they are so complex in their ramifications that they always make themselves felt in one form or another. Yield though they do in course of time to philosophical inquiry, they need to be rethought by each age in the light of its broader scientific outlook with a view to deepening our religious experiences. Better solutions can be arrived at through adoption of more ethical and religious methods. One who aims at studying philosophy just to understand the best of what it can vouchsafe should look for both fundamental and contemporary achievements that go together.

Now I turn to philosophy of language which might reasonably be thought of as comprising anything philosophers do when they think *qua* philosophers, about language. The philosophy of language is, it should be noted, even less defined and less in possession of a clear principle of unity than most other branches of philosophy. The problems related to language which are dealt with by philosophers constitute a loosely-knit collection and it is difficult for us to find any clear criterion that can separate it from problems related to language such as are dealt with by grammarians, psychologists and anthropologists. We can at least manage to obtain an initial sense of this collection by surveying various points of philosophy at which emerges a concern with language.

It is worth considering the ways in which problems related to language crop up in the various branches of philosophy. One of the branches of philosophy is Metaphysics which is distinguished from other branches in its attempt to formulate the most general and pervasive facts about the world, including, *inter alia,* an enumeration of the most basic categories in which entries belong and some depiction of their interrelations. We know of many philosophers who have tried to get at some of these fundamental features of the language we use to talk about the world. In Book X of the *Republic* we find Plato saying 'Whenever a number of individuals have a common name we assume them to have corresponding idea or form' (596). Plato is to spell out this rather cryptic remark, is drawing our attention on to a pervasive feature of language, that a given common noun or an adjective, 'tree' or 'sharp,' for example, can be truly applied in the same sense to a large number of different and diverse individual things, his position being that this is possible only if there exists some one entity named by the general term in question—treeness, sharpness—of which each of the individuals partakes. If this were not the case, it would be impossible for the general term to be applied in the same sense to a number of different individuals.

In this connection Aristotle appears on the scene, arguing in his Metaphysics as follows:

> And one might even raise the question whether the words 'to walk,' 'to be healthy,' 'to sit' imply that each of these things is existent, and similarly in other cases of this sort, for none of them is either self-subsistent or capable of being separated from substance, but rather, if anything, it is that which walks, sits or be healthy that is an existent thing. Now these are seem to be more real because there is something definite which underlies them (*i.e.,* substance or individual) which is implied in such a predicate; for we never use the word 'good' or 'sitting' without implying this. (Book *Zeta,* Chapter 1)

Here in the passage quoted, Aristotle tells us that we do not use verbs except in connection with subjects. We cannot go around saying 'sits,' 'walks,' and so on. Rather do we say just to bring home what we are driving at, 'He is sitting,' 'She is walking,' and so on. In fact Aristotle means to say that substances, 'things' have an independent kind of existence in a way actions do not. 'Sits' and 'walks'—they are themselves actions—have no such kind of existence independent of the substances, 'he' and 'she.' Thus it has become evident that substances are more fundamental ontologically than actions.

The nineteenth century German philosopher, Meinong affirmed that every meaningful expression which performs the function of referring to something must needs have a referent, inasmuch as short of a referent it gives nothing that has a meaning. Hence, when we have obviously a meaningful expression which refers to nothing in the real world, for example, 'the fountain of youth' as in the sentence, 'De Soto was searching for the Fountain of Youth,' we must suppose that it refers to a 'subsistent' entity which does not exist but has some other mode of being. This doctrine, as well as the Platonic position presented above, is based on a confused assimilation of meaning and reference. We shall discuss it a bit later on.

We had rather consider meantime certain words we often find occurring in the secondary language as well as in all higher languages but they rarely occur in the object-language. These words are characteristic of logic. It is quite likely that you will be interested to know something about the object-language and to know as well why the words characteristic of logic rarely occur in the object-language. I think you will get your curiosity satisfied when reading on down the paper. It should be borne in mind that logic warns us that such words as 'true,' false,' 'or,' some' and 'all' cannot be defined.

Bernard Russell explained the words 'true,' 'false' and 'not' clearly in his book *An Inquiry into Meaning and Truth*. He opines that it is unnecessary to have the two words 'false' and 'not,' because if p is a proposition, 'p is false' and 'not-p' are synonymous. The difference is, in fact, one of emphasis. If you want butter and looks in a cupboard and find cream cheese, you will say, 'this isn't butter,' but if the dairyman offers for sale a substance labelled 'butter' which you find to be 'margarine,' you will say 'you say this is butter, but that is false,' because you are more interested in his wickedness than in his goods. Thus it has become quite evident to us that 'false' and 'not' are synonymous.

In practice, as opposed to philosophy, we only apply the words 'true' and 'false' to statements which we have heard, read or considered before we possessed the evidence that would enable us to decide which of the words was applicable. Someone told you Manx cats have no tails, but he had told you previously Manx men have three legs, it is quite natural you did not believe him, for you did never see a Manx man possessing three legs. When he produced before you a Manx cat you would certainly exclaim 'So what you said is true!' When a newspaper says such thing has happened; but after carefully examining the evidence on the spot we got to know that such thing as was reported in the newspaper was false. When the statement comes first and afterwards the evidence, there is a process called 'verification,' which involves confrontation with the statement with the evidence. In the case of a statement in the primary language, the evidence must be enriched with a sensible experience or a set of such experiences. Speaking broadly, the process of verification is as follows: first you hear, read or consider a sentence 'S' then you have an experience 'E'; then you observe that 'S' is a sentence which describes 'E.' In that case you say that 'S' is true. This is certainly not a definition of the word 'true,' yet that is a description of the process by which you come to know that this word is applicable to a given primary sentence.

The word 'true' may be applied to a sentential utterance, in a sentence or proposition. Two essential utterances being instances of the same sentence, or two sentences being instances of the same proposition, are either both true or both false. Thus in determining truth or falsehood, it is the proposition that is relevant. A sentence or proposition is regarded 'true' when it has certain relation to an experience. In the case of verification, the sentence comes first and the experience after, but this is logically irrelevant; if the experience comes first, it equally proves the sentence to be 'true,' provided the sentence describes the experience.

It should be noted in this connection that all sentences in the primary language can be correctly said to describe a single experience. If you say something and say 'that is a dog' you are going beyond what can be seen at the moment. A dog has a past and a future, it possesses auditory and olfactory characteristics, and so on. All these are suggested by the word 'dog' which is a consideration of many inductions. Fortunately animals fit into natural kinds. If your dog proceeded to mew like a cat and give birth to a mixed litter of puppies and kittens words would fail you. In like manner the man who mistakes salt for sugar is making an induction: 'What looks like this is sweet.' In this case the induction is false. So long as a man avoids words which are condensed inductions, and confines himself to words that can describe a single experience, it is possible for a single experience to show that his words are true.

Everyone, whoever he may be, when he comes upon an unfamiliar word (or a phrase) he will have a sensation of derailment. Some process that usually flows smoothly has been interrupted. Some expected click of his mechanism has failed to occur. It is the task of a psychology of language to discover the nature of this click. The meaningful linguistic form must set off some characteristic linguistic effect in the person. What is the substantial nature of this effect?

This process takes us back to the process of reference. Whatever the nature of the comprehension effect it seems to be created in a person by his experiences of linguistic forms in association with referent categories. When a man hears uttered the word 'dog' in conjunction with dogs he learns to hear, read and consider the words with comprehension. It is difficult, though, to tell what the comprehension effect may be, because the effect is hidden away inside the organism. When a man absorbed a reference there occurred certain changes in his observable behaviour and the changes suggested the nature of the comprehension effect.

There are two major changes in overt behaviour that follows the experiencing of a linguistic form used to name referents and there are two principal notions about meaning which are founded on these changes of behaviour. The man who has heard 'dogs' uttered becomes able to identify dogs for himself and to distinguish them from other kinds of things. This performance has become possible owing to his having already formed a mental image of the dog which he can match against any other animals presented to his vision. The next step is to suggest that the meaning of the word 'dog' is the same mental image: the click of comprehension is the image the word evokes. However, there is a second change of behaviour to be seen in the man who has heard 'gods' uttered. He begins to respond to the word as he formerly responded to the referent to treat the word as a sign of the thing. If, for example, he has always run away from the animal, he may now run as soon as the word is shouted out. Ordinarily when we understand words in reading or listening to speech we do not make obvious response like running away but perhaps we do make some internal sign reaction, perhaps the click of comprehension is some subtle response of a muscle or gland. If there is an immediate effect that constitutes understanding of a meaningful form that effect must be neuro-psychological. There is nothing in consciousness or behaviour that is set off whenever the comprehended form occurs.

I have dealt in brief with the psychological aspect of word, since psychology is closely related to philosophy. Now we shall turn to discussing theories of meaning from a philosophical point of view. We shall concern ourselves with the nature of linguistic meaning. This is, so to say, a problem of philosophical analysis which can be best formulated as follows. What are we saying about a linguistic expression when we specify a meaning? It seems proper in this connection to attempt at an adequate characterisation of one of the uses of 'mean' and its cognate.

We generally come across other uses of 'mean' some of which are likely to be confused with our sense.

1. That is no mean achievement.

   Here the 'mean' is used as an adjective meaning 'insignificant.'

2. He is so mean to me.

   Here the 'mean' is used as an adjective whose meaning is tantamount to 'cruel.'

3. I mean to help him.

   Here the 'mean' is used as an intransitive verb meaning 'intend.'

4. The passage of the bill will mean the end of second class citizenship for the vast areas of our population.

   Here the 'mean' is used as transitive verb meaning 'result in.'

5. Once again life has meaning for me.

   Here the 'meaning' means 'significance.'

6. What is the meaning of this?

   Here the meaning of the 'meaning' is explanation.

7. He has just lost his job. That means that he will have to start writing letters of application all over again.

   Here the 'means' means 'implies.'

In these cases we find ourselves talking about people, actions, events, or situations rather than words, phrases or sentences. Rare are the cases in which we apply, or seem to apply, 'mean' to a linguistic expression, but where 'mean' does not have the same sense that we are examining, but it is here that confusion is most likely to occur.

8. Keep off the grass. This means you.

Here it seems possible to regard 'this' as referring to the sentence, 'Keep off the grass.' But it is clear that we are not saying what the sentence means. Here 'mean' means very much the same as 'refer.' It is more used of people as in 'Who do you mean?'—'I mean Baijayant.' But, as in 8 it can be used of linguistic expressions.

There is one sense in which we all know perfectly well what we are saying when we say what a word means. We succeed in communicating with each other by saying things like 'Procrastinate means put things off.' 'He doesn't know what suspicious means,' and so on. We know in general how to support, attack and test such statements, we know when such statements are warranted and when they are not, we know what practical implications accepting such statements would have, and so on. What we lack, in advance of a philosophical investigation, is an explicit and coherent approach of these abilities.

The literature on this subject contains a bewildering diversity of approaches, conceptions and theories, most of which can be grouped into three types, referential, ideational and behavioural. The referential theory identifies the meaning of an expression with that to which it refers or with the referential connection, the ideational theory with the ideas with which it is associated and the behavioural theory with the stimuli that evoke its statement and/or responses that it in turn evokes.

The referential theory has been attractive to a great many theorists, inasmuch as it seems to provide a simple answer that is readily assimilable to natural ways of thinking about the problems of meaning. It has seemed to many that proper names have an ideally transparent semantic structure. We generally make reference by means of words not only to mice and men and other substantive particulars which Aristotle rightly saw to be the primary object of categorization, but also to such things as truth and falsity, feeling and thought, belief and doubt, hopes and fears, necessity, impossibility, the nature of reality, the projected constitutions of a well-ordered republic, and even to such as square root of minus one. It has become a bit clear that if meaning is a complex concept, reference is by no means a simple one either. As with meaning, however, problems only arise when we fudge matters, neglect distinctions, and ignore complexity. It is not complexity that breeds problem, our neglect of it: especially our neglect of categorical complexity, and our consequent reduction of all categories—and thus all objects of reference—to the same logical status. One cannot lay hands on truth or necessity in the way a cat catches a mice or an angler catches a fish. Since all objects of linguistic reference have similar word status it is natural to think that they have—or to be unware they do not have—the same logical status, function or categorical level. When errors of this kind occur we stand in need of logical theory.

Logical analysis of the elements of discourse, known in the name of parts of speech, reveals the complexity of language, when it gets fully developed. When we considered the nature of symbolization we noted that language was quite complex from the start. The starting point of language is objective reference. In language objective reference comes about by the use of words which are associated with an object of external experience by social convention. Empirical reference of this kind is the sheet-anchor of language, the bond between language and reality on which depend all other uses of language. But the way in which language refers or related to reality is anything but simple. Linguistic reference is not like pointing at something with the finger. Moreover, the function of the symbol is not only referential, but also categorical and differential at the same time. In using a word to refer to an object we implicitly class the object with others similarly categorical, and obliquely differentiate it from others differently categorical. In addition, the symbol has mnemonic and heuristic functions which link this object to others previously experienced and facilitate the others yet to be encountered. Thus linguistic reference is a highly complex and open-ended affair from the start and becomes progressively more so since each speaker develops his own linguistic skills. Linguistic skill, suffice it to say, does not stay fixed at the stage of recognition and joyful designation of objects which delights and elates the infant as it learns to speak (Latin infans means 'non-speaker,' and like logos draws attention to early awareness of the importance of learning in the development of human intelligence). Linguistic reference is not restricted to mere designation—cat, dog and so on—but essays some more ambitious tasks: the cat is on the mat, the dog walks on its hind legs. This form of secondary reference, saying something about an object referred to, is traditionally known as predication, and it gives the infant little trouble, it has given the logicians a great deal. The reasons for this are the extreme range and diversity of characterization which can be described as a predilection—oral, imaginary, or even non-existent—which in grammatical terminology are said to be the subject of such predication.

The first form of the thing can easily be shown to be inadequate by virtue of the fact that two expressions can have different meanings but the same referent. Russell's classic example of this point concerns 'Sir Walter Scott' and 'the author of Waverley.' The two expressions refer to the same individual, because Scott is the author of Waverley, but they do not carry the same meaning. If they did, the statement that Scott is the author of Waverley would be known to be true by knowing the meaning of the constituent terms. It is a fundamental principle whenever two referring expressions bear the same meaning, for example, 'my only uncle' and 'the only brother either of my parents has,' then the identity statement with these terms as components, 'my only uncle is the only brother either of my parents has,' is necessarily true just by virtue of the meanings of these expressions. But this is not the case with 'Scott is the author of Waverley.' This statement is a particularly good statement, because the identity of the author of these novels was at first kept secret so that many people could understand the sentence 'Scott is the author of Waverley' without knowing whether it was true. In general, anything to which we can refer can be referred to by many expressions that do not carry the same meaning at all, for example, John F. Kennedy can be referred to as 'the President of the USA in 1962,' 'the US President assassinated in Dallas.' Such example show that it cannot simply be the fact that an expression refers to a certain object that gives it the particular meaning it bears.

There are other contexts in which expressions are used to refer to something, for example, in lists or in labels. But we may take the function of making explicit what a sentence deals with as the defining characteristic of referring. Types of expressions that normally have the function contain proper names like 'Jawaharlal Nehru;' abstract nouns like 'courage;' phrases combining a concrete noun or noun phrase with an article or demonstrative, like 'the pencil' as in 'the pencil is in my pocket;' and the concrete nouns in the plural, like 'pencils' or 'dogs.' If referring is one linguistic job among others and assigned only to some types of expressions, no account of meaning that presupposes that all meaningful units refer to something can be correct. More explicitly, it cannot be the case that to say a word has a certain meaning is to say it refers to something.

If the referential theory of meaning is based on the fundamental insight that language is used to talk about things, the ideational and behavioural theories are based on an equally fundamental insight—that words have the meaning they do only because of what human beings do when they use language. The theories focus on aspects of what goes on in communication, in an attempt to get at those features of the use of language that bestow upon linguistic units the meanings they carry about them. These theories are likely to find themselves saddled with the assumption fatally involved in the referential theory—that every meaningful linguistic unit stands for something, in some sense of 'stand for.' When they do make this assumption, as is often the case, they bring in association of ideas or stimulus response connections as ways of explicating this relation of standing for. Thus, one may suppose that a word stands for x by virtue of being associated with an idea of (ideational theory), or by virtue of having the potentiality of giving rise to responses similar to those to which x gives rise (behavioural theory). These theories, however, are not necessarily cast in this form.

There is of course a certain deficiency in the way the problem of meaning and theories of meaning are often stated. It is not the place to dwell upon them and it would jar on the patience of the readers of this paper. I would rather confine myself to discussing the ideational and behavioural theories.

The classic statement of the ideational theory was given by the seventeenth century British philosopher, John Locke, in his essay concerning Human Understanding, Section I, Chapter II, Book III. 'The use [...] of words is to be sensible makes of ideas; and the ideas they stand for are their proper and immediate signification.' This kind of theory is in the background whenever people think of language as a means or instrument for the communication of thought or as a physical and external representation of an external state or when people define a sentence as a chain of words expressing a complete thought.

What give a linguistic expression a certain meaning is the fact that it is regularly used in communication as the 'mark' of a certain idea; the ideas which marshal our thinking have an existence and a function independent of language. If each of us were content to keep all his thoughts to himself, language could have been no longer needed; we all have an intense desire to convey our thoughts to each other and so we have to make use of publicly observable indications of the purely private ideas which are coursing through our minds. A linguistic expression gets its meaning by being used in such an indication.

We won't be wrong in saying that ideas are involved in any intelligible bit speech. This is the sense 'idea' has in such expressions as 'I get the idea,' 'I have no idea what you are saying,' and 'He is not getting his ideas across.' The phrase 'get the idea' would have to be explained as equivalent to 'See what the speaker meant by his utterance' or 'know what is speaker is saying.' 'Idea' in this sense is derivative from such notions as 'meaning' and 'understanding,' and so can provide no basis for an explication of meaning. If we are to have an explication of meaning in terms of ideas, we must be using 'idea' so that the presence or absence of an idea is decidable independent of determining in what senses words are being used. Ideas would have to be introspectively discriminable items in consciousness. Locke was trying to satisfy this requirement by taking 'idea' to mean something like 'sensation' or 'mental image.' But the more we push 'idea' in the direction of such 'identifiability,' the clearer it becomes that words are not related to ideas required by the theory.

It should be mentioned clearly that even our most primitive empirical categories on which are based and modelled all categories have a normative function and it is, so to say, impossible to exaggerate its importance. The importance lies in the fact that, until understood, we are constantly liable to hypostasize this normative function of the categorical symbol in the form of concepts and ideas mysteriously lodged in our mind. It is not possible at all how they got there. This is a fruitful source of metaphysical idealism. When, on the other hand, rightly understood, this normative function is seen to be not only constitutive of our categorical concepts, but constitute thereby the first principle of logic: the principle of logical identity which is quite different and distinct from the notions of either physical or personal identity. Since all other logical principles presuppose logical identity, logic is not supposed to be discipline superimposed on language, but permeates its entire development. This same principle is also a basic principle of epistemology: the antique problem of universals disappears when we grasp the fact that the universal concepts are but the categorical symbols of ordinary language. Previous nominalist arguments to this effect, however, always foundered through ignorance of the complex nature of linguistic symbolization of its origins and of its essentially normative function. The problems to which classical philosophy drew attention but could not solve are the central problems of human psychology or mind, of logic and the nature of rational discourse, of epistemology or the study of this distinctive nature of human knowledge.

In dwelling on the categorical function of the linguistic symbol we should bear in mind that this function cannot be separated from its mnemonic and heuristic functions. To understand the use of the word 'fish' means that you can refer not only to fish now swimming but also to remote ancestors, and even identify fish in the future. You may later have trouble with eels and seals, but nothing that a little common sense and categorical refinement will not remedy. It is imperative for us to get rid of a common misconception. Not even a primitive empirical category, such as 'fish' stands for, is a class, a set of plurality of existent objects, since it refers to these along with others not yet in existence and yet others already extinct. This complexity present in our primary empirical categories focuses our attention on the points which help us avoid further misconceptions. First, our empirical categories, on which all others are modelled, must indeed be rooted in empirical fact, but are not restricted to it. Categories are not classes of given objects. Second, while any category whatever must be constituted by a linguistic symbol, this does not mean that categories are therefore 'free creations' of the human mind, as modern idealism frequently claims. Our basic categories are compounded of both psychological and empirical factors, and all higher, more abstract categories presuppose and rest on these more basic ones. The whole process of symbolic categorization is much more complex, but also far less mysterious, than is commonly supposed.

It has become clear to us that if empirical categories did not have some basis in empirical fact—in things—they do not exist. Likewise, if we did not manage to have some categories in our minds they would not form part of our knowledge. It was Plato who was the first to have grasped the essentially normative function of our categories and general ideas. They could not be placed on the same logical level as the changing phenomena of nature, nor could they be located in the volatile minds of giddy men, who constantly defend the most contradictory theses, convinced that they are in possession of truth. 'Human mind' is not believed to be an invariant entity, identical copies of which are lodged in all human beings, or more absurdly, in their genes. Plato grasped two obvious truths which seemed to have eluded most other labourers in the philosophical vineyard: that men differ psychologically as they differ physically; and that civilized life depends on the establishment of objective norms by which the thought and action of different individuals may be co-ordinated, in the interest of social harmony; and judged, when discrepancy of conflict arises. Thus, if generic ideas, as they enable us to correlate empirical data and co-ordinate human thought and action, are to perform their normative functions, they should be sought for on a different logical plane. In the *Republic* Plato explicitly correlates his generic ideas with category words of empirical language.

Now it is of paramount importance for us to understand the difference between the empirical and moral concepts. The term 'moral' should be treated, as it is in 'moral philosophy' in the broad sense and it should be used to cover all areas of inquiry in which human consciousness and action determine the very nature of the subject matter of empirical science. Moral concepts are those which refer to all things distinctively human, habits and customs (mores) included among others. It is not a place here to elaborate upon moral concepts, but it would suffice to say that they are quite different from empirical concepts and they flow mainly from the cognitive aspects. They are, as it were, categories in action, which not only refer to given objects and forms of behaviour but suggest new possibilities, guide and prescribe future behaviour. This is most obviously true of all procedural, legal and ethical categories, and more so of the rules, regulations and laws which embody them. These are future-oriented and designed not to describe the given, but to describe what is to be. These future-oriented concepts build on existent knowledge and forms of behaviour.

Now we find the door opened to behavioural theory of meaning now that we have discussed 'behaviour' from philosophical and psychological points of view.

The behavioural theory of meaning concentrates on what is involved in using language in communication, but it differs from the ideational theory in focusing on publicly observable aspect of the communication situation. There are several reasons for the attractiveness of such a project and the attractiveness is more or less highlighted by one deficiency, among others, of the ideational theory that stems from the fact that we do not, nor are we expected to, look for ideas in the minds of the speakers and listeners in order to settle questions about what a word means in the language or about the sense in which a speaker used a term on a given occasion. If I am not sure about the exact sense in which you used the word 'normal' in something you just said, it would be absurd for me to find out by asking you to carefully introspect and tell me what imagery accompanied your utterance of the word. It is not clear at all just what we look for in settling such questions, but the fact remains that there is a broad consensus concerning what various words mean, and it strongly suggests that meaning is a function of aspects of the communication situation, the success that psychology has already achieved in explaining some aspects of human behaviour in terms of regular connections between observable stimuli and responses gives rise to a hope of being able to give the same kind of treatment of verbal behaviour.

The simplest forms of the behavioural theory are to be found in the writings of linguists who take over ideas from behaviourally minded psychologists without bothering to delve deep into the complexities involved. The meaning of a linguistic form is the situation in which the speaker utters it and the response it calls forth in the listener. To mitigate the crudity of such definition postulated by linguists like Leonard Bloomfield, it necessitates the qualifying statement: we should discriminate between the non-distinctive features of the situation and linguistic (distinctive) meaning which are common to all the situations that call forth the utterance of linguistic form.

Psychologists and psychologically oriented philosophers have to a great extent confined themselves to dealing with responses to linguistic utterances and have started with natural signs, where there is no intentional production of the sign. Only in concentrating on responses they recognise that having a certain meaning cannot simply be identified with regularly evoking a certain overt response, for we can have meaningful utterances that evoke no response at all, and where there are overt responses, they can widely vary among themselves without any variation in meaning.

The behavioural theory is based on an insight that it perverts through oversimplification. Just as the meaningful use of language has something to do with reference to the 'world,' and just as in some way we do express and communicate our thoughts in using language, so it is also a significant fact that units of language get their meaning through being used by people, through the fact that they are involved in various sorts of behaviour. Behavioural theories err in conceiving this behavioural involvement in oversimplified terms. They suppose that a word or a sentence has a certain meaning by virtue of being involved, as response and/or stimulus, in stimulus-response connections which are basically similar, save for complexity, to a simple reflex like the knee-jerk. Unfortunately, no such connections have ever been found save for those that are obviously not determinative of meaning, like the fact that a sudden loud utterance of 'look out!' typically elicits a start. Some more adequate characterization of linguistic behaviour is called for, one that will get at the units of behaviour which are crucial for the meaning.

CONTRIBUTORS

Amiya Basu. Reader in English, Burdwan University, Burdwan, West Bengal.

Mallikarjun Patil. Department of English, Gulbarga University, Gulbarga, Karnataka.

Shailendra Kumar Mukul. Department of English, L.S. College, Muzaffarpur, Bihar.

Sharad Rajimwale. Assistant Professor, Department of English, Jai Narain Vyas University, Jodhpur, Rajasthan.

Avadhesh Kumar Singh. Professor of English, Saurashtra University, Rajkot, Gujarat.

S. Jagadisan. 48A, Tarachand Nagar, III St., Vivugambakkam, Chennai, Tamil Nadu.

S. Imtiaz. AH 198, III St. Anna Nagar, Chennai, Tamil Nadu.

Amar Nath Jha. Professor and Head of the Department of English, L.N. Mithila University, Darbhanga, Bihar.

Jaydeep Sarangi. Lecturer in English, Seva-Bharati Mahavidyalaya, Kapgari, Dt. Midnapore, West Bengal.

V.K. Jain. Assistant Professor, Govt. Girls' College, Khandwa, Madhya Pradesh.

Sandhya Rani Sahoo. Reader in English, DESSH, NCERT, Sri Aurobindo Marg, New Delhi.

P. Bhaskaran Nair. Department of English, Govt. Brennen College, Thalessery, Kerala.

Meenakshi Raman. Assistant Professor of English and Group Leader, Language Group, BITS, Pilani, Rajasthan.

Prakash Chandra Pradhan. Senior Lecturer in English, K.B.D.H.V. College, Nirakarpur, Khurda, Orissa.

Shubha Tiwari. Senior Lecturer, Department of English, A.P.S. University, Rewa, Madhya Pradesh.

Benson Agarwarker. Lecturer, Department of English, Shri H.K. Arts College, Ashram Road, Ahmedabad, Gujarat.

Pratibha Gupta. Department of English, L.N. Mithila University, Darbhanga, Bihar.

K. Balachandran. Professor of English, Annamalai University, Annamalai Nagar, Tamil Nadu.

R.P. Singh. Assistant Professor, Government College, Lal Bahadur Nagar, Rahnandgaon, Chhatishgarh.

Dipak J. Baruah. Senior Lecturer, Department of English, Jagiroad College, Jagiroad, Assam.

Sisir Kumar Chatterjee. Assistant Professor of English, Hooghly Mohsin College, Chinsurah, Hooghly, West Bengal.

Santosh Chakrabarti. Guest Lecturer, Rabindra Bharati University, Kolkata, West Bengal.

Mukta Mahajan. Department of Comparative Languages and Literature, North Maharashtra University, Jalgaon, Maharashtra.

Nandini Sahu. Lecturer in English, Institute of Advanced Computer & Research (ICAR), Prajukti Vihar, Rayagada, Orissa.

Rama Kundu. Professor of English, Burdwan University, Burdwan, West Bengal.

Madan M. Sarma. Professor of English and Head, Department of English and Foreign Languages, Tezpur University, Tezpur, Assam.

R.S. Pathak. Formerly Professor of English, Dr H.S. Gaur University, Sagar, Madhya Pradesh.

Bhaskar Roy Barman. Post Box 51, Agartala, West Tripura.